CW01509732

Body Confident You,
Body Confident Kid

Body Confident You, Body Confident Kid

Seven Steps to Feeling Good About Your Body so
Your Kids Grow Up Loving Theirs

Dr Charlotte Ord

BLUEBIRD

First published 2025 by Bluebird
an imprint of Pan Macmillan
The Smithson, 6 Briset Street, London EC1M 5NR
EU representative: Macmillan Publishers Ireland Ltd, 1st Floor,
The Liffey Trust Centre, 117–126 Sheriff Street Upper,
Dublin 1, D01 YC43
Associated companies throughout the world
www.panmacmillan.com

ISBN 978-1-0350-4898-4

Copyright © Charlotte Ord 2025

The right of Charlotte Ord to be identified as the
author of this work has been asserted by her in accordance
with the Copyright, Designs and Patents Act 1988.

All rights reserved. No part of this publication may be reproduced,
stored in a retrieval system, or transmitted, in any form, or by any means
(electronic, mechanical, photocopying, recording or otherwise)
without the prior written permission of the publisher.

Pan Macmillan does not have any control over, or any responsibility for,
any author or third-party websites referred to in or on this book.

1 3 5 7 9 8 6 4 2

A CIP catalogue record for this book is available from the British Library.

Typeset in Minion Pro by
Palimpsest Book Production Ltd, Falkirk, Stirlingshire
Printed and bound by CPI Group (UK) Ltd, Croydon, CR0 4YY

This book is sold subject to the condition that it shall not, by way of
trade or otherwise, be lent, hired out, or otherwise circulated without
the publisher's prior consent in any form of binding or cover other than
that in which it is published and without a similar condition including
this condition being imposed on the subsequent purchaser.

Visit **www.panmacmillan.com/bluebird** to read more about all our books
and to buy them. You will also find features, author interviews and
news of any author events, and you can sign up for e-newsletters
so that you're always first to hear about our new releases.

To the indomitable spirit in us all. May we use it to reclaim our love for ourselves and change the world for others.

Contents

INTRODUCTION: **Newborn Body Image**   1

CHAPTER ONE: **What Is Body Image?**   17

CHAPTER TWO: **Fit Your Own Mask First**   53

CHAPTER THREE: **Body Talk**   87

CHAPTER FOUR: **Self-Esteem and Body Image**   131

CHAPTER FIVE: **Scrolling for Self-Love: Balancing Body
Positivity and Pressures Online**   171

CHAPTER SIX: **Power in Motion: Transforming Body
Confidence Through Activity**   207

CHAPTER SEVEN: **Be the Change**   249

CONCLUSION: **A Body Confident Future**   277

RESOURCES   285

ACKNOWLEDGEMENTS   287

ABOUT THE AUTHOR   289

REFERENCES   291

INTRODUCTION

Newborn Body Image

'Everything has beauty. But not everyone sees it.'
Attributed to Confucius

We're all born with a body, and we all have a relationship with that body and a particular way of viewing, thinking and feeling about it. Our bodies are imbued with meaning, a physical entity we all share and yet are separated by through identity, age, race, class, (dis)ability, religion and gender. If our bodies meet societal expectations, then we can expect admiration, approval and social power. If they don't, we may be met with physical and psychological barriers in the form of stigma, discrimination and structural limitations. Beauty pays.

As a counselling psychologist, I've spent several years helping people who have been harmed by the war against certain body types, a war that I believe wounds us all. I've often found myself wishing that I'd been able to work with many of my clients when they were younger, before the belief that their bodies weren't okay became so embedded that it set them on a trajectory of self-loathing and harmful attempts at body manipulation such as crash diets, slimming pills, injections and even surgery. When I spoke to people about my intention to write this book, the most frequent reply I received was, 'I so wish that book had been around when I was a kid!' Having a poor body image can cause so much suffering, both physically and mentally, but it doesn't have to be that way. In writing this book, I hope to empower you with the knowledge and strategies that will help you heal your relationship with your own body and nurture body confidence in your children, setting them up for a positive relationship with themselves that will serve them in every area of their lives.

In this book, you will find evidence-based, practical guidance on fostering a positive body image both in yourself and your kids, along with insights on how to promote self-esteem and develop effective communication strategies. Each chapter contains exercises for you personally, along with age-appropriate activities and approaches you can take with your children. I'm aware that older kids especially might want to run a mile if they're invited to take part in body image exercises directly, so I've included ideas to open up conversations and foster critical thinking without being boring, 'weird' or too confrontational. Throughout the book, I'll share insights from parents who've faced their own body battles, along with experts in the fields of psychology, dietetics, visible differences, race, eating disorders and neuropsychology. I'll introduce you to some popular and most likely familiar childhood tales that, when looked at through a psychological lens, can help to illustrate important themes around body image, and I'll also share stories inspired by my work with clients, though all names and identifying details have been changed to protect their anonymity and confidentiality.

I hope this book is an invaluable and inspiring companion on your journey to a more body-accepting family environment.

Please know that however far you feel from a place of peace with your body right now, if you're willing to trust in and apply the strategies I've shared in this book, change can happen. I've worked with people of all backgrounds, of all body shapes and sizes, from a wide range of ethnicities, with a spectrum of physical health complications or disabilities, and contending with all types of stigma, and I've been able to help them all feel better about who they are, physically and psychologically. I have every confidence I can help you, too.

It's an inside job

The great news is that it isn't just external opinions of how attractive we are that influence how we get on in life, and that's why sharing this knowledge with you feels so important. I've been fortunate to work with people of all ages and backgrounds in my career, and what really struck me is how those who consider themselves to be attractive (regardless of what others think), or who value physical attractiveness less highly, are more likely to put themselves forward for high-end job roles and are also more likely to take advantage of social network opportunities. There is plenty of research to support this, too.[1] People who view their appearance positively tend to be more self-compassionate, have higher self-esteem and self-worth, are less prone to mental health issues like depression, anxiety and eating disorders, and are more self-caring. And that's where your role is so key. Regardless of children's physical characteristics, the influence of their caregivers and the level of attachment security they experience in their primary relationships make a tremendous difference to how they relate to themselves and, therefore, to the world. Kids of all gender orientations who grow up with emotionally warm, available, supportive and affectionate parents or caregivers consistently report higher body image satisfaction.[2] So, while we can't all win the genetic lottery, and can only have some sway over our appearance, the wonderful thing is these are not prerequisites to feeling happy in your body. In this book, I'll show you step by step how to find the peace you deserve with how you look and how you can foster a secure attachment with your child. In doing so, you'll arm them with a stable, valued sense of self, and that will include a deeper confidence in their appearance.

A widespread struggle

It's common for young people to worry about how they look, with around 50 per cent of children, particularly preteens and teenagers, reporting body image concerns.[3] This is a stark increase from ten years ago and a troubling indication of how the centrality of social media in children's lives and the persistent bombardment of narrowly defined body ideals erodes kids' confidence in how they look. The Covid-19 pandemic really didn't help. The various global lockdowns resulted in an increase in social media use of 70 per cent on platforms such as TikTok, Snapchat, Instagram, YouTube and Facebook, ensuring that kids prone to social comparison, fragile body image or rumination became increasingly exposed and, therefore, susceptible to mental health difficulties such as anxiety, depression and disordered eating.[4]

In addition, reliance on social media as a form of communication and connection became even further embedded in how we operate as a society. You could say it was the 'perfect storm' for exacerbating body image concerns; the need for adolescents to feel important among their peers interlaced with the cultural overvaluing of appearance, suddenly colliding with a hike in exposure to idealized images and quantifiable feedback from 'friends' on social media. It's no wonder so many kids struggle with the pressure to look a certain way, and children's mental health services are unable to meet demand. Nor is it surprising that eating disorder figures soared during the pandemic.

My story

When it comes to writing a book, most authors think about what they'd like to write about and choose their topic accordingly. I, on the other hand, feel that this topic has rather chosen me. My relationship with my body and other people's relationships with theirs have been central to my life since I was a kid myself. Fortunate to be reasonably athletically gifted and unfortunate to be (at least in my perception) the stockier, uglier one among my closest school friends, my body and appearance have felt like a double-edged sword for as long as I can remember. My childhood was hallmarked by an impossible tension between wanting to be fit, fast and strong to hold my own in various sporting pursuits and as thin as possible to meet beauty ideals. As soon as Sky television became a thing, Fashion TV, in the era of heroin chic and size 0, became my favourite channel. Not exactly the most ideal building block for a healthy self-view. I was eleven when I first learnt how to make myself sick by copying a friend at school and approaching forty by the time I regained some sort of a sense of peace around food. In the interim, I lugged around the kind of crippling shame one might expect of a health professional with an incredibly unhealthy secret eating disorder.

Along the way, my longing for acceptance of my own physicality led me through a seemingly successful career in the fitness industry as a TV personal trainer and international strength and conditioning coach, then, not quite so glamorously, through intensive eating disorder treatment. That was after I started to feel that the methods I had to use to maintain the 'perfect' body might actually kill me. As one journalist put it, I matched the image of a fit person so well that I looked like I'd been 'grown in a laboratory', and it came at a high price. I was split in two: a shiny beacon of health, fitness and togetherness by day; engaging in a frenzied and relentless cycle of bingeing and purging by night.

A big, fat overhaul

Being in eating disorder treatment led to a pivot in my fitness business. I stopped promoting weight loss and fat loss altogether, and started focusing on my clients' (and my own) genuine health and wellbeing. It was a tough transition when the prospect of a smaller, more toned body held so much promise for people and was so much easier to sell than self-acceptance, which no one was really talking about at the time. But I really believe that when you know better, you should do better, and ethically, it felt like the only way forward.

My passion for promoting health at every size (more on this to come), and my determination to do my part to dismantle the harmful impact of diet culture, ultimately led me to do my doctorate in counselling psychology. I've worked with others struggling with their own bodies ever since. From severely injured service people recovering from serious burns, amputations and war wounds at the Ministry of Defence rehabilitation centre, to young people struggling with eating disorders, to clients diagnosed with life-altering health conditions like multiple sclerosis and Ehlers–Danlos syndrome, to those immobilized by their high weight in NHS bariatric services. It is my life's work and privilege.

In this book, I hope to share everything I've learnt about how we, as adults, can help to ensure that the young people we care about feel peaceful in the only body they will ever have. How we can find the courage to say, 'This ends with me,' and give a hard *no* to the harmful influences that made us think it was normal to berate your body, so that the next generation doesn't have to. And if you have yet to find peace with your body, I also intend to help you do that, too.

Health at Every Size

The Health at Every Size (HAES) approach is a framework that's invigorated my professional practice with clients of all ages over the past decade and will underly this book, too. The HAES principles advocate for weight inclusivity; non-weight-focused health behaviours; equal access to healthcare; intuitive eating; ending weight bias, stigma and discrimination; and taking part in enjoyable movement. Originating in the 1960s when activists recognized the negative psychological and physiological impact weight prejudice was having on bigger-bodied people, it was more recently popularized by Dr Lindo Bacon in their book, *Health at Every Size: The Surprising Truth About Your Weight*.[5]

HAES respects the rich diversity of body shapes and sizes and rejects the idea that there are good and bad body weights, shapes or sizes. It also acknowledges that access to healthy foods and movement opportunities are not available to everyone and that health status shouldn't be used to dictate the value of a person, nor as a reason to judge or oppress.[6]

An overview:
Seven principles of body confidence

The chapters in this book are led by the seven guiding principles that will help you to support your child, and yourself, in building robust body confidence.

1. All bodies are good bodies: Body appreciation

We'll start by discussing what body image is, how it's formed and what influences it. Having a sound understanding of how your own and your child's body image are formed and function under-pins all of the other principles in the book, as well as the exercises and strategies I'll be inviting you to try. We'll draw on Attachment Theory to explore how body image is shaped by the emotional bonds between a child and their primary caregiver. And I'll also introduce you to neuropsychological understandings of body image development and how our childhood experiences shape the parts of the brain that create our self-view.

2. Fit your own mask first. This ends with me: Embracing broad perspectives of beauty

In Chapter 2, we'll gently and compassionately unpack your body image, including the culture, relationships and experiences that have impacted you. While I'll encourage you to be curious about your own positioning throughout the book, this chapter is particularly designed to help you gain a deep, warm-hearted awareness of how your body image has been shaped. Being conscious of your own influences, biases and beliefs about bodies, including your own, is helpful in understanding how your child's own self-view is constructed and how you can support them. We'll explore how the way your parents talked and behaved around body image impacted you and which beliefs and practices you'd like your children to inherit. We'll contemplate how you see, think and feel about your body, and how your perception is conveyed to yourself and others, including the young people in your life. We'll also consider common conceptualizations of beauty and their impact on your and your kid's body confidence.

I really want to stress here that this book, and my approach in general, is in no way about placing blame or shaming anyone. Not you, not your parents, and not your child. In my experience, blaming parents when their children are suffering from poor body image, or an eating disorder, for example, is not only often misguided but incredibly harmful and can result in appropriate treatment being delayed. There are, of course, instances in which parents cause trauma, which can result in mental health issues, including body image difficulties. But we also have to remember that our parents have been just as deeply entrenched in diet and wellness culture as we have.

I may not know much about you, but the fact you are reading this book already tells me that you care about the young people in your life and are willing to invest your time and means into supporting them. I also strongly suspect that you've been doing the very best you can with the knowledge and resources that you have, navigating an often conflicting and confusing bombardment of health information, which is all any of us can do. Whether you're aware that your own body image isn't great and know you don't want your child to have the same experience but aren't sure how to address it, or you've noticed that your child has a poor body image and you want to know how to help them improve it, I am on your side; I respect you and I intend to help you relate differently to any thoughts or feelings of self-blame or guilt that might crop up for you on your journey through this book.

I also aim to help you relate more compassionately to yourself and your own body and develop a deeper understanding of the mechanisms by which you've learnt to feel and behave the way you do around it. In turn, I hope you will finish this book with a sense of freedom and empowerment to change the script; after all, one of the most powerful ways to influence how your kid feels about themselves is through what you model to them. Indeed, part of the reason it felt important for me to share some of my own stories and struggles with my body is that I know what it feels like to carry deep shame and to feel stuck. My experience most likely won't be exactly the same as yours because everyone's experience is different, but I do know that no matter what lengths you've gone to or how much shame you've carried around it, you obviously had good reason, and change is possible. I have seen it time and time again, in people of all genders, body types and ages, and I am here to walk alongside you.

3. Use kind body language: Expression and acceptance of your body

You know how everyone loves to talk about how they and other people look, what diet they're on, and how much weight they've lost or gained? In Chapter 3 we'll be shining light on the ways in which adults and children are influenced by the narratives we hear around appearance and the historical origins of some of these discourses. I'll share some of my clinical experience working with a range of clients across the weight and eating disorder spectrums to illustrate how the moralization of food, narratives around healthy eating and societal issues such as thin privilege and pretty privilege can play significant roles in the development of body image issues. We'll hear from people whose struggles with their bodies have led them to the surgeon's table and offer evidence-based advice on how you can support bigger-bodied kids, kids from minority ethnic communities and kids with visible differences when they are faced with name-calling, bullying or any other type of stigma and discrimination. I'll provide you with suggestions on how you can adjust your own verbal and non-verbal language to promote body confidence in both you and your child and will take you through reflective exercises to raise your awareness of the impact of dominant discourses around physicality. We'll also be talking about how you can set boundaries around the language used to describe bodies both inside and outside of your home and how to talk to kids about their private and other body parts in a way that promotes safety, curiosity, consent and respect rather than shame.

4. Unconditionally good inside: Cultivating a sense of inner positivity and a whole-person view and appreciation

It's unsurprising that children, adolescents and adults who feel down about themselves generally are more vulnerable to negative messages about bodies and more likely to make negative comparisons between their own physical appearance and what they see presented as an idealized beauty standard. In Chapter 4, we'll focus on how body dissatisfaction and self-esteem are linked. Nurturing a sense of intrinsic and unconditional self-worth and acceptance is one of the greatest gifts any child can receive, and this chapter will equip you with practical steps you can take to boost your kid's self-esteem as well as your own. This includes advice on how and when to praise your child, how to set age-appropriate goals, and how you can use your child's failed attempts and struggles as an opportunity to convey unconditional love and reinforce in them a sense of real self-worth.

5. Media literacy: Eliciting support and positive exposure on- and offline and developing a critical eye

Our fifth principle focuses on helping you and your child navigate the ever-changing media landscape in a healthy way. Online platforms such as TikTok, Instagram, Snapchat and YouTube are now a central part of most pre-teenagers and teenagers' lives, and as such, they have huge potential to influence their psychological development. In Chapter 5 we'll unpack how the image-sharing and advertising pressures inherent on social media can serve to reinforce unrealistic body ideals, encourage unhelpful external validation-seeking, exacerbate our inherent tendency for comparison with others, spread unsubstantiated wellness rhetoric and leave children vulnerable to potentially harmful comments. More optimistically, we'll also look at how online platforms can provide access to inspirational models of body positivity, diversity, self-care, health at every size and body confidence, as well as serve as a useful resource to support you in the many challenges of raising children. I'll also highlight how the different ways in which kids engage with social media dictate whether it has a positive or negative effect on their psychological wellbeing. And we'll also look at what you can do to help your kid to understand the difference between helpful and harmful content and become more media literate.

6. Making movement fun: Working with and taking good care of your body

Having owned two gyms, spent ten years working as an international strength and conditioning coach, and twice been named UK Personal Trainer of the Year, you probably won't be surprised to hear that I consider movement to be an important part of developing body confidence! However, I've trained enough clients to know that one size definitely does not fit all, and, a bit like therapy, finding the right approach and motivation to create a fulfilling relationship with exercise is highly individual. For kids to want to move, it must feel good to them. It can't be a chore, or something to be endured. It has to genuinely feel good. Of course, what feels good varies from person to person. In Chapter 6, I'll introduce you to the concept of positive embodiment (that is, a sense of comfort, connection and agency between the mind and body facilitated through mindful movement) and why it's more important for adults and children than working up a sweat or burning calories. We'll look at various ways in which even the most reluctant kids can be encouraged to connect posi-tively with their bodies through physical activity and how tuning into their body, in turn, lays down new, healthy neural pathways in your child's brain. This is relevant to our task here as these pathways assist in promoting positive feelings towards ourselves. Also of great benefit is teaching children mindful self-care, bodily awareness and presence, and I'll guide you through how to use these tools yourself and how to introduce each of them to your kid.

7. Be the change: Focusing your energy on making the world a better place for every body rather than on trying to make your body something it's not

The seventh and final principle of *Body Confident You, Body Confident Kid* is understanding bodies in context and how we can all do our bit to make the world an easier place to be, no matter what type of body you have or what defining features you possess. We'll be taking a deep dive into your child's environment and considering how systemic, environmental, political, biological and social factors all play a role in influencing body confidence, considering questions like:

- *How can I support my child through potentially rapid bodily changes in puberty?*
- *How does the school curriculum impact kids' body confidence?*
- *What effect does traditional and digital advertising have on how children see themselves?*

Supported by reflections from other leading experts in child psychology and research, we'll look at some potential danger zones that may surround your child, as well as how to address them. I'll also bring in some strategies you can use to protect them against harmful influences, as well as amplify those that are more likely to lead to them to see themselves more positively.

We'll also explore how, in manageable, realistic and impactful ways, we can all play a part in reducing the discontent around our bodies that we see so often today in Western society. I'll highlight some of the amazing work already being done and how positive change is happening in the way we view and treat bodies as a society, as well as what you can do to support these movements. Even though progress has been made, however, we still need a lot more representation of people with disabilities, physical differences and diverse body shapes. Getting rid of stigma and discrimination entirely will probably never be possible, so arming children with the confidence and self-worth to be able to withstand these injustices is vital. Even if only in the smallest of ways, we can all do our bit to contribute to shifting beauty paradigms and promoting body inclusivity and diversity. In doing so, we will help make the world a safer place for our kids of all body shapes and sizes, races, abilities and gender expressions, and the generations that follow them. In Chapter 7, I'll discuss some ways in which you can be part of that incredible and empowering change.

A hands-on approach

Most people learn more from doing and experiencing than just reading and knowing things theoretically. That's why I've included many practical exercises and action points in this book for you to experiment with if you're willing. If there are any that you feel less inclined to have a go at, that's fine, they are all optional, but I would encourage you to be curious about what gets in the way for you if you decide they're not for you. It might be thoughts about having a lack of time, about coming back to it later, a scepticism about whether or not the strategy will work, a feeling of apathy, or something else. These are what we call 'hooks': things that show up and sometimes get in the way of acting in service of our values (I'm making an assumption here that you value being a supportive caregiver, otherwise you probably wouldn't be reading this book). We'll talk more about hooks and how you can respond differently to them when they do show up in Chapter 2. But for now, just be curious if you notice any resistance while reading along.

Wherever you are with your own self-confidence, no matter how deep the trauma wounds you carry around your own body, and however hard it seems to protect your child from harmful influences in their environment, please know that there is so much hope and possibility ahead of you. Thank you for allowing me to walk alongside you on this empowering journey.

CHAPTER ONE

What Is Body Image?

'Success is liking yourself, liking what you do,
and liking how you do it.'
Maya Angelou, author and civil rights activist

Before we get into the 'how to' of helping you, and your child, feel more confident in your own bodies, it's important to explain exactly what body image is, how it develops, and what shapes it. Having this knowledge is invaluable in understanding how your own body image came to be what it is, and what you can do to feel more at peace with it. It will also help you to understand body challenges from your child's perspective and developmental stage, which will then help them feel that you really 'get them', that you empathize with them, and from there build trust that you can help. Having this understanding will also give the exercises I suggest meaning and purpose.

Understanding self-concept

How we view our bodies is just one aspect of our overarching 'self-concept', our understanding of who we are as social, emotional, physical and spiritual beings. Carl Rogers, one of the founders of person-centred psychology, an approach which emphasizes individuals' inherent capacity for self-growth and development, suggested that there are three core components of self-concept:[1]

1. *Self-image – how you see and perceive yourself*
2. *Self-esteem – how much worth and value you feel you have*
3. *Ideal self – who you aspire to be and see yourself as*

When our self-image – that is, the way we see ourselves – aligns with our ideal self, we tend to have good self-esteem. But when there's a disparity between these two aspects, it feels incongruent, and we tend to suffer from poor self-esteem. That's why what you model to your kids, and what they see being represented positively in the wider world, are so instrumental in the formation of their own self-concept and, relatedly, their mental wellbeing. It's also why, if you grew up in the era of super-skinny models where an extremely thin, gaunt look was glorified, there may have been a lot of dissonance for you between your self-image and ideal self, and you may have gone to some lengths to try to align the two. It's also why it's essential that we call out fashion trends that perpetuate unrealistic and potentially unhealthy body ideals, like the 'thigh gap' ideal of the 2010s and the fashion currently for silicone butt injections and dermal lip fillers.

While it is possible to change our self-concept as we grow up, it's generally harder to do so as adults because we've already laid down the neural pathways that make negative thoughts and beliefs about yourself your default response. To change that, we have to be willing to lean into the discomfort of unfamiliar ways of being. That takes effort, practice and undoubtedly some courage, but don't be disheartened. If your brain tends to take a path straight to negativity, particularly about yourself, the chances are you've practised being negative a lot as a result of various factors that have influenced you in the past. Imagine what it would be like if you practised feeling and responding in calm, secure ways and appreciating the beauty in yourself and others instead? That's what I'll be helping you, and in turn your child, to do throughout this book.

Acting 'as if'

If you feel very stuck in a particular way of thinking about your body, weight or appearance, it can be helpful to think about it like a well-worn footpath. When we think the same thing repeatedly, it becomes quick and easy to just continue down the same path, as there is very little resistance. Taking a different route, one that hasn't been trodden down yet, will require more conscious thought to navigate. But, over time, the new path becomes more defined, and as the old path becomes disused, it grows over until it's no longer your go-to thought process. Sometimes, we have to commit to thinking and acting 'as if' we are accepting of ourselves in order to start really feeling it.

The building blocks of body image

Developmentally, the way we conceptualize our body in our mind forms over time, is continuously constructed and deconstructed, and is made up of four key elements. These are:

1. *Our perceptive experience – how we **see** our bodies*
2. *Our cognitive experience – the way we **think** about our bodies*
3. *Our affective experience – the way we **feel** about our bodies*
4. *Our behavioural experience – the way we **act** as a result of how we experience our bodies*

How we see our bodies, however, isn't always an accurate reflection of how we *actually* look, nor is it always constant. You may have found yourself feeling rather good about your body one day, and fairly awful about it the next, or you may have noticed your kid's perception fluctuate similarly. These inconsistencies in self-perception are often made worse by harmful diet culture, which encourages us to interpret normal bodily reactions to eating, menstruation, stress or illness, like a more rounded tummy, or higher water retention, as something unacceptable and unsightly. It also accounts for how we might suddenly feel different about our appearance when someone else draws attention to it or when we're trying on clothes in a store. We'll talk more about the impact of diet culture in Chapter 2, but for now, just try to notice if and how your own feelings about your body change from day to day and perhaps even hour to hour. You might ask your child about this too, encouraging them to be kindly curious about what influences how they feel about their body and normalizing everyday variations in how it looks and feels.

What influences body image?

The way we see and feel about our bodies is influenced by a number of intersecting factors.

* *The culture we grow up in*
* *How confident we feel about ourselves in other areas, such as our value as a person and self-esteem*
* *Our sense of belonging*
* *Our feelings of competence and security*
* *The attitudes and values our families hold around bodies*
* *Our society's construction of attractiveness and ugliness*
* *What we're exposed to in the form of marketing and social media*
* *Our personality and genetics*
* *Our previous or current experiences of abuse, trauma or oppression*
* *Our relationship with physical activity*
* *Our experience of puberty and bodily changes*
* *How similar bodies to ours are represented in the media*

Exploring how each of these aspects has affected your own relationship with your body is a bit like shining a light on a shadow. The more we look at it, understand it and become familiar with the more hidden, subconscious and often uncomfortable aspects of ourselves, the smaller the shadow tends to get and the less influence it will have on us. In psychotherapy, we call this 'shadow work', a type of therapy developed by the founder of analytic psychology, Carl Jung. Jung described shadow work as the means by which we bring the repressed, rejected parts of ourselves into consciousness and integrate them with our persona. Doing so improves our capacity to respond differently to challenging emotions and experience greater acceptance of both ourselves and others.[2] [3] But first, we're going to think about what is arguably one of the most significant influences on our self-image: our interactions with our primary caregivers.

Body image development within the family

You may have already heard of Attachment Theory, a concept developed by psychologist John Bowlby.[4] Its main premise is that, as part of our strategy for survival, people are born with an innate need to form emotional bonds with their parents and caregivers. This need for attachment continues throughout the lifespan, with early attachment experiences strongly influencing adult relationships with friends, partners, family and colleagues. Attachment Theory is particularly useful in helping us understand the role of parents and caregivers in developing children's body image, which sets the stage for how we feel about our bodies for our whole lives. Indeed, the very first attachment needs we experience as babies are the needs of the body.[5] Attachment Theory, therefore, suggests that if you struggle with your body image, an eating disorder or body dysmorphia, there's a possibility that you experienced a threat to your attachment bond and a subsequent feeling of loss (real or symbolic) when you were growing up, which could not be articulated. Instead, your body may have become a means of expressing what could not be said, or it may have become central to unhelpful means of coping, such as self-harm or disordered eating.

I've worked with many clients over the years who used food as a way of soothing themselves during childhood, and many recalled being punished for sneaking and hiding food and lying about what they'd eaten. This was especially the case for children who were considered to be 'too big'. Most carried a lot of shame around this and shared their story through an extremely self-derogatory lens. Yet, for kids who lack other emotion regulation skills, either due to age, education or lack of resources, food is one of the very few means of self-soothing they have access to, especially if their attachment bond with their parents is insecure. Food often has strong associations with love, comfort and safety. For example, feeding from our mother's breast, or bottle, is one of the very first experiences of comfort we ever have, and both tasting and ingesting food stimulates the brain's reward, or mesolimbic, system, to release the feel-good hormone dopamine. It's therefore unsurprising that food is where many of us turn when we don't feel good.[6] Unlike other substances that people often develop complex relationships with, such as alcohol, nicotine or other drugs, food is something we all have to partake in to survive. It's a lot to ask of an adult, let alone a child, to regulate their intake when it's not only their primary means of emotional coping, but a physical necessity, too. This picture is further compounded when children are shamed or bullied for their appearance, as this heightens their requirement for comfort and safety and, therefore, further increases the risk of developing a pattern of disordered eating.

Good enough care

When babies and children receive 'good enough' caregiving and experience their emotional and physical needs being sufficiently met, their true self can flourish. They feel safe, known and valued, and the foundations of a positive body image are laid down. These needs include being given enough food and shelter, as well as dependability, emotional warmth, containment, trustworthiness, having our emotions and expressions reflected back to us, and a sense of our caregiver being tuned in and receptive to our needs and emotions at least 50 per cent of the time.[7] I just want to reiterate that last bit: you do not need to be perfectly attuned to your child at all times to help them build a secure attachment! That is neither a realistic nor necessary goal for any parent. Indeed, Bowlby's work on Attachment Theory was heavily influenced by Donald Winnicott, a paediatrician and psychotherapist who, in 1953, coined the phrase, 'the good enough mother' (which has since been updated to 'the good enough parent'). He stressed that being 'good enough' is actually very different from being perfect. Winnicott highlighted that the good enough parent is attentive, sensitive and responsive to their children's needs, but as their children grow up, they also recognize that they can't possibly provide everything their child requires all of the time. Contrary to this being detrimental to the child, which many parents fear and subsequently blame themselves for, Winnicott believed that if kids are let down by their parents in manageable, developmentally appropriate ways, it actually prepares them for the imperfection of the real world and helps them to become healthier, more emotionally flexible and robust adults.[8]

If children's needs go repeatedly unmet, however, or if there is a great deal of inconsistency, volatility or neglect, the child's confidence in who they truly are becomes damaged, and they will begin to present a false self to the world. This false self is effectively a psychological mask or defence designed to protect the child from feelings of inadequacy, shame and rejection by allowing others to see only what they believe those others will find acceptable.[9] To some degree, the social rules that we are all conditioned by will lead us to act in ways we understand as being acceptable to the community in which we live. To be completely disregarding of these norms could be considered narcissistic or antisocial. The function of the false self-presentation, however, goes beyond this, and is an attempt to maintain a safe connection with the caregiver because the possibility of losing that connection feels deeply threatening to their survival. For example, Attachment Theory suggests that when a child imitates their parent's dieting or exercise behaviour, they are doing so in an attempt to maintain an emotional connection to that parent.[10] This is especially true if a child has been exposed to an environment in which a specific body type has been revered, in which case they are likely to want to emulate that as closely as possible to feel more acceptable, to belong, and therefore to feel safer.

When kids feel that their bodies are inadequate to their parents, caregivers or broader society, they are often extremely driven to try to change it, conceal it, or otherwise make it more acceptable. This can lead to serious problems if the child finds that they either have to go to extreme measures to achieve this, such as engaging in disordered eating behaviour, or if they have a perceived flaw that can't be hidden or changed successfully, such as weight, scarring or height. In these instances, it can result in the child feeling tortured and hopeless.

The four attachment styles

There are four attachment types. Here's a rundown of how each develops in childhood, and what effect each style tends to have on body image.

1. Secure Attachment

People with a secure attachment style find it relatively easy to be themselves, to give and receive emotional support, to share their emotions and display affection in relationships while maintaining their individuality and autonomy. They're able to work through conflict by maintaining a positive view of their partner while using clear communication and problem-solving to resolve disputes, and can move on from arguments easily. People with a secure attachment style tend to have established a stable sense of self-worth and self-acceptance from their early relationships. When kids receive responsive and attuned caregiving, they're more likely to view themselves positively, which sets the foundations for healthy self-esteem and a positive body image. Securely attached people are also usually more resilient to societal pressures to look a certain way and have healthy ways of responding to personal insecurities related to their body image.

How does it form in childhood?
Children develop a secure attachment when their physical and emotional needs are consistently met by their caregivers. This enables the child to trust in their bond with their parents or

caregiver and provides a sense of love and stability, which in turn gives them confidence to explore and engage with the world around them.

2. Anxious Attachment (also known as Preoccupied)

People with an anxious attachment style long for emotional closeness in relationships but experience intense fear of rejection and abandonment that often leaves them feeling anxious and clingy. They usually have low self-esteem, seek frequent reassurance, are prone to jealousy, and struggle to trust that someone would want to be with them. Because people with an anxious attachment style tend to rely so heavily on validation from others, they are often more susceptible to criticism and self-comparison, which can contribute to heightened anxiety about their appearance. This can exacerbate body image issues, especially if they feel their body doesn't meet societal beauty standards, making them feel vulnerable to rejection.

How does it form in childhood?
Children develop an anxious attachment style when their needs are inconsistently met, and their caregivers are generally unreliable. They feel uncertain about whether they will be looked after and doubt whether they are loveable.

3. Avoidant Attachment (also known as Dismissive)

People with an avoidant attachment style are often self-sufficient, fiercely independent, 'lone wolf'–type characters. They struggle with emotional intimacy and tend to find the emotions of others challenging to sit with. Those with avoidant attachment traits often feel uncomfortable with commitment and emotional vulnerability and are inclined to withdraw from conflict. People with an avoidant attachment style are also more likely to have poor body image, but for different reasons than those who are anxiously attached. Their fear of rejection and abandonment tends to lead them to become overly self-reliant, suppress their own feelings and sense of connection with their body, and instead experience it from an 'outsider looking in' perspective.[11] Because connection feels threatening to them, avoidantly attached people often refrain from discussing their body image concerns, which means that they often go unaddressed. This makes them more susceptible to resorting to unhealthy means of coping, such as food restriction or excessive exercise.

How does it form in childhood?
Kids with unmet emotional needs tend to learn that expressing their emotions is futile and they eventually stop trying. They often feel uncomfortable with their own emotions and the deeper feelings of others and will consequently try to avoid both. This is often the result of having parents who believe in a 'tough love' approach, who minimize, dismiss or ignore their children's feelings, or who are emotionally aloof or absent.

4. Disorganized Attachment (also known as Fearful Avoidant)

People who have a disorganized attachment style crave emotional closeness, but simultaneously fear it, which leads them to behave erratically and push people away. They frequently feel unworthy of love and find themselves acting irrationally in their relationships, making them feel unstable, insecure and like they can't trust themselves. They tend to avoid intimacy and difficult emotions, which often results in them ending relationships prematurely. Those with a disorganized attachment style are the most likely to experience their bodies as problematic and feel dissatisfied with their appearance, which places them at higher risk of developing disordered eating patterns and engaging in body-modifying behaviours such as cosmetic surgery. This is because when a child experiences a caregiver relationship that isn't sufficiently responsive to help them manage the physical and emotional sensations they experience, those sensations remain unprocessed in the body. This then contributes to a heightened preoccupation with the bodily self.[12]

How does it form in childhood?
Children who experience trauma, abuse or neglect often develop a disorganized attachment style. Children who have had to depend on a caregiver of whom they are afraid for their survival commonly develop a disorganized attachment style.

Changing your style

Understanding which of the four attachment styles most relates to you, and how you've come to hold the beliefs you have around other people's responsiveness to your needs, not only provides valuable information you can use to form a secure bond with your own kid, but can also make a significant difference to how you feel about your body.

Even if you currently have an insecure attachment style, it's absolutely possible to change that and reach a place of 'earned security'. Healing your attachment wounds involves increased self-awareness, doing the opposite of what your anxious or avoidant tendencies compel you to do, reviewing your beliefs about relationships, improving your communication skills, and surrounding yourself with people with healthy boundaries. Becoming more secure will help you feel less anxious or avoidant in relationships, both with yourself and others, which is a critical step in moving towards body acceptance. This is because you will no longer feel like you have to be anything other than what you are to be loved, valued and worthy.

While changing your attachment style is generally approached through the lens of how you operate in romantic relationships, with an emphasis on experiencing secure attachment experiences in those close attachment bonds, please rest assured that if you're not in a relationship, research has shown that you can still change your own attachment style of your own volition if you choose to.[13]

Is body image a social anxiety issue?

Our ability to identify similarities and differences is what gives us our capacity to problem-solve and make judgements about all sorts of things. It's something that makes us distinctly human, but it also makes us susceptible to self-criticism and sensitive to the potential judgements of others. Our awareness of how we look significantly impacts our experience of simply being in society, particularly if our body doesn't fit society's ideal body type and is more likely to be perceived as 'different'. Fostering a positive body image in kids is, therefore, really important. But it's not always easy.

As we've just discussed while thinking about Attachment Theory, developmental theorists believe that the images we hold about our bodies begin to form when we are just babies and create the basis of our sense of self. From just two months of age, babies are aware of their bodies through their sensory experiences of being held, fed, touched, cleaned and changed.[14] These tactile sensations help the baby to develop a sense of where their body ends and another's body begins, the first step in developing a body image. Research also shows that children are aware of other people's judgements and will modify their behaviour accordingly from just two years old, laying the foundations for how they think and feel about themselves for the rest of their lives.[15] Indeed, in 1902, the sociologist Charles Horton Cooley shared his concept of the Looking-Glass Self, a philosophy based on his observations that a child cannot develop a sense of themselves in the absence of others to reflect that self back. He famously noted, 'I am not who you think I am; I am not who I think I am; I am who I think you think I am.'

His theory highlights how what we come to know and believe about ourselves is the result of the attitudes, reactions and judgements of those around us. For example, imagine a nine-year-old girl at home enjoying a meal with her family. Her younger sister reaches for seconds, and the conversation continues as normal. However, when she serves herself some more, she notices her parents looking at each other before her father asks her whether she really needs more food. The girl is instantly moved from feeling happy in herself to feeling judged by her parents, negatively compared to her sister, ashamed of her appetite and/or enjoyment of the meal, and self-conscious about her body. Her parents might have looked at each other and asked if she was still hungry for several reasons: money might be tight and they were hoping to save leftovers for the following day; they may have been trying to encourage mindful eating; it could be an attempt to relieve their own anxiety about her weight; or something else entirely. But it's what the girl herself *thinks* their reason is that has the greatest impact. Now that there's a dissonance between what she felt about her body and what she now perceives her parents to think, she will do what she can to align her internal and external worlds by changing her behaviour. Depending on the robustness of her body image, self-esteem and relationship with food, she might simply think twice before she has seconds next time, or it could lead her to engage in disordered eating behaviours such as hiding or restricting food.

Body image in puberty

Concerns about what other people think and where one fits in the world tend to escalate for most preteens and teenagers as they approach and then navigate puberty, and this period can be particularly challenging for many kids. In his 1865 classic children's novel, *Alice's Adventures in Wonderland*, Lewis Carroll captures the trauma and struggle that many kids face in transitioning from childhood to adulthood. Alice finds herself repeatedly too big, then too small, to enter the garden. This unsettling fluctuation in body size is in response to her decisions around whether or not to consume mysterious food and drink, as instructed by the 'eat me' and 'drink me' labels. Invariably, she would then have to face the consequences of her actions,[16] much as we do, having been subjected to the huge buying power and political influence of mega-corporations in both the pharmaceutical and agricultural industries.

Later in the story, Alice loses control of certain body parts, such as her neck, which extends to a ridiculous length, and she is also faced with a variety of unsolvable puzzles, potentially symbolizing the loss of control and uncertainty that bodily changes during puberty present, along with the frustrations of a world that doesn't make much sense. I think many of us can relate to Alice's frustration and confusion of trying to fit in in the world, especially in a physical way; being told that how we look and what we weigh is in our control, and yet finding it largely uncontrollable.

How the brain builds body image

From a neurological perspective, relationships and the environment serve as the scaffolding for the healthy development of our central nervous system, which is linked to a region of our brains called the parietal cortex. This part of the brain is central in forming body image, allowing us to create a map of our body via sensory experiences. This map provides the basis of how you and your child ultimately see, think and feel about how you look.

The role a child's body image plays in both their mental and physical health, and indeed their experience of life, should not be underestimated. Research suggests that at every developmental level, how we feel about our bodies is a stronger predictor of self-esteem than any other variable, and that a healthy body image forms the basis of our sense of self and identity.[17]

A moment to reflect

I invite you to pause for a moment, take a breath, and consider what comes to mind when you think about your own body image.

* *Where does your mind take you?*
* *What does it focus on?*
* *Does an image of your whole body and how you feel about it or a particular part of your body come to mind?*
* *Are there parts that you like?*
* *Parts that make you cringe?*
* *Parts you rarely think about?*
* *What lens are you looking through when you think about your body? Do you tend to focus on what you see, how you feel, what you think or how you behave towards your body when you think about your body image?*

Write down your answers. Even if you're reading this book because you're more concerned about your child's wellbeing than your own, hold in mind that the way you see your body probably has a big impact on how your kid sees theirs (especially given that they may well grow up to have a body that's very similar to yours). It's also usually far easier to work with our own thoughts and feelings than someone else's, and doing so might mean that the body shame hot potato finally stops being passed down from one generation to the next.

Acceptance and commitment

You might recall that I introduced the concept of 'hooks' in the introduction. This idea comes from a model of therapy called Acceptance and Commitment Therapy, also known as ACT.[18] It's a behavioural model I draw on regularly in my clinical work, and many of my clients find it a useful approach given that it helps us to relate differently to upsetting or difficult thoughts and feelings. It also enables us to be more present and able to choose how we respond to what is showing up inside us. This allows us to act in ways that feel more aligned with the person we want to be and what matters most to us, regardless of what is happening inside. ACT encourages us to be more psychologically flexible in six different ways:

1. Contacting the present (being in the moment)

Being present in the here and now is notoriously hard, but we can improve our ability to notice what's happening in the present moment by developing our mindfulness skills. In doing so, we can notice what is showing up for us both externally, in the environment around us, and psychologically, in our internal world. Becoming more aware of our present moment is a powerful tool because it puts us in a position of consciously choosing how we wish to respond. This is in contrast to reacting in a subconscious way, which is usually driven by our attachment-related fears and needs.

2. Defusion (creating psychological space between you and your thoughts and feelings)

Defusion refers to creating distance between ourselves and our thoughts and feelings. It enables us to observe our internal experiences with curiosity and a non-judgemental stance and allow them to pass by in their own time rather than getting enmeshed with them. Steven Hayes, a clinical psychologist who developed Acceptance and Commitment Therapy, coined the phrase 'cognitive fusion' to describe how we can become entrenched with our thoughts and perceive them as fact rather than the collection of words or images that they really are. When this happens, we refer to those internal experiences as hooks, because we literally get caught up on them. Defusion is, therefore, the means by which we disentangle and effectively let things go. An example of cognitive fusion is when someone has the thought, 'I'm ugly and unattractive' and whole-heartedly believes this thought to be a hard fact, rather than recognizing it as a passing thought or symptom of self-criticism. Defusion techniques enable us to create distance between ourselves and the thoughts or feelings that show up inside so we can acknowledge them more objectively for what they are: a momentary experience, rather than a literal truth.

3. Acceptance (making space for your internal experiences)

Acceptance here signifies accepting our experience as it is without trying to change it or avoid it. It means leaning into painful, distressing, uncomfortable or upsetting thoughts, feelings, memories, sensations and urges rather than trying to get rid of them. It doesn't mean that we start liking these experiences or that we stop wishing they weren't there, but it does mean we stop trying to push them away. Doing so frees up our energy to do more of what matters to us, including getting our needs met in healthy ways.

4. Values (clarity on what matters most to you)

While most people think they know what is most important to them, the majority have never taken the time to really think about it, and even fewer have considered what living in line with those values would actually look like. Having clarity on our values puts us in a much stronger position to act in ways that feel consistent with who we want to be. This is fundamental to living a life that feels meaningful, fulfilling and aligned. We'll be exploring your personal values and specifically how they connect with your body image in Chapter 2.

5. Committed Action (acting in service of your values and who you want to be)

Committed action means *acting* in a way that chimes with our values regardless of what shows up for us inside. So, for example, you might notice anxiety and judgemental thoughts about yourself when you look in the mirror, but you say something positive about your body out loud in service of your values of self-acceptance and being a positive role model to your kids. In doing so, you are allowing the thought to be there without getting enmeshed with it or allowing it to dictate how you behave because you are using your values as your guide.

6. The Observing Self (pure awareness)

When we think about our mind, we tend to think about it as a single entity, but it actually has two distinct elements. There's the thinking mind – the part that generates our thoughts, memories, beliefs, plans, fantasies and judgements – and the observing mind – the part that's aware of all of these things going on inside you. As we go through life, our thoughts, feelings, bodies, roles and so on change, but the you that's observing remains the same throughout your whole life.[19] In practice, this might look like calmly observing your feelings of sadness, or anxiety or loneliness, without allowing those feelings to define who you are or how you behave.

Hooked on weight

Often when I ask people what comes to mind when they consider their own body image, they will tell me how they feel about their size or weight. This is usually accompanied by a crumpled face as they share their sense that their body is unattractive, 'too big' or 'overweight'.

Over what weight? I sometimes wonder, knowing that the answer to this question is often rooted in the fact that, in the

Western world, we are deeply embedded in a weight-centric medical system that randomly categorizes us according to body mass index (or BMI). I say randomly because this scale was never actually intended to measure health. It also wasn't created by a doctor, but rather by a Belgian academic called Adolph Quetelet in the early 19th century. Quetelet believed that the social ideal of a population could be determined by the characteristics of the average man, *l'homme moyen*, and that one could pinpoint this ideal by figuring out the population's mathematical mean. The resultant formula, a person's weight in kilograms divided by their height in metres squared, became known as the BMI scale. Remarkably, Quetelet was very clear that this formula was designed to measure populations, not individuals, and that it should not be used to assess an individual's body composition or health status. And yet here we are, 200 years later, still using it to evaluate individuals' health, size and associated value and morality worldwide. We've been taught we are worth less if we weigh more. BMI is also widely used to gatekeep access to various medical treatments and services. What makes the BMI scale's centrality in the way we assess our health all the more alarming is the fact that the studies it is based on were so racist. Based solely on the statistics of white European participants, by the turn of the century, it was used not only as a measurement of fitness to parent, but also for the scientific justification of eugenics; the immoral theory of 'racial improvement' that supported the sterilization of people of colour, disabled people, people with learning difficulties and migrants.[20] This is why it's so important that we start to uncouple weight from health and teach kids that health is a complex interplay of physical fitness, mental wellbeing, nutrition, lifestyle choices, environmental factors and genetics, all of which can never be reduced to a number on the scales or simplistic formula.

'Her BMI is normal, but . . .'
Laila's story

Early in my psychology career, I worked with a teenage girl, Laila, who was a very talented netball player. She was on the England development squad and wanted to pursue a career in professional sport. Of Black ethnicity, she told me that she built muscle easily, contributing to her weight being higher than average. The fact that her weight was higher than her white peers is also consistent with research findings that Black women tend to have more bone and muscle mass but less fat as a percentage of body weight compared to white women.[21] Laila came to work with me because her coaches were concerned that she wasn't eating properly, though she initially shrugged their concerns off. As our work evolved and her trust in the therapeutic relationship developed, it became apparent that she was struggling with a serious eating disorder that involved her heavily restricting calories, skipping meals, binge eating, purging, overtraining, abusing laxatives, and even limiting fluids. It was both astonishing and deeply concerning that she was able to still train and perform at the level she was given how malnourished and destabilized her body must have been.

Laila's BMI proved problematic on two levels. Firstly, despite losing weight, not only did the severity of her eating disorder go largely unnoticed because her weight never dropped to a threshold level, but her weight loss and increasing leanness were actually applauded. Secondly, as the daughter of a mother who was herself a professional dancer and held extremely rigid dietary rules and fatphobic beliefs, Laila felt unacceptable, unattractive and unworthy because of her higher weight, despite her family supporting her sporting aspirations. Her efforts to control her weight in an attempt to connect with her mother not only jeopardized her sports career but, far more importantly, her health. It's all very well telling our kids to ignore things that don't apply to them, in the way that BMI didn't apply to Laila. But when morals around weight and size are so deeply woven into the fabric of our society in such an unquestioning way, it's too much to expect young people not to be impacted by them. This client's experience was a worrying example of how eating disorder symptoms that would normally be a cause for great concern in a thin-bodied person are either ignored or actively encouraged in those who have a higher weight or BMI. It highlights why it's so important to focus on a person's behaviour and biomarkers rather than what they look like when assessing health concerns. That goes for adults as well as kids.

Your relationship with weight

If you notice that part of the story you tell yourself about your own, or your child's body, relates to being over, or indeed under, a certain weight, be curious about where that belief has come from and how well it really serves you or your kid. How you feel in your body and how they feel in theirs is a far more reliable indicator of your own and your child's health than a number on a scale, whether that be weighing scales, measurements or BMI. A systematic review of ninety-seven studies exploring death rates and weight found that, statistically, people who fall into the 'overweight' category on the BMI scale actually live 6 per cent longer than those who fall into the 'normal' category.[22] As is so often the case with medical 'facts', the conflation between high weight and poor health outcomes is unsubstantiated, rooted in racism,[23] and a fine example of intelligent guesswork becoming undisputed fact. So, at the very least, take the scale with a pinch of salt and remember that your and your child's healthy weight could fall anywhere on the scale of thin to fat.

Aside from our acceptance of the BMI scale as a basic truth, it's not surprising that we so often associate body image with size and shape, because we're reminded of its importance every single day. The weight loss, wellness and beauty industries are well aware that capitalizing on people's discomfort with themselves brings big gains. It's within these industries' interest to keep us feeling unhappy with ourselves, and what better way to do it than to sell a product that doesn't work and blame its failure on the consumer so that they keep coming back for more?

It makes me both sad and angry at the consumer 'health' industry to see people blaming themselves for being unable to control their bodies in the way big corporations tell us we 'should' be able to, despite so much evidence that it's difficult, if not impossible, for the vast majority of people. While research results vary, studies show that between 80 and 95 per cent of dieters will not only regain whatever weight they've lost, but will often end up at a higher weight than they began with.[24] What's even more devastating is that the very behaviours we're encouraged to engage with (dieting, over-exercise, health obsession, etc.) paradoxically worsen our health by destroying our intuition and trust in our bodies to tell us what they need.

Novelist and poet John Berger summed this up perfectly when he said, 'The publicity image steals her love of herself as she is and offers it back to her for the price of a product.'

I'm aware of the gendering of this quote and its implication that only females are susceptible, but having recently watched all four dragons on the Channel 4 entrepreneurship show *Dragons' Den* make significant offers on a make-up brand for men, War Paint, it's clear that no one is exempt. Research into eating disorders in boys also confirms this, with the National Eating Disorder Association estimating that one in three eating disorder sufferers is male. Marketing companies know that insecure people buy more stuff, and beliefs about the relationship between health and body mass index (BMI) only serve to compound further our insecurities around how we, and our kids, look and what we weigh.

Beyond weight and size

Body image and having confidence in our bodies is, however, about so much more than size and weight. How we think and feel about our bodies involves our relationship with our height, complexion, skin colour, the shape of our features, the size of our genitals, the texture, placement and abundance of our hair, the tone of our voice, scars, lumps and bumps, posture, and how your body smells and sounds. It's a sad reality that so many of us have grown up believing that, in order not to be a target of ridicule or discrimination, we have to change ourselves rather than dismantle the oppressive systems that enable these injustices to continue.

'This is not my shame to carry!' Sophie's story

One client I worked with, a sixteen-year-old girl called Sophie who was in recovery from anorexia nervosa, told me that her mum was constantly nagging her about her skin. While Sophie was very relaxed about the occasional outbreak of spots she experienced, attributed them (seemingly quite appropriately) to hormonal changes, and trusted that her skin would clear up in time, her mum was clearly terrified Sophie would be scarred for life. It was apparent that her mum had quite a strained relationship with her own body, was frequently dieting herself, and placed a huge amount of importance not just on her own appearance but also that of her daughter. Sophie shared her sense that her mum feared other people would think she looked dirty and unhygienic because of her skin breakouts and that this would reflect badly on her mum. In her completely understandable attempt to protect both herself and her daughter from the pain of rejection and criticism she herself was fearful of, Sophie's mum would make a stream of unhelpful comments about her skin, bombarding her with several potential 'remedies', many of which had been gleaned from unqualified wellness influencers and special offers at the local health store, and had little clinical evidence supporting their efficacy. She would also frequently recommend that her daughter visit a dermatologist for advice and offered to pay for any treatment required.

As well as helping her to stay steady in her eating in the face of this criticism, part of my work with Sophie involved helping her set boundaries around conversations about her skin so that she could retain a strong connection with her mum without internalizing her insecurities. It's so easy as an adult to transmit our fears to children, but in doing so we can unintentionally pass on the struggles, injustices and stigmas that we have suffered from. Being reflective about our own positioning will help to ensure that you're aware of what has influenced your own body image and beliefs about bodies generally so that you can make a mindful choice about what you want to pass on to your kids and how best to support them. Remember, this is not about finding blame. None of us get to choose the culture we are born into, the influences we're subjected to as kids, nor the intergenerational trauma that we inherit, and that includes our own parents and grandparents. This is about developing compassion and understanding, which in turn empowers us to choose how we want to move forward.

I remember when I was a kid I hated my freckles because people said I looked like Spuggie from Byker Grove, a bolshy redhead with a big attitude, not the pretty, conforming, perfect girl I desperately aspired to be thanks to some heavy-duty social conditioning. When we were around fourteen, my friend Ruby told me that I was too spotty to be a model and told another friend, Becky, that she was too fat to be a model, as if being a model was the only thing anyone would ever aspire to be. The sad truth was that, back then, I desperately wanted to be picked up by a modelling agency because I was convinced that that would mean I was really worth something. It was a reflection of just how highly physical appearance was valued and how it didn't really matter how kind, caring, smart, funny, entrepreneurial, sporty, empathic, determined, creative or loving you were; being thin and pretty was what mattered most.

Incidentally, years later, I rather surprisingly did end up on the front cover of a few health magazines and even featured in *FHM* and *GQ*, having made a name for myself in the fitness world. But, being totally honest, perhaps I wouldn't have if I hadn't spent several years eating in a disordered way to keep my weight down as a result of all those harmful early experiences. Indeed, by far, one of the most impactful and memorable moments of my entire childhood involved being weighed along with the rest of my class at the school sanatorium, and experiencing the most enormous shame as my weight was called out in front of everyone and then compared by my two best friends, both of whom were much lighter and daintier than I was. I remember that number as though it had been branded onto my soul with a hot stamp. To this day, I have a visceral reaction to discussing my weight with others, such was the level of judgement attached to that quite irrelevant number. I can only imagine how my friends who were bigger and heavier than me might have felt.

What is a positive body image?

So far, we've examined body image and its influences, but what actually constitutes a positive body image? Researchers in the fields of psychology and health sciences generally agree it includes the following dimensions:

- Feeling happy and relaxed with how your body actually is
- Feeling content with how you look

- Appreciating your body and the things it can do
- Recognizing that there's no such thing as a perfect body
- Rejecting those societal standards or ideals around physical appearance that don't serve you
- Understanding that who you are is more important than how you look
- Knowing that your health is more important than how you look[25]

It sounds simple, right?! And, in some ways, it is. Through my own experience and work as a fitness professional and psychologist, I've been fortunate to walk alongside thousands of people of all ages as they work towards a more peaceful relationship with their bodies. That experience has allowed me to develop a template for what actually works in helping people shift from a place of self-disgust to a place of self-compassion and acceptance, and this is what I'd like to share with you in this book and help you integrate via the exercises in each chapter.

EXERCISE

Body Confident You

A simple but impactful exercise to help you unhook from painful or unpleasant thoughts about your body is called 'I'm noticing I'm having the thought . . .'

Start by choosing a thought that you find particularly repetitive or troublesome. It might be something general, like, 'I look dreadful,' or more specific, such as, 'I have horrible legs.'

For thirty seconds, repeat that thought over and over in

your head, or out loud if you feel comfortable, and notice how it makes you feel.

Next, repeat the same process again, but this time, preface your thought with, 'I'm having the thought that . . .' So, I might say, 'I'm having the thought that I look dreadful.' Again, notice how you feel.

Finally, repeat the process again, but this time, preface your thought with, 'I'm noticing I'm having the thought that . . . (I look dreadful).' Repeat this statement for thirty seconds and note how you feel.

You may well notice that with each new statement, the thought loses its power, and you feel less entangled with it. This exercise helps you put some distance between the observing part of yourself, and the thought. It's in the space between that we have the opportunity to recognize whether this is a helpful thought for us to dwell on, and if not, how we want to respond instead.

As with most things, these strategies take practice, so try using it each time you notice a negative thought about your-self showing up by saying, 'I'm noticing I'm having the thought that . . .'

EXERCISE

Body Confident Kid

Emotional tolerance is an important skill for kids to learn, and there's a metaphor I find especially useful in helping children aged nine and upwards build a sense of resilience for their internal experiences.

First, explain to your kid that their thoughts, feelings and emotions are a lot like the weather, and they are like the sky. The sky can contain all sorts of different types of weather, including rain, sleet, snow, wind, thunder, lightning and clouds, and the sky is unharmed by any of it. In time, the weather always changes.

Then, invite your kid to doodle a picture of their own sky and some of the cognitive and emotional weather they experience. They might want to draw different types of weather and label them with specific thoughts or feelings, including those they have about themselves.

This can be a useful way of reminding your child that it's okay to experience lots of different types of internal weather, and even when it's not the weather you'd most like, such as torrential rain or gale-force winds, with the right tools and equipment, you can make space for it until it passes.

EXERCISE

Body Confident You and Kid

'Urge surfing' is a simple but effective technique that's really helpful in building our tolerance for difficult thoughts, emotions and feelings, including around how we look. It encompasses mindfulness, defusion and acceptance skills because it encourages us to be present with what we're experiencing inside, allow that experience to be there without trying to change it or push it away, and recognize our internal experience as something that might feel uncomfortable, but that ultimately can't harm us. Thoughts, emotions and feelings tend to rise and fall a lot like waves, and the more we're able to ride those waves like we would on a surfboard, the less they tend to pull us around and get us in a spin.

To practise this idea, I'm going to invite you and your child to set a timer and try not to swallow for one minute. As you read this, notice what thoughts or feelings show up for each of you. There might be some anxiety, trepidation and self-doubt; try to make space for whatever shows up inside.

When you're ready, go ahead and start your minute of no swallowing. Notice what happens in your body, and also what thoughts pop into your mind, and invite your kid to do the same. You might notice your mouth filling up with saliva and an urge to get rid of it. Or you might notice thoughts about looking silly if you dribble. Try to be curious about those thoughts and feelings and keep going. Be aware of how your thoughts and feelings change as the minute progresses. Does the urge to swallow intensify, stay the same or dissipate over time? There is no right or wrong here. The only aim is to notice and allow your experience to be as it is.

At the end of the minute, whether you managed not to swallow or not, congratulate yourself and your child for leaning into something new. Then think about how you can apply the same technique when an urge to respond in an unhelpful way to negative thoughts about yourself comes up. Can you surf those, too, and allow them to dissipate in their own time like a wave?

KEY REFLECTIONS

- Our body image is a multifaceted mental construct based on how we see ourselves and how we think others see us.

- The building blocks of our body image start being laid down from the moment we're born, and arguably even earlier, as our interactions with our primary carers build our understanding of ourselves as a separate, physical entity.

- The quality of our early interactions and several important environmental influences heavily shape the lens through which we see our bodies and how we think and feel about them. These key early relationships, especially with our caregivers, influence our sense of self-worth and safety, which in turn determines the security of our attachments. If a child experiences a secure attachment, they are more likely to develop a positive self-image, including body image. If they develop an insecure attachment, they may develop a negative self-perception, potentially impacting their body image as a central part of overall self-esteem.

- Helping your child develop a secure attachment doesn't require parenting that is perfect. A secure relationship is fostered in a supportive, emotionally responsive, openly loving and largely positive environment, with a fair amount of consistency.

- When the stories we're told about our bodies, and bodies in general, have been present from when we were young and reinforced by societal narratives, it's not surprising that we tend to become fused with these ideas and accept them as hard truths, without ever questioning their validity or usefulness. The purpose of this book is to help you disentangle from those stories that don't serve you so that you're free to choose new, more peaceful ways of relating to your body. In doing so, you will also change the stories passed down to your kids.

CHAPTER TWO

Fit Your Own Mask First

'Even I don't wake up looking like Cindy Crawford.'
Cindy Crawford, supermodel

If you've ever flown in an aeroplane, you'll have heard a safety briefing in which the flight attendant advises you to fit your own oxygen mask first in the event of pressure loss in the cabin. The reason behind this is that you won't be able to help others effectively if you run out of air yourself. I like this as a general metaphor for self-care and helping your children develop a more positive body image than you might have, but with one caveat: it's best not to wait until you're in an emergency situation before attending to your own needs and doing your own inner work!

If the idea of doing inner work evokes images of mystical trances and therapies or silent retreats in exotic locations, rest assured that there are simpler ways of gaining personal insight. Ultimately, inner work is a form of compassionate and deliberate self-reflection through which we can get to know ourselves and let go of harmful ways of thinking, behaving, relating and coping.

It's far better to begin this introspective work as early as you can so that, with a bit of luck (because no one's physical or mental health is entirely within their control), neither you nor your kids will require emergency intervention.

If you've struggled with your body image most of your life, you may believe that that's unlikely to change and that you're better off hiding it as best you can and focusing on helping your children have a different experience. Believe me when I say, I understand. But, at the same time, I'd invite you to consider the possibility that you can feel very different about your body without having to change anything about it. The prospect of being at peace with your body, let alone actively happy in the skin you're in, without dieting, pursuing weight loss or toning up, might feel completely alien, but it is the essence of self-acceptance and a powerful step towards better mental health. It's a shift from trying to change your body to literally changing your mind. It's about seeing your body in a new light, disentangled and healed from the harmful messages that made you feel bad about it in the first place.

It won't just be you who will benefit from your improved relationship with your body. It's very difficult to teach a child self-love and acceptance without having embraced it for yourself first. This is largely because kids learn a lot from what they see, rather than what they are necessarily told. I think of self-love as a skill we can all learn rather than simply a way of being that you either embody or not. If we're taught to relate to our bodies in a harmful way in the beginning and through the messages we receive as we go through life, then mastering this skill may take longer, but it is available to us all if we're willing to invest in it.

Working upstream

You might find it helpful to think about this like a polluted river. Downstream, the water is mucky and murky, and it's not really suitable for anyone to be swimming in. When we try to clean the water downstream, we are fighting a losing battle, because that isn't where the issue stems from. We're only addressing the consequences of the problem, rather than the problem itself. To clean the water once and for all, we need to go upstream, to the source, where the pollution is getting in. In the context of your body image, this means exploring the influences, narratives, experiences and subsequent thoughts and feelings that you both inherited and experienced about your body and those of others around you when you were growing up and as an adult. By working upstream in your own life, you will also help to ensure that your kid has clearer waters to contend with than perhaps you had when it comes to learning to love and accept themselves.

Why is this important to you?

In Chapter 1, we discussed the importance of having clarity over your values. This is especially true when it comes to changing your relationship with your body, because changing a longstanding habit of self-negativity requires a clear sense of why it's important to make this change. Very few of my adult clients, many of whom are in their forties and fifties, have ever done a specific values exercise before coming to therapy, despite our values acting as both a guide and anchor for the actions (and subsequent directions) we take in all aspects of our lives. Teaching kids how to identify their own values, rather than being taught what values they *should* have, is a key learning skill, because it's something we all benefit from. It helps us make decisions, set goals and create a life that is meaningful to us.

EXERCISE

Body Confident You

The following exercise[1] is designed to get you thinking about what really matters in your life and whether you're spending your time and energy on the things you really value, or whether things that you feel you 'should' find important, or that other people value, have taken priority. So, here's what you need to do:

1. Opposite, I have listed some common personal values people tend to hold, compiled based on various factors, including psychological theories, values research and empirical evidence. Spend 30 minutes, or more if you need it, reviewing these values and thinking about what each one means to you.

ACCEPTANCE	FUN	NON-CONFORMITY
ACHIEVEMENT	GENEROSITY	NURTURANCE
ADVENTURE	GENUINENESS	OPENNESS
ATTRACTIVENESS	GOD'S WILL	ORDER
AUTONOMY	GROWTH	PASSION
BEAUTY	HEALTH	PLEASURE
CARING	HELPFULNESS	POPULARITY
CHANGE	HONESTY	POWER
CHALLENGE	HOPE	ROMANCE
COMFORT	HUMILITY	SAFETY
COMMITMENT	HUMOUR	SELF-ACCEPTANCE
COMPASSION	INDEPENDENCE	SELF-CONTROL
CONTRIBUTION	INNER PEACE	SELF-ESTEEM
COURTESY	INTIMACY	SELF-KNOWLEDGE
CREATIVITY	JUSTICE	SERVICE TO OTHERS
EXCITEMENT	KNOWLEDGE	SEXUALITY
FAITHFULNESS	LEISURE	SIMPLICITY
FAME	LOVED	SOLITUDE
FAMILY	LOVING	SPIRITUALITY
FITNESS	MASTERY	STABILITY
FORGIVENESS	MINDFULNESS	
FRIENDSHIP	MONOGAMY	

2. Notice what shows up for you as you consider each one, and whether it's a value that you hold personally or one you feel you 'should' hold but don't. If you notice 'should' thoughts or self-criticism emerging through this process, try to allow those thoughts to pass by in their own time and observe them with kind curiosity. Remember: there is no right or

wrong with this. If you value attractiveness or beauty highly, for example, as with each of your values, be curious about what it is about those values that feels very important. You might value beauty because you associate it with feeling loved and accepted, or with self-care. Or you might value fame because you want to feel recognized and accomplished. In this way, our values can give us helpful insight into our most authentic needs and desires.

3. Categorize the values that resonate most clearly for you into one of three columns: Very Important to Me, Important to Me or Not Important to Me. As you do this, remember that this is based on what really matters to you, not anyone else, and not what you think you ought to find important. It's absolutely fine if you notice you do (or don't!) share values with your family, partner, friends or wider society; the important thing is that you place each value according to your personal relationship with it. Be mindful that you're making your selections based on what matters to you, not what you currently spend the most time on. So, for example, if I held my health as a very important value but did literally nothing in my life in service of my health, that would still go in my 'Very Important to Me' pile. Likewise, if I spend all my time working and earning a large salary but don't value wealth, that will go in my 'Not Important to Me' pile.

	Very Important to Me	Important to Me	Not Important to Me
1			
2			
3			
4			
5			
6			
7			
8			
9			
10			

4. Now, look at your 'Very Important to Me' list and rank each value, from most important (1) to least important (10).

	My Most Important to Me
1	
2	
3	
4	
5	
6	
7	
8	
9	
10	

5. Next, turn to the bullseye diagram overleaf or recreate the image in a journal, and plot each of your top ten values depending on how much you think you are/are not currently

fully living that value. So, if I value the environment and feel I'm living my life as far as I can in service of that value, I'd place that in or near the centre of my bullseye. Or, if I value my fitness but can't remember the last time I did any exercise, that will go on an outer ring.

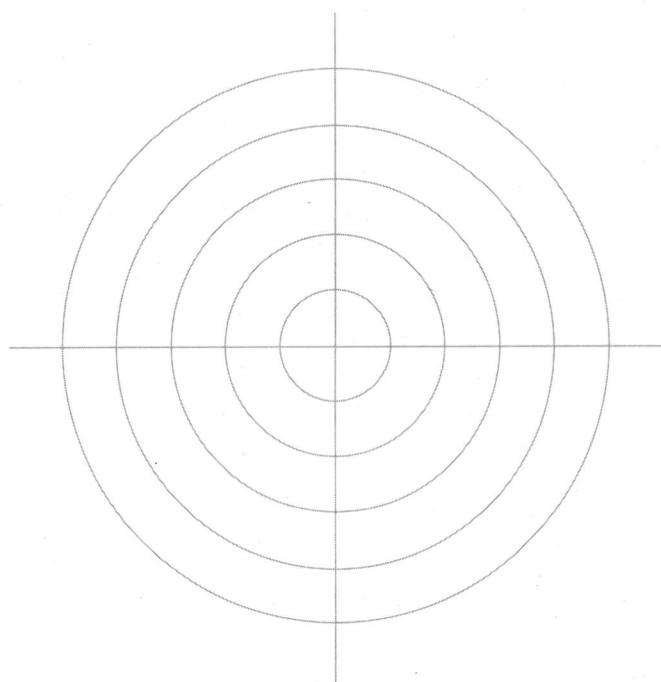

6. For those values that are important to you but currently fall on the outer rings, consider and write down in the table opposite one specific thing you could do to move yourself closer towards living each value more fully. Doing this places emphasis on what action you can take to move you towards what matters most to you, a focus on behaviour that is often

much more within our control than what thoughts or feelings we have. So, if I value self-acceptance but spend my time and energy trying to change myself (the opposite of self-acceptance) by dieting, spending lots of money on cosmetic procedures and berating myself in the mirror, I might start by committing to only verbalizing positive things about myself. Or by making a new habit of applying moisturizer daily so that I feel more caring and loving towards my skin. This might seem like a drop in the ocean, but the aim is to identify small, easy steps you can take that will add up over time, rather than big ones that are less likely to be sustained.

Value	Action

7. Finally, consider if and how your values relate to your body image. If you have a value of being a loving parent, it might be that modelling self-care is in service of that value by teaching your child how to love and respect their body. It will also send them the message that treating your body kindly and body acceptance is the norm, that it's good to appreciate and celebrate yourself, and that they can trust you won't judge them for how they look.

Body Confident Kid

A useful question to ask your kids aged 10 years and up to help them think about what really matters to them is to ask them what they would like their friends to say about them at their 21st or 30th birthday party. For younger children, the exercise can be simplified by asking them what they'd like others to appreciate about them at the end of the school year. Remember, it's important that, whatever their answer is, you respect it. If they say something that concerns you, make space for your own feelings and also remember this is a valuable opportunity to explore what really matters to your child and help them find healthy ways of living their values. So, if your child values being popular, as many children do, you might ask them what makes them feel popular, what it means to be popular, how people become well-liked, what feeling they get when they consider themselves to be popular, who they want to be well-liked by, and so on. In this way, we open up the conversation and support our kids in finding their own understanding around their feelings, rather than simply telling them how they should or shouldn't feel and what they should or shouldn't attach importance to.

The impact of diet culture
on your body image

If you're someone in your thirties to sixties, the chances are you grew up right in the midst of something called diet culture. We didn't call it that back then, but diet culture was everywhere, and it was sneaky. We barely knew it existed, and yet it was tightly woven into almost every aspect of everyday living. Diet culture is essentially a societal phenomenon that emphasizes and privileges thinness not only as the ideal body type, but also as a sign of health and moral virtue. Stemming right back to Ancient Greece, where the concept of food and calorie restriction gained popularity as a means of pursuing better physical and mental health, the 19th century saw the concept of dieting shift from a focus on a holistic approach to wellness to a means of gaining social approval via weight loss. In the process, the dieting trend moved away from genuine mental and physical health, instead promoting harmful stereotypes around weight and appearance that associated thinness with goodness. It also pushed the colonial belief that everyone has full control over their personal health, weight and shape, determined by what they eat and how much they work out. As a result, diet culture led to the demonization of some foods while glorifying others, as well as the oppression of those who didn't fit the thin bodily ideal.

Diet culture continues to encourage the idea that fatness is the problem and dieting is the solution, despite a significant body of evidence showing that weight loss is incredibly difficult to sustain long term through dieting, and that even if it wasn't, it isn't always beneficial to a person's health. Indeed, a report published on behalf of the US Department of Health and Human Services looking at the social determinants of health estimated that only 34 per cent of a person's health can be attributed to their lifestyle choices and behaviours, such as what we eat, how much we exercise, or whether we use drugs or alcohol.[2] It makes sense, of course, to focus on those aspects that are in our control, while remembering that eating a healthy, balanced diet and engaging in regular physical activity is no guarantee of a specific weight for most people. Regardless, research findings suggest that a much greater percentage of our health can be attributed to factors that are often out of our control, such as our environment, housing, food access, transportation, social services connections and, the big one, access to healthcare.

The quality of healthcare we receive is, paradoxically, strongly influenced by our body size, given that medical professionals aren't immune to diet culture and, therefore, often hold stigmatizing beliefs about weight. It stands to reason, then, that bigger-bodied people have poorer health outcomes when they don't receive the same healthcare provision as smaller-bodied people. I remember putting a post about inequalities in healthcare on my Facebook page a few years ago and being inundated with people sharing their experiences of being fat-shamed or stigmatized at the doctor's. One bigger-bodied friend of mine wrote, 'I swear I could walk into my doctor's office with a 9-inch nail through my palm, and they'd still blame it on my weight.' This was following several experiences of being told she needed to lose weight when seeking support for various symptoms over the years, including panic attacks during a particularly stressful time in her work life, unexplained memory loss, tonsilitis, and tendonitis in her forearm. These are all symptoms a thinner-bodied patient might receive treatment suggestions for beyond 'Have you thought about losing weight?' Understandably, my friend, like so many other higher-weight people, eventually stopped going to the doctor altogether, which, of course, skews health data as it pertains to weight.

Constant, unchecked and completely normalized exposure to diet culture unsurprisingly leads many people to engage in a soul-destroying cycle of food restriction, weight loss and regain, frustration, despair, anger, and negative body image, all of which is a far cry from the improved health and self-esteem that said diet culture promised to deliver.

How diet culture ate away at us from birth

Along with genetic factors, we all inherit certain values, beliefs and traditions from our parents, and unfortunately for many of us, that included being handed down toxic diet culture beliefs. To be fair to our parents, they didn't really stand a chance. From the 1960s to 1990s, it wasn't uncommon for mothers to be told to watch their own weight to facilitate a healthy birth, but also to feed their babies less to manage their weight. This meant that even newborn babies ended up being restricted by well-meaning parents and doctors who thought they were doing the right thing. Concerns about children's weight tend to escalate even further from the age of two onwards, as the correlation between a child's size and their eventual adult weight increases. This is despite research showing that childhood BMI is a poor predictor of adult health and that many higher BMI adults were not high BMI children. Data also suggests the strongest predictors of weight gain in children are weight-based teasing and being put on a diet.[3] This is because, just like for adults, restrictive dieting and problematizing of their weight often leads children into cycles of bingeing and restriction, weight cycling, food preoccupation and a departure from the intuitive, trustful relationship with food that we are born with, all of which, paradoxically, contribute to weight gain.

Indeed, while writing this book, I was queueing up at a petrol station behind a mum and her three kids, each of whom had a chocolate bar and packet of crisps in their arms. I was just thinking how cute and endearingly cheeky-looking the three kids were when their mum turned around and apologetically explained that the family had been poorly recently and barely eaten, so she'd promised them a treat before reassuring me that they didn't usually eat like that. I smiled and told her it sounded like they all needed to get their strength back and hoped they were all feeling better soon, but what I really wanted to tell her was that I wasn't judging her, or her kids for their size, and there was nothing wrong with what they had chosen to eat. It was a perfect, albeit heart-wrenching, example of a mum doing her best to take care of her family but feeling like she was under constant scrutiny because her kids weren't thin.

If you grew up in an environment where your weight, size or appearance were criticized and you felt ashamed of your body, or you witnessed other people's bodies being criticized, it's completely understandable that you'd want to protect your kids from suffering in the same way. Add to that protective instinct a relentless bombardment of disinformation about the relationship between health and weight, and it's not surprising that so many parents endeavour to keep their bigger-bodied child's weight 'in check'. Even now, from toddlerhood onwards, the cultural messaging we receive about bodies supports the idea that fatter bodies are bad and thinner bodies are good. As the late writer and political activist Upton Sinclair ruefully remarked, 'It is difficult to get a man to understand something when his salary depends on him not understanding it.'[4] The diet and wellness industries are big business, and their influence starts young.

Children as young as two have been found to hold anti-fat attitudes, which not only has negative social consequences for larger children, but also leads to poor self-perception in children of all body sizes.[5] Children's attitudes, strongly influenced by those around them of course, play an enormous role not only in the self-esteem trajectory of those kids they hold negative attitudes towards, but also their own. It's a mistake, then, for parents of naturally thin children to think weight stigma and discrimination aren't a problem for them or won't be in the future. Nobody wants to be part of a stigmatized group, and susceptible kids will go to great lengths to try to get out of or avoid becoming part of one. Exposure to body prejudice, whether direct or indirect, therefore puts children of all shapes and sizes at risk.

Part of the work in changing your relationship with your body and forging a new path for younger generations is harnessing the courage to look deeply inside yourself at the messages you've internalized over the years. For example, the reason why kids (and adults) hold value judgements on body size in a way that they might not for other visible differences can be at least partially explained by attribution, a theory which was first proposed by social psychologist Fritz Heider.[6] It describes the fact that people generally endeavour to work out *why* something has happened, either to themselves or others, and put the cause down to either external, situational circumstances (over which we have little to no control), or internal, dispositional factors (over which we do). When we apply this to body image, it suggests that when people view someone else's negative attribute as being under personal control (an internal fact), they're more likely to stigmatize that individual than if the attribute were considered uncontrollable. So, while we wouldn't necessarily cast negative judgement on someone because of how tall they are, the same cannot be said when it comes to being in a heavier body. That's why, as individuals and as a society, we need to be open to reviewing our own beliefs and experiences about how much anyone can control their weight and use compassionate scepticism and critical thinking when assessing information that might influence our own and our children's health behaviours.

At this point, of course, you may well be thinking: But everyone knows being 'overweight' is bad for your health, right?

Separating fat from fiction in the weight–health connection

Let's pause for a moment and think about how you came to the belief that being of a higher weight negatively correlates with health. Usually, we come to believe something through being repeatedly exposed to it, in a process known as habituation. The first time we hear something, it takes our brains quite a lot of effort to process it, but with each time we hear it after that, we become more and more accustomed, our brain's response diminishes, and unless new, novel elements emerge to challenge our belief, it remains embedded in our brain with very little effort.[7] To put this in context, the likelihood is that you heard your parents' beliefs about weight and health as a child, along with those of your grandparents, teachers, peers, as well as all kinds of media and public health messaging. When we hear consistent messaging of this nature, most kids won't dispute it, let alone explore the actual evidence, and so we come to 'know' things as facts that might actually have little reliable evidence to back them up. For example, being of a higher weight is generally accepted as a precursor to health conditions such as type 2 diabetes, despite the fact that people of all sizes can develop the condition and some larger-bodied people never do. There is evidence to suggest that yo-yo dieting and associated weight fluctuations are linked with the development of type 2 diabetes, and that high insulin levels themselves encourage the body to store more fat, as do certain medications used to treat the issue. It is therefore a two-way street. One study of more than 3.8 million adults found that people who weight-cycled the most were significantly more likely to develop diabetes within the study's four-year follow-up period than those who weight-cycled the least, irrespective of their baseline BMI.[8] Whether we develop a health issue like diabetes is a far more complicated and nuanced process than a simple weight equation.

It's important to remember, then, that weight is just one of many factors that contribute to our health, and you cannot determine the status of someone's health simply by looking at the size and shape of their body. People of high weight can have excellent health markers, just as lower-weight people can experience various health issues. In fact, there is no health condition that high-weight people experience that thinner-bodied people do not. People naturally come in all shapes and sizes and it's often, paradoxically, attempts to change our normal, healthy weight that contributes to people developing unhealthy relationships with food and exercise. That, in turn, can lead to significant weight gain, further perpetuate the stigma that higher-weight people experience and discourage them from engaging in healthy behaviours. The more comfortable we can become with body diversity, therefore, the more accepted people will feel, and the less likely they'll be to engage in destructive behaviours that will ultimately threaten their wellbeing.

Health goals

Surprisingly, many of the most common health goals people strive for today are either based on scant evidence or plain bad science. These include the BMI-based notion of a 'healthy weight', as we discussed in Chapter 1, and the 10,000-steps-a-day challenge. The latter was popularized by a hugely successful marketing campaign to promote an early pedometer device before the 1964 Tokyo Olympics. The idea came from the Japanese symbol for 10,000, which looks like a person walking, so the pedometer itself was named Manpo-kei ('Man' meaning 10,000, 'Po' meaning steps, and 'Kei' meaning metre)[9] Its creator, Dr Yoshiro Hatano, a young academic at Kyushu University of Health and Welfare, sought to encourage the Japanese away from what he considered to be an increasingly sedentary lifestyle. Aside from the handy walking symbol being associated with an easily remembered 10,000 figure, Dr Hatano also rationalized this recommendation by proposing that increasing someone's daily step count from 4,000 to 10,000 would equate to an additional 500 calories per day expenditure. Using more bad science, he therefore predicted that this would help the people of Japan stay slim. So, essentially, even the innocent-sounding 10,000-steps-a-day recommendation is rooted in fatphobia. It wasn't until 2022 that a study published in the *Journal of American*

Medical Association (*JAMA*) directly explored how effective – or otherwise – step-based goals were on our health, including mortality, cancer and cardiovascular disease. This large-scale study concluded that taking up to 10,000 steps a day may be associated with lower mortality and cancer risks. Due to its design, the study could not make causal claims, and it also suggested that any increase in steps, up to 10,000, was likely to be beneficial. Beyond that, the associations were less evident. This is not to discourage anyone from pursuing an active lifestyle, but a useful illustration of how an idea based on zero research can become widely accepted as the global standard for how much we should walk each day, despite the fact it wasn't until 2022 that a paper was published actually assessing its validity.[10]

Similarly, the five-pieces-of-fruit-and-veg-a-day recommendation, derived from a 1991 US marketing campaign set up by a collaboration of fruit and vegetable companies in California (a rather glaring conflict of interest), is one of several different number-a-day campaigns across various countries. Much like the 10,000 steps idea, the number five seems to have been selected simply because it's memorable, achievable and aligns with the number of digits on one hand.[11] This is worth remembering if you notice yourself feeling guilty or stressed about what or how you are feeding yourself or your family. The likelihood is that every individual's body will respond differently to certain nutritional protocols, and many of those recommendations that are now considered gospel truth are based on archaic beliefs or marketing campaigns and are not the outcome of rigorous research, investigation and evidence. Adding fruit and vegetables into your diet and exercising regularly are of course positive health practices, but the message here is to hold rigid guidelines lightly and do what works for you and feels best for your body.

'I was trying to protect them from suffering like I did.' Annika's story

Annika, a mum of two, shared how she was a very slim child whose thin physique was a concern until she gained a lot of weight during puberty. 'They made a big deal of it at primary school, and they put me on Complan, a nutritional supplement, because I was too thin. Then I hit puberty, and my weight became a concern for a different reason.' She explained how most of her family are bigger-bodied, apart from her mum, and that concerns about how her weight was impacting her health plagued her for most of her life. This, she told me, was reinforced by medical professionals telling her that issues such as a painful hip and frozen shoulder were a result of her weight and that she needed to lose weight before any other treatment options would be considered.

Annika, like so many women, found herself on a hamster wheel of weight-loss attempts. 'My entire life, I have dieted, done hypnosis, kinetic food testing, counselling, everything to try to help me with this weight problem, right up until last year when I was on Ozempic [a diabetes medication delivered via weekly injection, which induces weight loss and has subsequently gained huge popularity in recent years]. She described how the pressure to try to lose weight led her to take measures that ultimately harmed her body and metabolism, including having a gastric band fitted that she eventually had to have removed and weight-loss injections, for which at the time of writing, very limited research on their long-term effects exists.

'I'm now fifty-one and I've come to terms with [my body size] and I worry about my health more than I worry about my body,' Annika told me. She shared that having her health markers tested and using the health data monitor Whoop has been helpful for her in realizing that the non-weight-focused measures she has been committed to, such as regular exercise and improving her strength and fitness, have been beneficial to her health. 'I'm a size 18 and my visceral fat is absolutely fine. It's quite freeing.' While exercise, strength and fitness have long been hijacked by diet culture as code for ways to lose weight, it's helpful to remember that these activities have enormous non-weight-related health benefits and that your body might naturally respond to them with weight loss, gain or no change at all.

However, Annika's own battle with her weight made her determined to be a perfect parent, serving her kids only organic food and ensuring they didn't have access to sweets and chocolate, which she felt had been central to her own struggles. 'It went disastrously wrong,' she reflected. 'My daughter's school bus would pick her up from outside Sainsbury's, and she was going into school with a big bag of crisps and fizzy drinks every day in secret. She would lie about it. It was worrying because I could just see her going down the same path as me, eating for joy, sadness and stress; it wouldn't be one biscuit, it would be the whole pack of biscuits. It's just a horrible repeating pattern.'

Like Annika, many parents try to protect their children from the stigma and battles with their bodies that they have faced, using the same harmful approaches that caused them so much suffering in the first place. This is completely understandable because an alternative approach has not been available, and the persistent narrative is that we could all control how we looked if we just tried harder. This is not in any way parents' fault. It's the outcome of a trillion-dollar diet and wellness industry that capitalizes on people's shame and fear around health and weight and convinces us that if we just try hard enough, or if we don't let our kids get fat in the first place, we can control our weight and have perfect health. The irony, of course, is that the research shows that the more we try and control our own or our kids' weight through restriction, the more likely we all are to develop disordered eating and ultimately gain weight.[12]

To add further complication, as body-positive (BoPo) and Health at Every Size (HAES) movements have gained traction, diet and wellness brands have appropriated the terms used by these campaigns for their own gain. Research shows that body positivity has not only been commercialized and packaged into services and products for our consumption, but has also deviated from its original, inclusive objectives.

A recent study[13] on how body positivity is represented in physical cultures on Instagram found that only certain bodies were visible in the data: those of cis-gendered (people whose gender identity is consistent with their sex registered at birth), lean, white individuals. They observed a distinct absence of Black, Indigenous, People of Colour (BIPOC), fat/thick/curvy, disabled, LGBTQAI+, gender non-conforming, and older representations. This is concerning given that weight bias and discrimination are strongly linked to other forms of oppression, particularly racism. The health of 'overweight' Black people is disproportionately impacted by the focus on weight-centric healthcare, continuing the racial discrimination from which current-day fatphobia stems. This is important for all of us to recognize, both in terms of its impact on how our own relationship with bodies and appearance is shaped, but also what needs to be done for things to improve on a societal level. We'll explore this more in Chapter 7.

The morality of fat in kids' culture

If you cast your mind back to your own childhood, you might recall reading or watching *Charlie and the Chocolate Factory*, Roald Dahl's beloved piece of children's literature that is bursting with fatphobia and anti-fat messaging. Those messages went completely over my head as a kid despite watching the movie countless times, and this is the insidious nature of anti-fat bias. It sneaks in and infiltrates our belief systems before we are even old enough to realize it has happened.

One of the central themes of the story is a cautionary tale about the seven deadly sins, many of which are symbolized by the children's relationship with food. Most of the children display greed. Four of them were given their just desserts for wanting or expecting too much: Augustus, whose sin was gluttony and who struggled to stop eating; Violet, whose sin was pride and was greedy for chewing gum; Mike, whose sin was laziness, who was too greedy for television to eat at the table; and Veruca, whose sin was greed and who demanded pretty much everything.[14] Charlie, on the other hand, notably thin, is pious in his attitude to food; he makes his annual birthday chocolate bar last an entire month and demonstrates restraint of his desires around food throughout his visit to the factory, despite his hunger – a symbol of esteemed integrity that Willy Wonka handsomely rewards in the end. The narrative strongly reinforces the good/healthy/virtuous versus bad/unhealthy/sinful perspective around food, which can be so damaging for kids.

The virtue-signalling of thinness was also reinforced by the stigmatizing treatment of Augustus Gloop, who was mocked for his stupidity, appearance, immaturity and unworthiness of love and affection. Indeed, the Oompa Loompas' song suggested he ought to change into something that would make other people happy, which was, rather confusingly, fudge![15] What is also curious in this story is that, as consumers, we are invited to judge Augustus for delighting in the very thing we are supposed to be excited by in the book – chocolate – and which Charlie himself longs for more than anything.[16] The Oompa Loompas, meanwhile, make it quite clear who is to blame for the children's greed – the parents of course! With messaging like this hallmarking our childhoods, it's no wonder we're a generation who struggle not only with our own body image but a conviction that we're also bad parents who constantly fall short of the perfect parent expectation.

A focus on workability

Let's take a moment now to reflect on your own experience of controlling your body size, shape, weight, skin colour or physical appearance. How determined were you to change? What motivations did you have? How much effort went into it?

Suppose, for example, you're anything like the hundreds of men and women I've worked with who were desperate to free themselves from weight stigma, shame and health-related fears and simply fit in. In that case, the chances are you could not have been much more motivated or had stronger willpower to change your weight, shape or appearance. If personal responsibility and drive were really that influential on body size and weight, I daresay few people would be in bigger bodies.

Instead, the diet and exercise regimes that were meant to offer you the promised land of self-confidence, acceptance and contentment, almost without exception, result in rebounding weight, self-blame and frustration. Though opinions about the best way to lose weight waver as frustratingly as the needle on the scale, no specific diet plan has been definitively proven to facilitate long-term change without compromising health. That's largely due to our bodies' compensatory physiological mechanisms and remarkable capacity to maintain a stable weight; a set point that is unique to each individual. And the real sting is that what the longer-term research demonstrates is that weight-loss attempts made through dieting (and by that I mean protocols that encourage calorie-restriction or cutting out food groups, rather than a more flexible style of eating that might suit your body, such as generally following a Mediterranean diet, for example) harm your health, because they invariably lead to ping-ponging between rigid restriction and hitting the 'sod it' button. The resultant weight cycling (that is, repetitive ups and downs of weight loss and regain, or the 'yo-yo effect') and the impact of stress associated with experiencing weight stigma are both well-documented to have negative health consequences, independent of weight itself.[17] [18] Both have been found to contribute to increased caloric intake and weight gain, as well as depression, anxiety, poor sleep, low self-esteem and eating disorders.[19] [20]

Like most people, I came to the realization that you can't just white-knuckle your way to sustained weight loss through my own experience. I mentioned earlier that, years ago, I was a fitness trainer on the TV show *The Biggest Loser* and had, purely coincidentally, started filming very soon after reaching my physical peak in a bodybuilding competition. Bodybuilding, even in the bikini class I competed in that demands less muscular definition and leanness than other classes, is still a sport that requires meticulously planned nutrition and training to be ready for a specific event. I had never intended to continue that demanding regime after my competition. But, following the event, I was approached by an agent and was swiftly cast in one of the biggest fitness trainer roles on television. It felt like a dream come true to be given this opportunity at a rare moment in my life when I actually felt good about my body. In hindsight, I realized that was possibly the main reason I got the part in the first place. In that painfully brief snapshot of time, I symbolized society's vision of what fitness looks like, despite it being completely unrealistic even for me. I felt compelled to try to maintain that unnaturally lean physique for several months longer than planned, with fairly disastrous consequences.

One might think that with my training and nutrition background, all the equipment and resources one could ever need, and the motivation provided by five million viewers, it would be a fairly easy task to keep my weight in check. I even had my own fridge on set! All I had to do was maintain what I already had and keep doing what I was already doing. But I literally couldn't. I ended up bingeing, purging, obsessing about food, piling on weight, ultimately becoming the biggest gainer *The Biggest Loser* had ever seen. That confirmed to me once and for all that people's almost universal struggle to lose weight and maintain weight loss had little to do with willpower or motivation and everything to do with the body's hardwired mechanisms for protecting us from famine. There I was, positioned as the fit, lean expert that would swoop in to 'rescue' the bigger-bodied folk from the supposed errors of their ways and enlighten them to a more virtuous way of being, when the reality was, we were all fighting the same futile battle. The only difference was that, veiled in thin privilege, my body didn't give it away.

Choosing another way

For many of the clients I've worked with, being critical and negative about their body and making various attempts to change it feels so ingrained that it often seems like an impossibility it will ever change. This is often the case, even when you know dieting doesn't work for you. If this resonates, I'd like to introduce you to a concept called the Choice Point.[21] This is a model that we use in Acceptance and Commitment Therapy (ACT) to help people identify what is showing up for them internally in the form of thoughts, feelings, sensations and memories. The choice point is the moment where you pause to notice what is showing up inside, and with that mindful awareness can decide to respond in a way that aligns with your values or moves you away from them. Having increased awareness around our internal experiences in a given moment (i.e., being mindful and aware of our thoughts and feelings in the here and now) means that we can make a more conscious choice about how we want to respond. That way, we can decide to accept that the difficult thoughts or feelings are there, even if we wish they weren't, and, rather than trying to avoid them, consciously make space for them and act in a way that aligns with our values and long-term goals. This is in contrast to when we aren't very aware of what's happening inside us, which is when we are most likely to react subconsciously in ways that don't always serve us. When we react rather than consciously respond, we're more likely to behave in ways that are unlike who we want to be, moving away from our values, in an attempt to avoid the difficult thoughts or feelings we're experiencing. We call this experiential avoidance. We'll work through the choice point concept using an example from your own life in the exercise that follows.

Body Confident You

Spend a few minutes answering the questions below to help you identify some of the strategies you tend to default to when faced with challenging thoughts or feelings. This will help you to notice them quickly when they do show up, giving you a chance to press pause and consider your Choice Point. You might also want to remind yourself of the personal values you identified earlier in this chapter so they're fresh in your mind as you work through this exercise.

1. *What are the frequent uncomfortable thoughts, feelings, urges, sensations or memories that you notice show up for you around your body?*

This might include thoughts such as, 'I'm ugly' or 'Why can't I lose weight?', or feelings such as anger, sadness, shame or despair. You might also recall being rejected or criticized in the past. These are the hooks we discussed earlier (see page 36), the experiences showing up inside us that trigger us to act in unhelpful or destructive ways

2. *What do you tend to do when confronted with unpleasant or painful feelings about your body?*

This might include restricting your food, following strict diet rules, wearing clothes that hide your body, bingeing, purging, exercising to 'earn' your food, weighing yourself frequently, calorie counting, spending long amounts of time applying make-up, avoiding social situations, etc.

3. *Do those actions feel like they take you away from or towards the things that matter most to you?*

For example, avoiding going to social events might temporarily neutralize social anxiety, but it could move you away from values of friendship, connection, fun or adventure.

4. *Do those actions stop the thoughts or feelings from coming up again? Or do they just delay them for a short while?*

Do they actually work in the long term?

Once you've answered these questions, you can use some of this information to help you fill in the Choice Point diagram on page 82. Bringing a specific challenging situation you've faced to mind, note down what 'hooks' you recognize showed up for you. Then, under 'away moves', write down any actions you took to try to relieve the discomfort of these hooks. Under 'helpers' you can also fill in those actions that would have helped you to make space for and accept the uncomfortable thoughts and feelings and act more in line with who you want to be. Under 'towards moves' fill in how you would like to respond to the challenging situation if those hooks were no longer an issue for you and you were acting in line with your values.

CHALLENGING SITUATION

This will be personal to you but could be anything: a social event, weight gain, conflict with a loved one, a hurtful comment, etc.

_____

_____

_____

CHOICE POINT

HOOKS

Difficult or uncomfortable thoughts, feelings, memories or sensations that you notice showing up in response to the challenging situation

_____

_____

_____

HELPERS

Values you want to live by that you can use as a guide. Mindfulness and defusion techniques as covered in this book.

_____

_____

_____

EXPERIENTIAL AVOIDANCE

'AWAY MOVES'

Moving away from the outcome you want, acting ineffectively, behaving unlike the person you want to be.

_____

_____

_____

EXPERIENTIAL ACCEPTANCE

'TOWARDS MOVES'

Moving towards the outcome you want, acting effectively, behaving like the person you want to be.

_____

_____

_____

Getting familiar with what internal experiences you find difficult to make space for and the away moves you use to try to avoid them (whether that be dieting, self-berating, withdrawal, bingeing, drinking, lashing out, or something else) is key to healing your relationship with your body. It will help you to identify what stories you tend to get hooked by, and what you need to work on accepting to live life more in alignment with who you want to be, including being a parent who models body acceptance. This is a different approach to traditional cognitive behavioural therapy (CBT) in which one might aim to challenge, dispute or discredit unhelpful thoughts or feelings we might be having. Instead, in third-wave CBT models like ACT, we aim to accept what is out of our control (including the thoughts or feelings that show up in us), and make a conscious choice about how we wish to respond based not on whether that thought or feeling is *true* or not, but rather on how helpful it is for us to get enmeshed with it. So, instead of getting into a battle with your own mind over whether the other school mums will judge you for having gained weight, you might just reflect on whether it's helpful to you, and in service of your values, to invest time on this thought, or whether there are more constructive actions you can take to help you move towards being the person you want to be.

EXERCISE

Body Confident Kid

The above exercise can also be adapted to help your child (and you) gain a clearer sense of what they tend to do when difficult thoughts or feelings show up for them too.

First, ask your kid what they would like to change if you were able to wave a magic wand: what their life would look like, what they'd be doing, or how they might be feeling differently. This will give you and them insight into both what matters to them and what they feel is getting in their way.

Then, ask your child what they have tried, or perhaps they've noticed you trying, to help them with the problem or difficulty they're facing. You can then think together about how well those strategies have worked and whether they feel like they've moved them towards or away from the things that matter most to them.

The key thing to focus on here is workability, or how well their current strategy is helping them feel the way they want to feel. If it isn't, then you can brainstorm alternatives with your kid, which might include making space for difficult thoughts and feelings and responding to them in a different way.

KEY REFLECTIONS

- Get clear on your personal values and revisit them regularly. This will help guide your behaviour and keep your values at the top of your mind, especially in challenging situations. It might be helpful to write them in a prominent place at home or work or keep them in a note on your phone – anywhere you will see them often.

- When you notice difficult thoughts or feelings showing up, try to press pause for a moment and think about the Choice Point. What is hooking you, and what are you usually inclined to do when these hooks show up? What can you do now that will take you towards your values, rather than away from them?

- Be mindful of the thoughts and feelings that you most frequently get hooked by and try to notice how you have tried to avoid this discomfort in the past. If you can, be curious about what it's like to allow those thoughts or feelings to simply be there, noticing them with curiosity without trying to push them away. What happens to them when you do this? Do they pass? Stick around? Become more or less intense? Notice what happens, taking as non-judgemental a stance as you can.

- When you notice yourself being hooked by thoughts around your body or needing to change your appearance, remember to think about workability. What has worked for you in the past? If you recognize what you usually do (for example, extreme dieting, berating yourself, hiding yourself away or engaging in excessive exercise) doesn't serve you well in the longer term, think about what alternative action you could take that might take you closer to your values in a different way.

CHAPTER THREE

Body Talk

'Our own physical body possesses a wisdom which we who inhabit the body lack. We give it orders which make no sense.'
Henry Miller, author

I'd like to start this chapter by inviting you to make a mental note of how often, over the next twenty-four hours, you hear people talking about bodies, whether in terms of weight, health, dieting, appearance, exercise, skin texture or colour. While I appreciate that I have a particularly keen ear for body talk and undoubtedly have an attentional bias towards it, I'm often struck by just how much we humans talk about our physical selves. In some ways, perhaps this shouldn't be surprising given that it's one of the very few things every single one of us has: a common ground on which we can all share our trials, tribulations and opinions over, regardless of age or circumstance.

Whether we notice how much bodies are spoken about or not, exposure to constant messages about what makes them good, bad, healthy, unhealthy, acceptable or otherwise influences our own beliefs and subsequently impacts how we feel about our own physicality. So, while it's impossible for any of us to control what we hear about bodies all of the time, we can be mindful of how we talk about them, be selective about what narratives we expose ourselves and our kids to, and be conscious about how we choose to respond to less helpful perspectives.

Belonging

Feeling like we don't belong or don't fit in is an almost universal fear. We use many old adages to describe our feelings of being an outcast: the black sheep, a fish out of water, the runt of the litter, a square peg in a round hole, a lone wolf. Each of these metaphors describes our difference from others, often in a way that suggests alienation, inferiority and loneliness.

Hans Christian Anderson's story of the ugly duckling[1] illustrates how powerful the way we speak about bodies and our attitudes towards difference can be. Criticized and ostracized because he didn't look the way a duckling is supposed to look, the ugly duckling suffers from low self-esteem and feelings of inadequacy as a result of his peers' misunderstanding and intolerance of difference. This leads him to withdraw and isolate himself, a common defence strategy. The ugly duckling symbolizes our psychological journey of self-discovery and quest for identity, acceptance and self-worth. Through perseverance and personal growth, he ultimately realizes his value, beauty and sense of belonging despite the narrow-mindedness of the other ducks and animals, who represent unrealistic societal norms and expectations.

Ugly Duckling Syndrome isn't a clinical diagnosis, but it does describe the trajectory people often take when they develop a belief they're unattractive or don't fit in during their formative years. Even if they grow up to be a proverbial swan, ultimately meeting societal standards of beauty like the bird in this story, early experiences of rejection or inadequacy can in any case set the stage for psychological difficulties such as social anxiety, body dysmorphia, self-doubt and pervasive feelings of inadequacy. This highlights why setting a tone of acceptance and appreciation of individuality in your home is so important in helping your child build body confidence.

Around the kitchen table

Let's think about how bodies are spoken about in your home. Usually, when I'm sitting with clients who really struggle with their body image or who are recovering from an eating disorder, they talk about how one or both of their parents grappled with ongoing body dissatisfaction. They also reflect how their childhood home was often filled with diet talk or discussions about the latest exercise regime their parents were embarking on in a bid to bring their bodies into some sort of socially sanctioned line. Others remember the unspoken messages they received at home, from the absence of certain types of foods, the types of bodies that were shown on the walls or the front pages of magazines lying around, or their parents being engrossed in 'earning' their food by religiously monitoring their steps, counting calories, or intermittently fasting. Some of my clients even recall being told that no one would love them if they were fat. We only have to look around us at all the people in all different body sizes walking around in couples to know this isn't true, and the saddest thing of all is that telling kids that they're too big rarely leads to them losing weight, but it does lead to them losing their self-worth.

If this evokes uncomfortable feelings because you realize some of these things have shown up in your own household, maybe even via you, I am sending you the biggest, warmest, most compassionate hug right now. We all make mistakes, all of us are learning as we go, and very few of us, me included, have managed to emerge completely unscathed by the formidable power of diet culture. So, be gentle with yourself. You are doing your best, and that is good enough. Very little is irreparable, and what's really important is what we do with newfound insights. So, if you have a perfectionist part, give it permission to stand down, put your kindly curious hat on, and let's explore where you discovered these ideas yourself.

Breaking bread

In Latin, the phrase *'con panis'* means 'with bread'. It's where the words 'company' and 'companion' originate, and means someone who shares your dining table, who sits next to you and is close enough to be privy to the intimate details of your life. Years ago, when I was going through eating disorder treatment myself, I worked with a dietician called Jane. In one of our sessions, I remember Jane explaining that in years gone by, the way families used to check in on each other was to gather together to eat around the kitchen table. It was the way everyone knew that you were okay, and if you didn't show up to eat, it was a clear sign that something was wrong. Breaking bread together isn't just about eating. It's about looking out for and supporting one another. Perhaps one of the great challenges of the digital era is that communal meals and gatherings, such a vital source of a sense of belonging and kinship, are being edged out in favour of more convenient, remote activities.

While it might not be feasible to break bread together with your family every day, setting an intention to do so at least a few times a week and making those gatherings (even if there are only two of you!) a safe space in which everyone can eat together free of judgement, share food stories and benefit from mutual support, is a great place to start.

Clear your plate! But don't get fat!

Take a moment to think about the questions over the page and notice what shows up for you as you read them. Do they remind you of instances when you were growing up? Are there phrases that strike you, that you or your family members use now? Do they align or jar with your own beliefs? Reflecting in this way will not only help shed light on some of the views you were exposed to during your childhood, but will also help identify what might have been inherited that isn't necessarily serving you or your family well.

- *What types of bodies do I consider to be healthy or unhealthy?*
- *How do I react to media portrayals of diverse bodies?*
- *Do I believe there are 'good' and 'bad' foods?*
- *What do I believe constitutes a healthy diet?*
- *How do I feel about food being left on a plate?*
- *What are my beliefs about comfort eating?*
- *How do I feel about hunger?*
- *Do I speak differently about people based on their body size or appearance?*
- *Are my views on different body types influenced by my religious or cultural affiliations?*
- *How do I talk about my own body, both to myself and in front of others?*
- *How do I feel about the idea of body positivity?*
- *What beliefs do I hold about different body types in romantic relationships?*

For me personally, working in NHS weight management and bariatric (weight loss surgery) services for five years challenged many of the beliefs I held about higher-weight bodies, health, disability, ethnicity and body image. During this time I worked with thousands of very large-bodied people, and what really struck me was that the most common reason people shared for considering this invasive, life-altering and high-risk surgery was often not poor health, immobility or fears over their longevity, as one might expect, but rather because they didn't want to be judged by others, or stereotyped; they didn't want to be an embarrassment to their kids, or feel humiliated when they couldn't fit into public seats and spaces. So many of the patients I assessed had no health issues whatsoever, but were terrified of developing an awful illness because they had been told their weight was a danger to themselves. This begs the question of whether it's the weight itself that's a major threat to health, or the chronic impact of stress that one experiences being constantly told that the only body you have is a ticking time bomb.

The research here is interesting; virtually none of the studies that show a causal link between weight and health control for the impact of stress and weight stigma. However, studies exploring the direct relationship between weight stigma and health found that being exposed to weight discrimination and fatphobia is an independent health risk factor.[2] That means that, irrespective of weight, people who are subjected to weight-based inequalities have poorer health outcomes. One study found that individuals who experienced weight-based discrimination were twice as at risk for chronic stress and associated symptoms, including metabolic issues and inflammation. The researchers concluded that focusing on eliminating weight stigma may reduce the health issues often associated with, but arguably not caused by, being of a higher weight.[3]

What I also noticed during my time working in bariatrics was just how similar many of the patients' childhood experiences were. Many recalled witnessing their bigger-bodied parents jump desperately from one diet to another, or being taken to weight loss clubs or programmes because their own body was deemed to be a problem. Several were bullied at school for how they looked, or were denied food, which evoked immense guilt when they were caught stealing and hiding it. I personally had a few bigger-bodied childhood friends who I remember being paid for every pound they lost; even if only on a subconscious level, the message that sent those kids, and everyone who witnessed it, was that their bodies were so unacceptable, their relatives would literally pay them to change. I doubt many people who have had such a shaming experience of larger bodies growing up, and whose childhood has been hallmarked by a relentless battle to try to lose weight, make it to adulthood without at least some inclination to do whatever it takes to escape that punishment. It's perhaps no wonder that more and more people of all ages are putting themselves on the waiting list to have part of their stomachs amputated, despite the extremely variable long-term outcomes.

How to put boundaries around diet talk

Working on your own language around bodies is one thing, but what do you do when Aunt Joan is round for tea and won't stop talking about her recent weight loss following a juicing plan, or your brother-in-law has just discovered intermittent fasting and wants to share how great he's feeling? Navigating diet talk with friends and relatives can feel like a sticky wicket, so it's a good idea to be prepared.

- Be clear on what your values are around this. You might care deeply that your child develops a peaceful relationship with food and avoids weight-loss diets, which are proven to put kids at risk of eating disorders,[4] but don't feel inclined to debate the ineffectiveness of dieting with your relatives. In that case, focus on your child by saying, 'We don't talk about diets in our house.' If anyone questions why, you can explain that restricting food intake and cutting out food groups increases the risk of kids developing eating disorders. In this way, you honour your value of protecting your child from the harms of dieting, without sharing personal opinions on other adults' dieting behaviour, which may make them defensive.

- Be firm about your family's boundaries around food and bodies so that if a visitor makes a remark about someone else's appearance, weight or food, your kids hear you holding this boundary with a 'We have an agreement that we don't comment on other people's food choices in our house.' If this feels difficult, you can also neutralize the comment. The most important thing is that your child hears you advocating for their body. That might mean saying something like, 'Their body is just fine, and we have no reason to be concerned about their eating or exercise.'[5]

- Give yourself permission to also simply leave the conversation or change the subject if you're dealing with a particularly confronting or defensive person, or if you just don't have the energy for a debate. It's not your responsibility to educate everyone around you; it's a shared task for us all to address as and when we have the resources to do so.

Why the 'O' words are harmful to our health

I rarely use the words 'overweight', 'obese' or 'obesity' in my writing, and if I do, I put them in quotation marks to indicate that these are words used by some but not by me. The reason for this is that, when we look closely at the origins of these words, we find that they're rooted in racism, problematize certain body shapes, and encourage weight stigma and discrimination. This contributes to inequalities in employment and in the quality of both physical and psychological healthcare.

As previously discussed, the standard method of categorizing someone's weight is via the BMI scale; a measure that was never intended to provide information about someone's health, was based only on a white male sample group, and doesn't account for varying body compositions. Yet, despite this, as activist Aubrey Gordon highlights in her book, *What We Don't Talk About When We Talk About Fat*,[6] the subsequent weight categories, including the 'O' words, are used to perpetuate anti-fat bias and make assumptions about people's health status based on their size.

The origin of the word 'obesity' is itself inherently problematic, stemming from the Latin *'obesus'*, which literally translates to the morally laden 'having eaten oneself fat'. Using these words maintains the harmful view that being in a fat body is not only your fault, but assumes that there's something wrong with you. As therapist and co-author of *Beyond a Shadow of a Diet*,[7] Judith Matz, emphasized when I spoke to her for this book, people are told that the marginalization they experience as a result of their body size is in their control, if they would just lose weight. So, it's understandable that kids and adults are still highly motivated to attempt to do so even though the evidence shows that the more people diet, the higher their weight eventually becomes.

So, if the 'O' words are harmful, what descriptors should we use instead? A 2020 systemic review exploring preferences for weight-related terminology found no single term or phrase that is universally accepted across diverse demographics and cultures but that neutral descriptors such as 'higher weight' or 'plus size' are generally preferred by those in larger bodies. The study concluded with the recommendation that for conversations about weight-related health, it's best to ask individuals how they feel most comfortable referring to their body size and then honouring that.[8]

How to have awkward conversations

Some of the most challenging and uncomfortable conversations parents have with their kids centre around bodies. Conversations around sex, private parts, bodily functions, consent, contraception and puberty; these are topics that many adults find incredibly awkward to discuss, often because their own parents avoided it like the plague, too. Looking back, I never had these discussions with my parents, presumably because they also found such subjects difficult to talk about. As a result, I grew up feeling pretty uncomfortable discussing anything to do with bodies at all and also found other people talking about their bodily functions pretty jarring. The problem with this is that if children grow up never talking about bodies, they also grow up never talking about body issues, including health, body boundaries and body safety. If they miss the opportunity to learn that it's okay to say no when Grandma Georgina or Uncle Simon want to give them a kiss and they don't want them to, then how can we expect them to feel confident saying no if more serious physical advances are made towards them that don't feel right? It's important, then, that we learn to make space for our own discomfort and anxiety around having these tough conversations so that we don't end up having to have even tougher ones further down the line.

As a psychologist, and depending on the age of my client, I try to be mindful of leaning into my own discomfort and saying the sometimes hard-to-say words like sex, orgasm, masturbation, discharge, death, racism, scarring and fat, because doing so makes it clear that it's safe for clients to talk about whatever it is that's troubling them. It also reassures them that any feelings of embarrassment or shame will be held gently and compassionately and explored with kindness, respect and curiosity. This is the essence of therapy; building a safe and trusting enough relationship between client and therapist so that together we can shine a light gently over what lies in the shadows. Only then can those parts that have been ignored, rejected and pushed into the subconscious be reclaimed so that we can feel secure and whole again.

In an age-appropriate way, your child requires the same gentle and compassionate curiosity.

Body talk

You can help your kid feel confident about body boundaries and how to keep their body safe in the following ways, which are informed by the American Academy of Paediatrics guidelines.[9]

1. Use the proper names for body parts, including genitals: vagina, penis, breasts and bottom. This may well feel uncomfortable, but that's probably because many of us were given messages that certain body parts were shameful or secret. So much so that they had to be given made-up names, or simply not talked about at all. Kids also need to know which

are their private areas and that those parts covered by a swimming costume should not be looked at or touched without their permission. (In the latter instance, that also includes the mouth.) If your child asks why certain body parts should be kept private, it's important to stay calm to normalize questions about bodies and use simple language that is age-appropriate. For younger children, you might say, 'Some parts of our body are private because they are personal and special, just for you. We keep them private to help us stay healthy and safe.' You can also add that there might be specific times when it is okay and safe for someone to see your private parts, such as when Mum or Dad are helping you wash or visiting the doctor with a parent or trusted adult present.

2. Ensure that family members respect each other's modesty when requested. This includes teaching younger siblings to give older siblings space when needed, laying the foundation for good social behaviour and an understanding of modesty.

3. Teach your kid the difference between 'Okay touch' and 'Not okay touch'. Make it clear it's okay to say 'No' to any form of touch that doesn't feel comfortable, is scary, confusing, painful, is in areas involving their private parts, or that they don't like. Respecting their decision not to be hugged or kissed, even by close relatives such as grand-parents, is important. There are plenty of other ways to show affection or appreciation without being physically intimate, including fist bumps, high fives, thumbs up, or a good old wave. This is essential in instilling body autonomy in your child, teaching them that their body is theirs to make decisions about.

4. Ensure your kid knows that if they experience 'Not okay touches', they should tell you or another trusted adult, and you will be there to listen, support and protect them. This includes if they are inappropriately touched by a trusted adult, which can feel extremely confusing to a child.

5. Try not to assume that having these conversations once is enough, because new situations and potential challenges often arise at different developmental stages. Review body boundaries and what to do if someone makes them feel uncomfortable with touch regularly so that they are well prepared to respond to inappropriate situations should they need to.

Talking to kids about social injustice around bodies

Social injustices around body appearance are real and can significantly impact someone's experience in virtually all areas of life. Numerous studies have shown that people are more likely to attribute positive, moral traits to those they consider to be conventionally attractive.[10] The ugly truth about 'pretty privilege' is that people who are considered attractive are perceived as more intelligent, sexually healthy, mentally stable, warmer and more sociable.[11] On the flip side, it's also not uncommon for people deemed very attractive to feel that others are drawn to them for superficial reasons and, therefore, can be prone to feeling like they lack authentic connection based on more than just their looks. To pretend to ourselves or kids that this phenomenon doesn't exist and that looks don't have any impact is essentially a form of gaslighting, however well intended, in the same way that trying to convince someone that racism, ableism, sexism or fatphobia doesn't exist would be inappropriate. The good news, however, is that by being transparent with your family about societal prejudices in an age-appropriate way, whether it be racial inequality, pretty privilege, weight bias, disability access or trans rights, you simultaneously validate their experience and teach them valuable lessons about fairness and the importance of caring for a range of different communities, including ones they don't personally belong to.

'You're not fat, you're beautiful!' – Jess's story

A client I worked with, Jess, a mum of two girls, shared how sad and angry she felt when her nine-year-old daughter came home from school very upset because one of her classmates had called her 'fat'. Like most parents with a strong drive to protect their young, Jess was instantly compelled to reassure her daughter and try to make her feel better by telling her, 'You're not fat, you're beautiful!' While this is a perfectly natural maternal response, and one that has been heavily conditioned into us thanks to fatphobia, there are more helpful ways to respond to your kid if they get name-called around their appearance.

Firstly, we need to be sure that the words a child has used have been imbued with the same meaning that older generations would ascribe. 'Fat' can, and should, be used as a neutral descriptor, and many children are learning to use it in that way.

Even if you believe your child has been name-called unkindly and you believe they are not fat, reassuring them that they are not perpetuates the idea that being fat is the problem and somehow bad. It also implies that you can't be fat and beautiful.

Rather than reacting to her urge to reassure, Jess took a moment to pause and centre herself before responding. Instead of dismissing her daughter's feelings by trying to convince her she wasn't fat, she said this: 'I can hear how painful it was for someone to call you names like that; it's a really unkind thing to do. Can you tell me more about what happened and how it made you feel?' In doing so, Jess avoided falling into the trap of unintentionally positioning certain body types as bad and something so awful it has to be denied. Instead, she validated her daughter's feeling that the name-calling was unkind and hurtful. It made clear that the friend's behaviour was the problem and not her daughter's body, and she also created a safe space for her daughter to say more about what the incident meant to her.

Kids can only learn to regulate the emotions that we allow them to have, so however painful it is to see them hurting, it is so helpful if we are able to stay open and curious about what they're experiencing rather than shutting their feelings down by telling them they shouldn't feel that way.

Owning our privileges

For many of us, acknowledging our own privileges can be quite an uncomfortable experience. As a slim, white, middle-class, able-bodied woman, I possess characteristics that have undoubtedly opened doors for me, and I'm lucky to be able to take things like fitting in a bus seat or having a public toilet available to me, or not having to think about my race, for granted. At times, owning the advantages I have has been an uncomfortable and sobering experience. That's not to say that being privileged means that you haven't worked hard or haven't faced hardships in your life, but it does mean acknowledging that the playing field isn't level.

While it's been a challenge at times to recognize my unearned advantages, it nevertheless feels vital I do so in order to advocate for a more inclusive society. Most of us have privileges of one description or another, whether age, race, ability status, religion, sexual orientation or socioeconomic status. And we all have a choice as to whether we ignore or deny we have it, accept we do, or go ahead and advocate for those in minority groups. Many age-appropriate resources are available to help you navigate this with your kids, such as kid's podcasts and YouTube videos, young social justice activists, and books on activism for young people.

Why food morality is toxic for body image

I had a slightly unorthodox home situation during my teens in that I continued to live with my step-mum after my dad passed away suddenly when I was fourteen. This was an unexpected and destabilizing time for both me and my step-mum and, unsurprisingly, as I came to terms with my grief back then, I got even more sucked into diet culture. Over the years that followed, I embarked on a whole range of diets, including some really quite extreme ones like the ridiculously restrictive cabbage soup diet and various 'cleanses'. There was also a clear sense of what constituted 'good' and 'bad' food both at home and outside it. Foods were categorized into 'healthy' and 'unhealthy' and I was often congratulated for 'being good' when I was cutting out certain food groups, limiting my food intake, or burning (or 'earning') calories on the treadmill at home. This moralizing narrative wasn't unique to our household; it was almost everywhere at the time.

Of course, there are several problems with this virtue-signalling perspective, which, in my experience, does more harm than good to people's physical and mental health.

Firstly, all foods have nutritional value, can be broken down by our bodies, and contain nutrients that our bodies can utilize. All foods can, therefore, form part of a healthy, balanced diet.

When we start to categorize foods as good and bad, we tend to attach value not only to the food itself, but also to the consumer. We start to believe that *we* are bad because we ate one type of food, or virtuous because we ate another. This is where it becomes really important *not* to tell your kids, 'You are what you eat.' While, in a literal sense, we are influenced by the nutrients we ingest from food and use them for energy, repair and various bodily functions, our value and identity as human beings extend way beyond what we consume.

Navigating ultra-processed foods

So, how do you encourage your child to develop an easy, varied and intuitive relationship with food while ensuring their nutritional needs for healthy growth and development are met?

Over the past few years, we have been made increasingly aware of the dangers posed by ultra-processed foods – foods that bear little resemblance to their original ingredients and have undergone extensive industrial processing, often containing many different additives and preservatives and being low in nutritional quality. In UK adults, 57 per cent of energy intake is derived from ultra-processed food, with this figure rising to 66 per cent in adolescents [12]. Consumed regularly at high levels these types of foods have been linked to chronic diseases like heart disease and type 2 diabetes, but it's also important to remember that ultra-processed foods such as wholegrain bread, baked beans and high-fibre cereals are often affordable, accessible and nutritious and can be included in moderation in a healthy diet.

Below are some simple guidelines for encouraging a healthy relationship with food in an environmental context that promotes dieting on the one hand and the consumption of highly processed, lower-nutritional-value foods on the other. Later in the chapter, we'll dive deeper into what intuitive eating means and the nuances of applying it in your home.

- **Focus on variety:** Depending on your budget, encourage your kid to try a wide range of foods from different food groups, including lean proteins, fruit and vegetables, whole grains and dairy or dairy substitute products, which will help to ensure they receive a nutritionally balanced diet.
- **Promote balance:** Talk to your kid about balanced eating and explain how all foods can form part of a healthy diet.
- **Education without judgement:** Providing your child with age-appropriate information about nutrition and how the body uses food to support our energy needs, growth, repair and wellbeing will help emphasize the benefits of whole and

minimally processed foods without attaching moral value to different food types.

- **Involving kids in meal preparation:** Encouraging your child to take an active role in food shopping, cooking and even growing fruit, vegetables or herbs can be useful in developing their sense of connection to what they're eating, as well as autonomy and ownership over their food choices.

- **Model enjoyable, healthy eating:** This may be a work in progress if you are healing your relationship with food, which is fine. Be compassionate with yourself and try to lead by example in making food choices that are satisfying, enjoyable and feel good for your body. That is likely to mean letting your kids see you eating various foods from different food groups.

- **Cultivate a positive food environment:** Try to create a relaxed atmosphere around mealtimes and avoid making negative comments about specific foods or food choices. If you notice yourself making judgements about food, be kind to yourself and name it. No one expects nor needs you to be perfect at this and it can take a while to move away from deeply engrained habits such as commenting on certain foods!

Relatedly, when we start to believe that we are better or worse people depending on what foods we eat, we are much more likely to restrict so-called 'bad' foods for both ourselves and our kids. As therapist Judith Matz reflected, it's natural for parents to want to reduce the likelihood of their kids being shamed or picked on for their appearance. It's also very common for parents to fear their child's weight being judged as a reflection of their parenting because that's the message that diet culture promotes. Diet culture tries to pin blame on the individual, including both parents and kids, to preserve itself. It does that by turning normal body diversity into a problem and by revering thin body types. In many families, what often tends to happen is that the heavier child is put on a diet and isn't allowed to eat the same foods as their thinner siblings, or they might be encouraged to exercise more than the others. Both of these enforcements, albeit almost always well-meaning, are shame-inducing and are likely to interfere with respect for and healthy trust in one's own body.

What's more, when foods are restricted, a scarcity mentality is created around them, often leading to those food types being perceived as more highly valued. This makes us all much more susceptible to behaviours such as binge eating, stealing and hiding food, purging, hyper-fixation of restricted foods, and a further increase in feelings of guilt and shame after eating them. While having a 'sweet tooth' is seen to be a downfall in many cultures, mainly because of the tenuous link between sugar, weight gain and health, which I'll come back to, the irony is that we're hardwired from an evolutionary perspective to find sweet foods most attractive. That's because sugary foods are often a sign of ripeness in fruit, a valuable source of nutrients and carbohydrates, particularly back when our ancestors were out on the savannah searching for food. Conversely, bitter or sour foods are often a sign of spoilage or toxicity, and our sensory systems are designed to help us eat defensively so that we don't get poisoned by foods that have gone off.[13] In this way, sweetness signifies safety. To therefore shame ourselves or others for being drawn to sweet foods goes against our biological make-up in the same way that food restriction and dieting do more broadly; our bodies are designed to keep us alive and to react fast to potential famine situations by consuming nutrients as quickly as possible. Restricting food groups and calorie intake creates a rebound effect, a bit like a bow and arrow; the further you pull back on the bowstring by cutting calories, the further the arrow will fly. That means that when your body decides it's at risk of famine and overrides your motivation and willpower to control your weight, you'll be much more susceptible to binge eating.

The unsweetened evidence on sugar

You might be wondering about the impact of sugar on your and your kid's body. While diet culture has demonized sugar and thrives on setting good and bad food trends, making us believe that certain foods, like sugar, have catastrophic implications for our health, the reality is that sugar can absolutely form part of a healthy diet, just like all other types of foods. As dietician and journalist Christy Harrison writes in her book *Anti-Diet*,[14] nutrition research is seldom carried out in a controlled, rigorous laboratory setting. That's because having a sample of people eating under a microscope for long enough to yield meaningful data is expensive, time-consuming and totally impractical for the people taking part. Christy explains that, instead, researchers will ask participants to self-report, relying on subjective appraisals and accurate recollections. Unlike the gold-standard randomized controlled trials performed in labs, these types of studies can't provide information about causation (that is, whether a particular food actually causes or prevents disease). It's also important to note that studies on varying degrees of sugar consumption don't control for factors such as having an eating disorder, chronic dieting, or being exposed to weight stigma, all of which can contribute to people consuming large amounts of sugar and are each independently associated with poor health outcomes.[15] [16]

The idea that sugar causes hyperactivity has also been disproven by several research studies. The 'sugar-high' myth you may already be familiar with originated from one case report in the 1970s, in which a doctor removed sugar from a child's diet and observed improvements in that child's behaviour. Since then, studies have found no link between sugar consumption and hyperactivity, but they have found that parents are more likely to perceive their children's behaviour as hyperactive when they think their child has had sugar, even when the child has not.[17] [18] That is, when we *expect* kids to be more hyperactive, that's what we tend to perceive. If you think about it, most kids will find going to a party with their friends exciting, especially if there are foods on offer that are not usually permitted, like cake and sweets. They might also be more inclined to become over-tired. While it might be your kid's environment rather than what they're eating that's causing them to bounce off the walls, some studies even show that sugar has a calming effect on kids due to its effect on the production of the feel-good neurotransmitter serotonin,[19] while others report improved memory and classroom performance following consumption of a high-sugar drink.[20] Another interesting finding came from a double-blind controlled study that compared twenty-five school-age (6–10) kids who were thought to be more sensitive to sugar by their parents, with twenty-five pre-school-age (3–5) children who were considered to respond normally to sugar. Each child's family was assigned one of three diets: one high in sugar with no artificial sweeteners, one containing aspartame as a sweetener, and one containing saccharin (a placebo) as a sweetener. The study found no significant differences between the diets on any of the thirty-nine behavioural and cognitive variables they tested. It concluded that even when sugar or aspartame levels exceed typical levels, they don't affect children's behaviour or cognitive function.[21] The notion of an energy crash following sugar consumption also has very little scientific evidence, with several studies, including a meta-analysis of 31 randomized controlled trials finding no statistical difference in mood between subjects who had ingested carbohydrates versus a placebo at any time following consumption, and only a very small decrease in alertness.[22]

While I'm not suggesting it's a great idea to allow kids to live solely on sugar, and I'm sure their dentists would agree, it also isn't necessary to exclude or vilify sugary foods from your family's diet unless there's a specific health reason to do so. In these instances, seeking the support of a Health at Every Size registered dietician can be helpful. The World Health Organisation recommends limiting added sugars to 10 per cent or less of total energy consumption for a healthy diet for adults, and the NHS recommends up to 5 per cent of daily energy calories from sugar for children[23] [24].

How to encourage intuitive eating

With so much confusing and often contradictory nutritional information out there, it can be a challenge to help your kid develop a peaceful, easy relationship with food. Intuitive eating is an approach to nourishing yourself that reconnects you to your body's natural cues for hunger and satiety, honours your individual preferences and respects your body's innate wisdom for what it needs. The ten principles of the weight-neutral, intuitive eating model were originally devised by dieticians Evelyn Trebole and Elyse Resch in 1995, and the approach now has a significant body of research supporting it. While exploring the principles of intuitive eating in detail is beyond the scope of this book, I will briefly outline them here, based on Evelyn and Elyse's work,[25] and recommend their recent publication, *Intuitive Eating, 4th Edition: A Revolutionary Anti-Diet Approach*, for a more comprehensive description and guidance on implementing the principles in your home.

The principles of intuitive eating

1. **Reject the diet mentality:** Clear your home of dieting books, magazines, or anything else that gives you false hope of losing weight quickly and easily. Choose to actively reject the diet industry and refuse to let it steal any more of your love for yourself, your peace with your body, and your enjoyment of food.

2. **Honour your hunger:** Listen to your body's signals for hunger and do your best to respect them. This may require you to do some inner work around how you relate to hunger and fullness and whether these natural cues have been hijacked by diet culture in your mind. (You'll know if this is the case if you feel virtuous or reassured by a feeling of hunger or feel guilty or down about yourself when you feel full). Remember that allowing yourself to become excessively hungry will likely lead to your brain's alarm system detecting a potential famine, ultimately making you more inclined to overeat.

Nourishing your body regularly is essential to rebuilding your confidence in your body's ability to regulate itself.

3. **Make peace with food:** Notice when you fall into moralizing attitudes around certain types of foods and permit yourself to eat all foods freely, trusting that once your mind and body recognize that there is no scarcity and that it will be fed regularly, there is no need to overeat.

4. **Challenge the food police:** Be aware of when your brain turns into the food police and starts judging your own or other people's food choices. The thoughts we have aren't always in our control, but if we stay conscious, we have the choice whether or not to engage with them.

5. **Rediscover your love of food:** We're designed to take pleasure from food, and experiencing satisfaction from a wide array of foods is a key part of healthy eating.

6. **Allow yourself to feel full:** Practise being present when you eat and notice when you start to feel comfortably full. This may mean eating slower than usual so that you can recognize the cues as they arise, and it may mean adjusting your eating environment so that you're less distracted by what's happening around you. This is to increase the pleasure you experience while eating and tuning in to your body's sensations, not to prevent you from eating 'too much'. It is also worth holding in mind that the absorption rate, rate of energy uptake and glycaemic index are modified in ultra-processed foods, meaning that you may need to eat more of these foods to experience a feeling of fullness.[26]

7. **Meet your emotions with kindness:** Experiencing a wide range of emotions is a normal part of being human, even though we sometimes might prefer it not to be! It's also

natural that when we feel lonely, bored, stressed, anxious or sad, we sometimes turn to food for consolation. While emotional eating is normal, and there's no shame in it, it won't help you work through those feelings and might ultimately create more of a problem if food becomes your only source of coping. Eventually, the source of the emotions will need exploring if they're to be healed.

8. **Accept your personal body signature:** None of us can defy our genetic blueprint, and just like you wouldn't expect to be able to shrink a 6-foot person to 5 feet, nor is it realistic to hope to change your body size in a major way. All bodies are good bodies, and putting your efforts into accepting and caring for yours rather than trying to change it is ultimately more likely to take you to a place of contentment in the long run.

9. **Movement:** Exercise doesn't have to be gruelling to have major benefits for your health and promote body confidence (see Chapter 6 for much more on this).

10. **Honour your health:** Make food choices based on what you enjoy and what feels good in your body. Remember that healthy eating is not about one meal, snack or day, but rather how you eat regularly.

The Division of Responsibility in Feeding Method (DOR), devised by dietician and family therapist Ellen Satter, is an approach suitable for children of any age, from babies through to teenagers, and it provides a useful framework for encouraging intuitive eating in young people. The DOR recommends that parents take responsibility for deciding what food and when, advocating for a wide variety of tasty foods across meals and snacks, and the kid gets to decide which of the provided foods they would like to eat and how much. The benefit of this approach is that it honours children's food preferences as well as helping them stay attuned to their hunger and fullness signals. This sets them up for a great relationship with food and the ability to select appropriate portion sizes for their body, as they grow. As with all dietary protocols, however, one size does not fit all and if your child is a picky eater, is showing signs of disordered eating, or is displaying behavioural or growth concerns, it's important to seek advice from your GP or paediatrician.

Parenting through puberty

Many children will experience a significant gain in weight either just before or early on in puberty, which is why normalizing all different sorts of body shapes and weights can be particularly helpful. This can be dropped into everyday conversations about how some people are tall, short, brunette, redhead, thin, fat, have a visible scar, use a wheelchair, have varying colour skin, and that body differences are normal. Discussing more stigmatized differences alongside more neutral traits in this way helps position each characteristic as just another example of beautiful body diversity.

It's also why committing to not using body-shaming language is important, because not only does berating your body reinforce your own negative beliefs around how you look, it also sets up your kid to think that weight gain, stretch marks or curvy bits are bad, too.

If you're stuck in a body-shaming loop, not talking about your body in a negative way or berating yourself for eating certain things can require a lot of conscious effort to begin with, but most people find that not being negative about their bodies out loud leads to less negative thoughts about it in general. As with most new habits, repetition is key and will make speaking more kindly about yourself easier over time. The research supports this, with several studies demonstrating that self-affirming, kind and compassionate self-body-talk improves self-acceptance and reduces feelings of disgust towards our appearance.[27]

So, be kind to yourself, accept there might well be days that you forget and accidentally call yourself 'naughty' for having seconds, and keep permitting yourself to let your child see you living unapologetically in your body. This includes being mindful about the non-verbal messages you send to your kids, too, like your exercise and dieting behaviour, and why modelling intuitive eating is such a key part of helping your child develop a positive body image. If adjusting the way you speak about your body feels hard, I would strongly encourage you to consider enlisting the support of a psychotherapist who specializes in body image and who will be able to help you on this much-deserved healing journey.

Growing older sooner: puberty and ethnicity

It is widely accepted that the onset of puberty is influenced by race and ethnicity, and that Black girls tend to develop earlier than white girls. Given that race is a social construct with no genetic or biological basis (most genetic diversity exists within, not between, racial groups meaning that two individuals from the same 'race' can be genetically as different as two people from different 'races') it's unclear whether these developmental differences are due to Black girls generally having a higher amount of adipose (fat) tissue, which is associated with more oestrogen and is linked to starting puberty earlier. Research suggests that environmental factors such as food insecurity, stress, socioeconomic factors and exposure to racism can all contribute to higher body weights and adipose tissue in Black children. Psychologically, reaching puberty early is significant, as it increases the likelihood of kids being treated as more mature and subject to higher expectations than their same-aged peers.[28]

Dr Joy Cox, a researcher, social justice advocate and author of *Fat Girls in Black Bodies*,[29] shared how Black girls are especially at risk of being subjected to adultification and objectification. Dr Cox told me that tween and teenage girls of all skin colours whose bodies are more developed are quickly seen as 'fast' or sexually forward, with blame frequently attributed to the child's desire for attention and deliberate enticement of men rather than the absolute inappropriateness of the male gaze upon them. This raises an additional challenge for parents of more developed Black girls, who not only have to navigate keeping their children safe by discouraging them from wearing clothes that are popular with their peers, such as short shorts or crop tops, but also make sure they don't feel to blame for other people's racist and inappropriate reactions to them. This may partly account for why studies have found that Black parents are more likely to use more authoritative parenting techniques and behaviours.[30] The threat level Black children face is often higher. Research shows that an authoritative parenting style may involve more direct guidance and behavioural expectations rather than extensive verbal negotiation or reasoning, which can result, for example, in kids simply being told what they can and cannot wear, often without explanation[31].

In terms of that child's body image, however, the lack of explanation creates a problem. When a kid is told they're not allowed to wear a certain piece of clothing that their friends are wearing without a clear rationale, they will try to work it out for themselves. Many will conclude that their body is different in some way, that it is 'bad' because it prevents them from fitting with their peers and feeling acceptable and included.

This is where being willing to lean into uncomfortable conversations is helpful. I know it can be difficult sitting down with a tween or teen and explaining that they can't wear a fashion trend like their friends because it might attract the wrong kind of attention. Depending on their age, they may or may not have a concept of sexual grooming or assault. You're likely to be met with feelings of disappointment, anger and frustration that can be tough to make space for and be compassionate towards, especially when you're just trying to do the best you can by them.

In these instances, kids need to know that there is nothing wrong with their body and that it's your job to help them stay safe while also respecting their right to dress in a way that feels right for them. It's understandable that you'd want to protect your kids from potential harm and judgement given the reality of a society where, unfortunately, appearance can attract unwanted attention or negative assumptions. Here's an example of how you might start a conversation around this with your child:

Parent: '*I know you're at an age where you want to choose your own clothes to wear and that's awesome! Your clothes should feel good to you and like an expression of who you are. But sometimes people have different ideas about what certain clothing means, and though it's not fair, they might make assumptions that aren't accu-rate. For example, they might think someone is trying to attract their attention or act older than they are. You should be able to wear what you want to, but because not everyone thinks that way yet, we just need to be thoughtful. I want you to feel confident and safe in what you wear and I'm always here to talk it through if you're not sure or need help picking.'*

Remembering why this is important to your child can be useful. Kids often want to dress the same as their peers because it serves the same subconscious mechanism as when an infant mirrors their mother. When we see aspects of ourselves reflected back in someone else's appearance, we feel a sense of twinship, reassurance and safety. To look the same as another and to recognize shared characteristics is affirming, and it gives kids a feeling of belonging and self-esteem that's fundamental to the development of a healthy sense of self.[32] So, it makes sense that it feels jarring for kids to be told they're not allowed to match their friends' clothing in the way they'd like, especially because of their own body shape or because of how someone else might react. It's easy to see how the body can quickly become a source of frustration and contempt if diversity is not sufficiently celebrated. Validating your kid's feelings by acknowledging how frustrating and difficult it is not to be allowed to do something many of their friends are doing will help them to feel heard, understood and listened to.

Growing up is hard, especially for kids who don't fit in or are picked on because of their appearance. While stepping in and trying to fix the problem for them might feel intuitive, it can often lead to an increased sense of victimization and powerless-ness. However, there are many things that you can do to help your child feel like they belong and build their self-confidence, resilience and social skills.

At home in your body

As a parent or caregiver, perhaps one of the most powerful things you can do to support your child is to give them a secure base to rely on. Linking to Attachment Theory, that means creating a reliable home environment in which they feel loved, safe and accepted exactly as they are. As we discussed in Chapter 2, that might require you to address your own feelings around certain types of body types, as well as consider the messages embedded in conversations about bodies and food that may have been passed down through your family for generations. Children who experience home as a secure base they can depend on for love, reassurance, acceptance and soothing tend to grow up to be adults who have internalized that sense of security and can draw on it when faced with challenges, setbacks and rejections.

The seeking and finding of the secure base and feeling of belonging symbolized by home can be considered a central theme in L. Frank Baum's *The Wonderful Wizard of Oz*. The story, regarded as the earliest truly feminist American children's novel owing to the fact that the only characters able to wield actual magic in the story are female, and its male characters all turn to Dorothy for rescue,[33] follows Dorothy in her quest to find a way back home to Kansas. Just as Hansel and Gretel travelled through the forest and Alice travelled through Wonderland, Dorothy journeyed through Oz in search of home; an idealized notion of safety and belonging.[34] In the same way that our fast-paced, often stressful lives and exposure to stigmatizing messages lead to a disconnection between our bodies and minds, Dorothy is separated from her safe base and realizes that there really is 'no place like home'.

If you've struggled with your body image most of your life, you, too, may be on a journey to find your way home. Unlike a physical home, our bodies are the only ones we will ever have; we can't simply move to a different body when we want to. Reaching a place of comfort and safety in your body means learning to accept its quirks and flaws, decorating it in a way that feels good to you, and performing necessary maintenance to help it provide shelter for you for as long as possible.

Just like a physical home, we can help to keep our bodies structurally sound by nourishing ourselves well, being physically active, engaging with healthcare when we need it, and allowing our bodies to rest. But there's also something about accepting the parts that can't be fixed. The parts that you wish were different but cannot safely be reconfigured. Re-establishing your connection with your body often begins with acknowledging it as your home and committing to speaking kindly about it.

Disentangling from your own self-stories

One of the things that makes us distinctly human is our ability to tell stories, to make links between the past, present and future, in ways that other mammals cannot. Our ability to make associations between words, sounds, objects and ideas, along with our unique capacity for expanding and generalizing those links from specific experiences to much broader contexts, is what enables us to learn and understand in a way that far exceeds any other species' capacity. It's also one of the reasons we suffer in unique ways. We're able to create stories about the world and, perhaps most importantly, stories about ourselves, that have the potential to evoke considerable distress. These stories usually do have some grounding but are often generalized extensively. If we become enmeshed and hooked by these self-stories, they can quickly influence our behaviour and become self-fulfilling prophecies.

'No one will be attracted to me so I won't even try.' Max's story

Max, a client I worked with who described himself as a bigger-bodied divorced father of three who has always struggled with his weight, came to therapy strongly attached to the story that he was unattractive and would never find love again. Max explained that he had been hurt badly by his very first girlfriend when he was sixteen and that he doubted whether he would ever feel that way about anyone again, especially after his marriage didn't work out. Alongside his belief that love was dangerous, having been so badly hurt during his teens, he explained that part of the problem was that dating apps seemed to be the only way people meet these days, and that prospective dates would take one look at his photo and swipe past. It's no myth that people often treat each other with less humanity on dating sites than they might in the physical world, with behaviours like ghosting considered appropriate ways of ending a relationship. However, Max's attachment to his story also ensured that he was unwilling to take anyone who *was* interested in him seriously, convincing himself that they must be gold diggers or catfishers. He was also reluctant to be open to the possibility of meeting a potential partner offline because he experienced social anxiety and avoided social situations unless it was for work. Unsurprisingly, Max's experience of dating, or lack thereof, reinforced the story he held about himself, which itself compounded his avoidant behaviour. He shared his concern that his teenage children had also started commenting on their own and other people's romantic desirability based on their appearance.

In therapy, we explored how Max had become hooked by limiting thoughts and beliefs about himself, assessed how well they were working for him and began to develop his ability to lean into difficult thoughts and feelings. I encouraged Max to remember why this was important for him, his values of romance, companionship and adventure, and modelling acceptance and worthiness to his kids. Doing so could never guarantee that Max would meet the love of his life, but it dramatically increased the odds over doing nothing at all. In the end, he did go on to meet a woman he felt deeply connected to for the first time since his divorce several years earlier.

The benefits of acknowledging our conceptualized self

Noticing the stories we have about ourselves and who we think we should be (referred to as our conceptualized self in ACT) is useful in several ways. Firstly, it is part of developing our ability to zoom out and look at our thoughts, feelings and behaviours from a more objective place and connecting with what we call our observing self. This is the part of us that's able to look at a situation with a wider lens so that we can identify our patterns, triggers, emotions and behaviours in a less entangled and reactive way and reflect back on events with awareness and compassion. In doing so, we become more able to identify thoughts and beliefs that don't serve us well and change the way we relate to those thoughts when they do show up. As I mentioned before, we call this defusion, and it means using specific techniques to see thoughts and feelings in a more objective, distanced and less impactful way. I'll introduce you to a couple of quick and easy defusion techniques shortly.

Secondly, acknowledging our conceptualized self (that is, the stories we tell ourselves *about* ourselves) helps us to accept ourselves as we actually are. It nurtures our ability to experience difficult thoughts and feelings and not be knocked off track by them or drawn away from our values.

During my counselling psychology training, I had a professional placement in an NHS bariatric service. In this service, I worked with a number of patients who loved swimming and who desperately wanted to take their children to the pool but avoided swimming themselves because of their fear of being judged or humiliated. The story many of them were fused with was that they were 'too fat' or 'too embarrassing' to be seen in a swimsuit. Often, these self-stories were based either on previous personal experiences where they'd been shamed, or witnessing others in similar bodies being spoken about in hurtful ways. While these stories undoubtedly had some grounding in terms of fatphobia and weight stigma being very real issues, they were profoundly limiting for each of these patients. On deeper exploration, many of them realized that staying enmeshed with their self-stories around swimming and exercise might allow them to avoid the discomfort of thinking someone might judge them, or stare, or even fat shame, but it prevented them from doing things that they realized felt much more important to them, like enjoying active time playing with their children, the wonderful feeling of swimming like a fish, the fun and social opportunities of aqua classes, and a general feeling of health and wellbeing. This realization helped many of them feel more willing and able to lean into those difficult feelings, allowing them to overcome their fears of wearing a swimsuit in front of others.

Gaining awareness of our conceptualized self also allows us to develop a more stable sense of who we are. People can feel destabilized for a number of reasons. These might include changes in circumstance (moving house, switching jobs, becoming unemployed, having children, developing an illness, ageing, losing or gaining wealth), trauma, experiencing dissociative states (feeling disconnected from yourself, uncertain of who you are, or, at the extreme, having dissociative identity disorder[35]). We can also become destabilized when we're hooked by rapidly changing thoughts about ourselves, such as one minute thinking, 'I'm a good mum' and the next, 'I'm an awful mum.'

EXERCISE

Body Confident You: The Documentary About YOU

The mind as a documentary-maker[36] is a defusion exercise I find useful in helping clients get a sense of the stories they hold about themselves and unhooking them from those stories if they no longer serve them.

First, I'd like you to reflect back on the last documentary you watched on TV. For example, I recently watched *My Octopus*

Teacher, which told the story of a filmmaker, Craig Foster, who forged an unlikely friendship with an octopus in a remote underwater kelp forest in False Bay, South Africa. The documentary shared how, over a year, Craig's bond with the octopus grew, giving us, the viewers, an insight into how the octopus eats, sleeps, hunts and defends herself from predators. Through this window into their world, we get a sense of knowing Craig and the octopus, understanding who and what they are, as well as an appreciation of the enchanting underwater wilderness of South Africa's largest bay. However, the documentary is not Craig, and nor is it the octopus, or even False Bay – it is merely a snippet of what each might be like. No matter how truthful the depiction, no documentary could ever get past the inevitable bias inherent in showing a tiny piece of a very big picture. *My Octopus Teacher* was likely compiled from the very best bits of hundreds if not thousands of hours of footage, which were then stitched together in potentially jumbled chronological sequences to present the most enticing story.

As human beings, we are also documentary makers. Our thinking mind trawls through a whole lifetime of experiences, carefully selects a few particularly powerful memories, and edits them together to create the captivating story of 'This Is Who I Am!'

Think about your own documentary. Which experiences has your mind selected as the most important, and do those capture you and everything that you are in a way that really represents you? When we become overidentified with a particular narrative about who or what we are, it can often prevent us from acting in ways that feel congruent with what we value most and who we really want to be.

For example, for many years my own documentary told the story of a not-very-intelligent, psychically fragmented, emotionally avoidant workaholic who was only good at things because she overworked and didn't deserve any credit for anything because she'd had a fairly affluent upbringing.

Thankfully my current documentary is a lot warmer and more uplifting! It goes something like:

This is the story of someone who has overcome a lot of adversity and shown courage and tenacity in healing her own inner wounds. She is passionate about helping others do the same and is constantly learning. She is full of zest for life, is loveable, adores animals and while she has flaws just like everyone else, she is at peace with herself (most of the time!).

If you were to create a different 5-minute documentary about your entire life, what would a more compassionate, less-biased documentary maker prioritize in the edits? What documentary would your best friend make about you?

EXERCISE

Body Confident Kid

If the documentary-maker exercise resonates with you, you might like to introduce it to your child. For older kids and teens, you can encourage them to think about what their documentary would look like if they were to make it themselves and whether their best friend or family member would emphasize the same or different parts of who they are.

For younger children, you might invite them to write a story about themselves (or create a self-portrait if they enjoy arty projects). The aim of this story or portrait is for them to express aspects of themselves that can't be seen, such as their thoughts, feelings, preferences, values and hobbies, as well as some of their visible characteristics.

When doing this, remind your kid that there are no right or wrong ways to do this or things to include and that the aim is to recognize the strengths and vulnerabilities that make them their unique and special selves. Once they've finished, encourage them to show their story or artwork to others if they feel comfortable doing so and talk through what they've noticed or learnt about themselves during the activity. This is a great opportunity to offer validation and support as well as emphasize both self-expression and acceptance.

EXERCISE

Body Confident You and Kid

Another simple but powerful defusion technique you can practise with your kid is to change the tone of the internal dialogue. Doing so helps you and your child recognize that, a bit like the weather passing through the sky, your thoughts can't harm you. They are just a collection of words that happen to be passing through your mind. What usually makes them feel important and intolerable is that they're often accompanied by a serious, often angry or anxious tone, so this exercise focuses on helping you gain space from the thought by changing that tone. Here's how:

1. First, notice and name the difficult thought that's showing up for you or your child. Let's use, 'I'm so ugly' as an example.

2. Either out loud or in your head, sing the thought or say it in a funny voice. I like to use the theme tune of *Star Wars* or 'Happy Birthday' for this, but I've also heard people use the voices of Daffy Duck or Kermit the Frog.

3. Repeat this several times and notice if there is any shift in the feelings you or your kid experience in relation to the thought. The idea isn't to get rid of or push the thought away, but to change our relationship to it by voicing it in a different way.

KEY REFLECTIONS

- Clarify your family's values around food and body talk so that everyone in your home knows the boundaries and why they're important in creating a safe space. Depending on the age of your child, get them involved in choosing these values too. In a way that feels comfortable for you, uphold these boundaries with visitors by either stating your family values around diet talk clearly, or simply diverting the conversation if that feels more manageable.

- Eat together as often as you can without the distraction of screens.

- Be mindful of the way you describe different types of bodies and try to keep in mind what messages are imbued in the words you use to talk about bodies. If you're unsure how to describe someone's appearance and need to for any reason, the next thing to do is respectfully ask! Few people are offended by respectful curiosity.

- Make discussions about bodies, body parts, body boundaries, body safety and body consent a regular conversation in your home. If it feels really uncomfortable and you're struggling to lean into it, be kind to yourself and talk to a trusted partner, friend or therapist about what support you need to have these important conversations with your child.

- If you're concerned that your kid wants to dress in a way that might compromise their safety, remind them that it's your job to help them feel safe and strong, no matter what. It's important to emphasize that they should and do have the right to dress as they wish, and that your advice is about reinforcing their comfort, confidence and wellbeing, not about controlling their expression.

- If you notice that your most enticing docu-film called 'This Is Who I Am!' is screening in your mind and showcasing some of your most powerful, painful experiences, try to meet it with playfulness. Thank your mind for being such a great editor and for putting on such a captivating show. This is in no way to undermine your past experiences but to help you remain grounded in the here and now, able to observe your own thoughts and feelings without getting enmeshed by them.

CHAPTER FOUR

Self-Esteem and Body Image

'No amount of self-improvement can make up for a lack of self-acceptance.'

Robert Holden, founder of The Happiness Project

As a psychologist, I've noticed there's a troublesome thought that's almost universally experienced by my clients regardless of their age or reason for coming to therapy.

It's the thought of not being good enough.

The reason many of us are prone to self-doubt, self-depreciation and fear of not meeting expectations is that we're hardwired to be alert to the possibility of rejection. Rejection threatens survival, particularly thousands of years ago when even adults were unlikely to last very long if they were cast out of the tribe. Fitting in, belonging, being valued and being accepted by your peers wasn't just ideal – it determined your longevity.

We may no longer depend on the acceptance of others quite

like we did hundreds of thousands of years ago, when resources were scarce and conditions were more brutal. But while you can take the people out of the Stone Age, you can't take the Stone Age out of the people.[1] Our brains are still perfectly designed to help us survive, and that means being vigilant to the risk and threat of being an outcast.

So, how do we assess whether we are good enough or not? Comparison.

The thief of joy

As Theodore Roosevelt once said, 'Comparison is the thief of joy', and not only do we compare ourselves to others, but to the glorified stories we tell ourselves about them, along with a myriad of impossible ideals. We effectively compare our insides to others' outsides without fully understanding their starting point, feelings or values. We forget that the playing field is never level, even if you grew up in the same family as someone else.

The function of this comparison, however, isn't quite as self-defeating as it might sound. The idea of there even being a 'good enough' standard to obtain suggests that there's a benchmark that one can succeed or fail at reaching. The trouble is the 'good enough' benchmark is ill-defined in many areas. That means we sometimes struggle to differentiate what can be usefully quantified (demonstrating sufficient skill to pass your driving test, or perform open-heart surgery, for example), versus aspects that are much more subjective – beauty, talent, intelligence, wealth, helpfulness, kindness and so on. Which is unsettling. How can we know if we're good enough without a clear yardstick against which to assess ourselves? To resolve this issue, we look to the closest thing we have to measure ourselves against: other people. As long as we feel we are matching up to or exceeding others, in theory, we should feel safe. Except that's rarely how it works. External validation might reassure us temporarily, but without our own self-approval and without meeting our own needs for love and acceptance, it's usually short-lived.

In addition, we have our brain's negativity bias to contend with. This primes us to err on the side of caution when it comes to self-appraisals to stay safe (after all, better to mistake a stick for a snake than the other way around). That means that, faced with the uncertainty of whether you are good enough or not, your mind is most likely to go with the latter.

Why is this relevant to body image? Because research shows that body image and self-esteem directly influence each other, and a positive body image is the most significant predictor of high self-esteem, especially in adolescents.[2] [3] Children and adolescents who feel down about themselves are also more vulnerable to negative messages about their bodies and more likely to make unfavourable comparisons between their own physical appearance and what they see as an idealized image. This is even more problematic when we consider that everyone who uses the internet is not just exposed to an *idealized* image of attractiveness, but an image that, thanks to filters and doctoring, doesn't even exist. The trouble is, though, that we think it does. AI only exacerbates this issue, creating the possibility of not only presenting you with an unrealistic image but one that you, specifically, desire. Unfortunately, it isn't in the interest of many businesses to change that. Self-contentment isn't good for the economy. People need to feel unhappy with themselves to buy stuff, whether it be slimming pills, slimming pants, make-up, cover-ups, anti-ageing lotions or hair dye.

In this chapter, we'll explore where self-esteem comes from, signs that you or your kid might be struggling with low self-esteem, and what you can do to nurture self-confidence in yourself and your family.

Where does self-esteem come from?

Several factors influence our self-esteem, including our childhood experiences, the society we're brought up in, the influence of media in all its forms, and the people around us, including our parents, friends, family and colleagues. The extent to which these factors influence us depends on our personality and our life stage. A young child's self-esteem will be most impacted by their relationship and attachment to their parents, whereas friends may more strongly influence a teenager. Those friends may help to build up, or unfortunately bring down, how that teenager sees and feels about themselves. As adults, our work colleagues, romantic partners and friends notably shape our lives, yet the attachment styles we developed in our early years continue to have an enduring influence.

'Deep down I felt like a terrible, unlovable person.' Lucy's story

Lucy came to therapy hoping to break free of a binge-eating pattern that had caused her tremendous shame since her teens. Now in her forties, her self-esteem was very low and she felt at constant war with her body. Feeling hopeless, she was seriously contemplating weight-loss surgery. Lucy was also plagued with guilt and anxiety about the impact her low self-confidence and destructive relationship with food might have on her eleven-year-old daughter. She held a strong belief that she was deeply flawed and unacceptable, and every time she binged it reinforced her conviction that she not only engaged in bad behaviours, but that *she* was fundamentally bad.

During our work together, Lucy and I explored how growing up with a highly critical and verbally abusive mother, and being bullied at school because of her weight, had led her to feel safer relating to the world from behind a mask. She became adept at moulding herself to meet the needs of others and accustomed to hiding her own thoughts, feelings and personality in an attempt to fit in and avoid criticism and rejection. Consequently, Lucy became increasingly lonely and distrustful that anyone would accept her for who she really was, let alone care enough to look after her in the way she longed for. She experienced an intense hunger for the love and acceptance that were absent during her childhood and tried to fill this emptiness with food – a common strategy, given food's availability and connection with care and nurturing. Food became both Lucy's best friend and worst enemy – on the one hand, comforting her, numbing her and helping her regulate her emotions when she felt happy, sad, anxious or lonely, but on the other, leading her to feel more and more ashamed and unacceptable as her weight escalated. Her deeply rooted fears about living in a larger body made her struggle with food even harder, as her attempts to restrict what she ate almost always gave way to compensatory binges.

Lucy and I mined deep beneath the surface of her eating disorder to help her understand that her turn to food was a survival mechanism, a means of coping and meeting her own needs for love and security when she had few other resources available to her. She was able to develop compassion towards her child self by imagining her own daughter dealing with the rejection, abuse and isolation that she had experienced. She found this deeply painful but also transformative. Therapy helped her to experience the safety, support and containment that was missing in her childhood so that she could learn to be the parent she needed, both for herself and her own child. She began experimenting with allowing herself to have a voice and setting boundaries that served her, at first in the safety of therapy and then in the wider world. She learnt how to sit with her emotions, offer herself loving kindness, and seek nurturance from those close to her, allowing her to put food back in its rightful place.

In the end, Lucy opted not to have weight-loss surgery, instead choosing to continue on her journey towards greater self-acceptance and healing her relationship with food. She came to realize that self-esteem came not from changing her body, nor from other people's opinions of her, but from the decision to give herself her own love and approval.

The original influencer of unrealistic body standards

One of the key ways in which we learn about social norms, values and roles is through play, and as such, the toys we have access to as kids have a big impact on how we see ourselves. If you grew up somewhere between the 1960s and '90s, you may have been part of the Barbie and Cindy youth, in which case it is understandable that many of us internalized the two main values of these iconic figures: beauty and homogeneity. If the 1990s Barbie had been a life-size adult, she would be 5 foot 9 inches tall, with an 18-inch waist, 39-inch bust, 33-inch hips and size 3 shoes.[4] With these dimensions, '90s Barbie would have been unable to stand and would have likely moved around on all fours. She would also weigh 110 lbs, which would give her a BMI of 16.24, well within the criteria for anorexia nervosa.

Given that 1990s Barbie's ancestors included 1960s Slumber Party Barbie, who carried around a set of scales permanently set to 110 lbs and a book entitled *How to Lose Weight* (with the sole instruction 'Don't eat' inside), it's hardly a surprise that '90s Barbie's proportions, and values, remained completely unrealistic.[5]

It's important not to underestimate the influence dolls have on children's sense of self, even with the recent introduction of more inclusive and relatable figurines. The Barbie collection, for example, now includes physically disabled, Down syndrome and wheelchair-using models, tall, petite and curvy (which scales up to a UK size 6–8, an improvement on the original Barbie's size 2 proportions, but still well below the average size of a 16–24-year-old woman in the UK, which is a size 14).[6]

Dolls act as socializing agents, exposing kids to the values of wider society within their private playtime. A study published in the *Journal of Body Image* found that their racially diverse sample of young adult women reported significantly lower body appreciation and a higher inclination to compare their appearance when looking at different Barbie figurines compared to looking at Lego Friends. This suggests that despite the reinvention of toys like Barbie to reflect more realistic body shapes and promote healthier values like fitness and functionality, the reality is that these dolls still emphasize a thin, largely white ideal which many kids will never hope to live up to.[7]

While toy manufacturers such as Mattel, who created Barbie, have reinvented their dolls to promote health and wellbeing in response to criticism that their toys encouraged unrealistic body ideals, studies show these toys still negatively affect kids' body satisfaction and appearance-related self-esteem. Researchers suggest it's because we still so strongly associate wellness with a thin, and now also muscular, body type that many people simply don't have.[8] So, while the 2023 *Barbie* movie sported a fantastically diverse cast, including plus-size lawyer Barbie, played by actress Sharon Rooney, the dolls themselves still have a lot of catching up to do. It's therefore important to be mindful of the messages your kid's toys and digital media are sending them.

It may take some time to undo the harmful narratives that Barbie and similar toys embody.[9] A study exploring the attitudes of 3–10-year-old girls towards Barbies of different shapes and sizes found that the girls generally demonstrated negative views towards curvy Barbies (remembering that curvy Barbie would be a scaled-up size 8) and positive attitudes towards thinner-bodied Barbies. Those girls with higher levels of body dissatisfaction were more likely to display positive attitudes towards the original (scaled-up size 2) Barbies, and across the sample, Curvy Barbie was the doll they least wanted to play with.[10] This aversion to fatness is likely to reflect parents' anxieties about weight and desire to be thin, as well as general exposure to positive attitudes towards thin bodies and negative attitudes towards fat ones.[11]

Kids between 2 and 6 years old have yet to develop their analytical ability and are extremely receptive to new information. This means that they readily accept what they're told without questioning it, laying the foundation for the attitudes and beliefs they will hold as they grow up. This is consistent with the findings of studies showing that bigger-bodied kids are not only excluded by their peers but are often overtly disliked and rejected, posing a significant risk factor for their social development and making them more susceptible to an array of mental health challenges, including depression, anxiety, loneliness, eating disorders and physical illness.[12] [13] These studies highlight just how important it is, along with anti-bullying strategies in schools, for kids of all ages to have continual exposure to bodies of all shapes and sizes, not just token appearances that do little to address existing stigmatizing attitudes.

Signs of low self-esteem

It's clear that high self-esteem has a positive impact on kids' mental health and development and that poor self-esteem is strongly linked to physical, psychological and social challenges. These consequences can potentially impact a child's longer-term trajectory, including their employment, financial status, mental and physical health and even their propensity to commit criminal behaviour.[14] But how do you know whether someone has low self-esteem in the first place? Before we get into spotting signs of low self-esteem in kids, let's start with you.

Take a look at the list below and note how many of the following statements you agree with.

- *I constantly compare myself negatively to others.*
- *I find it difficult to maintain relationships.*
- *I'm a people-pleaser.*
- *I struggle to accept compliments.*
- *I doubt myself a lot.*
- *I'm not very good at maintaining boundaries.*
- *I'm often self-critical.*
- *I'm afraid of failing.*
- *I often feel out of control.*
- *I find it difficult to ask for help.*
- *I worry a lot.*
- *I believe that I <u>shouldn't</u> feel the way I feel because I have relatively good circumstances.*

If you resonate with several of these statements, you likely have low self-esteem. We'll think about how you can support yourself in improving your own sense of self-worth and self-confidence shortly, but before we do, let's also think about how you can identify low self-esteem in your kid.

Children, like adults, tend to use defensive strategies to reduce their feelings of inadequacy and worthlessness. These provide useful indicators that your kid is struggling with their self-esteem and include behaviours such as:

- *Refusing to take part in or quitting activities to avoid the possibility of failure.*
- *Blaming others when things go wrong to protect them from feelings of shame associated with getting or doing something wrong.*
- *Putting themselves down with self-critical comments such as, 'I'm stupid.'*
- *People-pleasing, which negates the fear of being a disappointment or disliked.*
- *Negatively comparing themselves to others.*
- *Bullying others to feel more powerful in compensation for feelings of powerlessness or inadequacy.*
- *Acting the clown or trying to be the 'funny one' to direct attention away from aspects of the self that feel shameful, such as appearance.*
- *Minimizing the importance of things to protect against painful feelings of rejection. For example, 'I didn't want to be her friend anyway,' or 'I don't care what anyone thinks.'*
- *Withdrawing socially.*
- *Making excuses for poor results or mistakes rather than accepting responsibility.*[15]

If you recognize some of these behaviours in your child, please don't despair. All children go through periods of low self-esteem and lack confidence at times, and this can often be linked to specific events like exam results, a parental split, falling out with friends or being bullied. Some of these things are not in their control, or yours for that matter, and that is a part of life. However, you can take some powerful steps to support your kid, and you might be surprised to hear that trying to change or bolster their self-esteem, at least directly, isn't one of them. Why? Let me explain.

Fostering a positive self-view

Self-compassion is actually far more important than self-esteem for our psychological wellbeing, and acts as a middleman between self-esteem and body image. Self-esteem is based on our feelings of self-worth, usually derived from our accomplishments, abilities or external validation. Without self-compassion, we're left on shaky ground if we aren't winning, achieving, being the best or receiving praise. That's why so many high-achieving people have very low self-worth.

A quick internet search on celebrities who have openly talked about their struggles with depression and feelings of worthlessness demonstrates how no amount of money, success, fame or external validation provides immunity from negative thoughts about yourself. Conversely, the reality, in many cases, is that the better your circumstances are, the worse symptoms of depression can sometimes become.[16] The reason for this is that when how you feel becomes further and further removed from how you think you *should* feel, it leaves fertile ground for self-criticism to escalate. I've sat with many teenagers and adults who have told me they simply don't deserve to feel sad or unhappy because they have a nice home, loving parents, supportive friends, great kids, financial security and so on. I have said the exact same thing to my own therapist and struggled to believe that anything I achieved could be attributed to anything but my extremely fortunate circumstances and charmed life (incidentally, another common characteristic of people with low self-esteem is overemphasizing how easy you've had it while minimizing the challenges you've faced). In my experience, having positive things around you can simply create a wider gap to fall into if you're someone who is struggling with low self-esteem and/or depression.

Years ago, I did some training with world-renowned hypnotherapist Marisa Peer, and it really stuck with me when she noted that fame doesn't damage people; damaged people are drawn to fame because they don't feel like they're enough, and they think fame will fix that for them. Of course not everyone who becomes famous does so because they feel inadequate. Many will gain recognition simply for being outstanding at what they do. But there are certainly plenty of people who yearn for acceptance and seek to meet that need by chasing the spotlight. So, they get brilliant at their craft, go on stage, and everyone adores them, but then they go home again, and they still feel lacking. They believe that people might love their voice, humour or performance, but that persistent feeling of the 'real them' not being enough remains. From this perspective, it might be fair to say that many of the most wonderful, inspiring and impactful things we humans do are, in fact, *because* of our suffering, not despite it.

Fostering self-compassion, then, is crucial in helping us not only internalize external validation and the fulfilment of success when we get it, but still feel worthy, valuable and 'enough' when we do not. Self-compassion involves showing ourselves loving kindness regardless of whether we win or lose and independent of external praise. It recognizes our value regardless of our number of friends, followers, or the amount of recognition we receive. It involves understanding and accepting when we are hurting or feeling inadequate. It also acknowledges that we all suffer at times and that we are not alone or defunct because we suffer. So, while self-esteem and self-compassion are important, only the latter provides a stable scaffolding for self-worth independent of our successes and failures.[17]

Embracing your flawsomeness

As a parent, one of the best things you can do for your kid's self-esteem is to model self-compassion and acceptance of your own perceived flaws. Show them how flawsome (that is, flawed but awesome) you are and they will learn how to embrace their flawsomeness, too! Being flawsome is all about celebrating your strengths, accepting your weaknesses and living authentically. Here are just some of the ways you can do that:

1. **Own your uniqueness:** Embrace the parts of yourself that make you feel different or self-conscious. Personally, I have a particularly round and muscular bottom that I spent much of my life trying to conceal in baggy clothing. It's a strong trait on the maternal, Viennese side of my family, so instead I now make a point of commenting on the strength and power in my butt muscles and how they've helped me be good at sports, which shifts my perspective to one of gratitude.

2. **Learn to laugh at yourself:** Approaching our imperfections with affectionate, playful humour makes them much easier to accept. For example, referring to your stretch marks as personal lightning bolts that prove that you've survived growth spurts and childbirth and have lived a little!

3. **Be vulnerable:** Sharing your vulnerability is a sign of strength and is the antidote to shame. Research shows people tend to bond over pain and shared struggles far more readily than shared successes because it fosters a

sense of belonging, solidarity and safety.[18] For example, you might share that you've often felt uncomfortable in your own skin and found yourself focusing on all the things that seemed wrong when you looked in the mirror. It can then be helpful to explain that you recognize that wasn't healthy for you and that now you work hard at self-acceptance and being kind to yourself instead.

Leaning into anxiety

Making space for your child's anxiety about whether they are good enough or attractive enough without trying to fix the problem immediately is an essential, albeit challenging, part of parenting. It goes against maternal and paternal drives not to relieve discomfort, reassure and problem-solve when your child is distressed. But learning to tolerate, understand and make space for difficult emotions is a life skill all children require.

My colleague Dr Jenny Draisey, a clinical psychologist specializing in helping children and adolescents who are struggling with anxiety, depression and low self-esteem, emphasizes that while society encourages the idea that we should feel happy and confident all of the time, that idea is wholly unrealistic. She explained how parents understandably want to skip straight to the part where their child no longer feels anxious or self-doubting, because it's hard not only for the child to tolerate those feelings but also for the parent to witness. However, without first teaching kids why they feel anxious or low, normalizing the full range of emotions, and helping them develop the skills to relate differently to difficult feelings when they show up, we actually deny children (and ourselves) a valuable opportunity. That is, the chance to build resilience and skills to cope with tough experiences, which are an unavoidable part of being human.

'You can't be happy all the time and sometimes, by sheltering kids from going through anything difficult, they then don't know how to cope,' Dr Draisey reflected. She also highlights how helpful it can be for parents to share their own vulnerabilities when their kids are facing tricky circumstances that might be impacting their self-esteem. For example, if a teenager has fallen out with their friends and feels excluded, you might offer an example of when something similar happened to you, how you felt about it, and what helped you to get through it. While it's important not to shift the focus away from your child's concerns or make assumptions that their experience is the same as yours, normalizing both their experience and feelings by sharing your own reinforces their sense of connection and belonging and reassures them that it isn't just them, and they can and will find a way through their difficulties. It can also be helpful to remind your kid of their shared struggles and that the likelihood is their friends will also be having to navigate tricky feelings that they're not sure how to handle. Explaining this can help kids to realize that just because they are being excluded, for example, doesn't mean that they are the problem, even if it does feel pretty horrible.

Supporting kids who don't want to talk

Many parents will identify with the upset and frustration of recognizing that their child is struggling and wanting to help them, but feeling unable to get them to talk about what is happening inside. This is especially common for older children and teenagers who are moving towards greater independence or who may find it challenging to find the words to articulate their concerns. They may also be worried about burdening their parents. Pulling away from parents and developing autonomy is a normal part of adolescence, but there are things you can still do to encourage open communication.

Focusing on laying the foundations of a trusting relationship and looking at things from a longer-term trajectory can be helpful when your kid just doesn't want to talk. This requires patience and involves letting your child know that they can come and speak to you and that you will offer them a safe space, even if your kid doesn't want to use that space right now or rejects it. Dr Draisey encourages parents in this position to be self-compassionate when it happens and to keep the channels open, ensuring that your child knows that it's fine if they don't want to talk today or tomorrow, but that you're always there for them if they change their mind. Working with your child to establish boundaries, family rules, values and expectations can help to build a relationship based on mutual respect, which may include permitting your child to pull you up on it when you don't behave in line with family values. This reinforces your child's value and autonomy within the family structure and develops their trust that you will listen to and respect them.

When your kid *does* choose to confide in you, it can be powerful to remember the following three phrases from clinical psychologist and founder of the parenting community Good Inside, Dr Becky Kennedy:

1. **'I am really glad you told me about this'** – which reminds your kid that you are a safe person to talk to, even if you don't like what they have to say.

2. **'I believe you'** – which validates their feelings and conveys respect, compassion and support.

3. **'Tell me more'** – which helps them feel listened to and understood. While it can be tempting to jump straight into problem-solving mode or provide reassurance, it's helpful not to overlook this step. Asking your kid to describe more about their experience demonstrates that you are someone who can tolerate whatever they are feeling. Eventually, they will be able to tolerate their own feelings as well.

It can be tough as a parent to sit back and allow your child to feel what they're feeling without offering the band-aid of reassurance. But if you can tolerate your own feelings around it, support your child in understanding their physical and psychological symptoms, and assess what resources they can draw on to help them through it, the more courage and resilience they will build. This might involve allowing your kid to communicate in a way that feels most comfortable to them, for example, via text message, even if they're sitting in the next room!

While in an ideal world your kid will turn to you if they are in need of help or support, the reality is that there are many reasons why this might not happen. I know plenty of people who described having good relationships with their parents growing up but who found it difficult to confide in them over certain things. In this instance, it can be helpful to consider whether there is a trusted adult, such as an aunt, uncle or family friend you can rely on to provide a safe space for your child should they need it. Dr Draisey acknowledges how tough it can be as a parent to place this trust in someone else and rely on them to honour your child's confidentiality if your child doesn't want you, or anyone else, to know what they are struggling with. At the same time, however, it's essential that that trusted person understands your parameters and can support your child in finding a way to speak to you if they are experiencing something serious that the adult feels you need to know about.

The hidden art of reassurance

Offering reassurance and praise are important, albeit nuanced, aspects of supporting your child's self-esteem and body confidence. However, when we constantly try to mitigate kids' concerns about their body image, or anything else, by reassuring them, they lose the opportunity to recognize and name what they're feeling and tolerate that discomfort. Without at least some ability to tolerate tough feelings, anxiety-prone kids tend to become adults who use avoidance strategies whenever difficult thoughts and feelings show up. Those strategies, including using drugs, alcohol, food, dieting or work, usually create further suffering rather than alleviating it.

We might think of this as clean and dirty pain. When we try to avoid our organic feelings of anxiety (clean pain) by burying ourselves in work or general busyness, for example, we often create further suffering, such as feeling disconnected from our loved ones, stressed, overwhelmed, and like our own needs aren't being met (all of which are examples of dirty pain). So, while there's a place for reassurance, it's also important that you sit alongside your child as they learn to tolerate and build resilience for the full range of human emotions.

The praise paradox

Giving praise can, of course, be positive for kids (and adults!), but there are some instances to be aware of in which it can be less helpful to a child's self-esteem. It's interesting to note that in more traditional cultures worldwide, praise is discouraged for fear of making children arrogant, over-confident and ego-driven. Conversely, Western industrialized cultures tend to consider praise as a valuable tool for reinforcing good behaviour and boosting kids' self-esteem. But what does the science say?[19]

Research shows that well-delivered praise can help children develop a positive and compassionate self-narrative, encouraging them to try hard, be persistent and cooperate. A simple, single-word exclamation such as, 'Wow!' or an encouraging gesture such as a high five or fist bump evokes positive feelings and motivates children to work on improving their performance and persevere with challenging tasks.[20] [21] This fosters a growth mindset, which is the belief that you can improve your most fundamental abilities through dedication and hard work.

Research also shows that being clear about what exactly you are praising, rather than general encouragement like, 'Great job!' or 'Well done!', can help develop kids' sense of competence and self-esteem. For example: 'It was so kind of you to help me bring the shopping in; I really appreciated it.'

A study on 3,000 ten-year-old Japanese children found that those children who received more praise for prosocial behaviour, such as helping and supporting others, showed fewer symptoms of depression between the ages of ten and twelve, even after the researchers controlled for confounding factors.[22]

It's clear, then, that praise can help bolster self-esteem, but there's also evidence to suggest it can have a negative impact. Praise can be detrimental for kids who feel uncomfortable receiving it, dislike attention, or feel embarrassed by it. Similarly, if kids perceive praise as insincere, they tend to feel misunderstood, pitied and even patronized. This is especially true for older children who can analyse the motives and beliefs of those around them.[23]

How to make praise positive

The way a child responds to praise is both individual and context-specific, but there are some general guidelines that can help ensure that it has a positive impact on your kid, as well as other members of your family, including yourself![24]

1. **Build the supportive framework:** Remember that to feel securely attached, we all need to feel loved, supported and accepted, regardless of what emotions we're experiencing or how well we have done. Praise, then, needs to fit into a

broader framework of supportiveness so that family members feel approved of as people all of the time, not just when they've accomplished something.

2. **Praise them for the hard stuff:** Offer praise for endeavours that have challenged your child somehow, not for things that come very easily to them. Praising children for things they find easy sends the message that either we have low expectations of them or don't understand the lack of challenge involved in the task, neither of which is conducive to improving their self-esteem.

3. **Don't go overboard:** While it might seem encouraging, excessive encouragement can feel disingenuous and/or like an impossible standard to maintain, especially for older children who have more of a concept of their future performance. Extreme praise – 'You're perfect!' 'You're the absolute best at this!' – can create anxiety in kids who don't want to lose their parents' respect or approval (we call this Golden Child Syndrome), leading them, paradoxically, to be less likely to try the next time they face a challenging situation.

4. **Praise effort, not ability:** It's good to praise kids for what is in their control, not what isn't. That means celebrating effort and their use of resources rather than having special abilities or natural talent. Research by developmental and social psychologist Dr Carol Dweck, a leading expert in motivation studies, has shown that when kids are praised for seemingly fixed attributes, such as talent or intelligence, it can give them the message that making mistakes is a sign of innate weakness that they have no power to improve on, which is the opposite of a growth mindset.

5. **Pay attention to tone:** Be as descriptive, warm and admiring as you can when delivering positive feedback so that your kid knows exactly what you're acknowledging and in a tone that feels sincere and non-analytical.

6. **Avoid praise that's in relation to others:** Steer clear of social-comparison praise and emphasize individual mastery. Social comparison theory, proposed by psychologist Leon Festinger, suggests that when we compare ourselves to others and find we're superior in some way, the result is a boost to our self-esteem. However, no one can finish first, be the most popular, prettiest, or best at something all the time. As and when kids inevitably lose their competitive edge, if their self-esteem is based only on how they match up to others, they're potentially going to start feeling inadequate or unworthy. In addition, praise based on social comparison promotes social standing as a value over individual mastery. Praising individual mastery avoids the pitfalls of comparison by emphasizing the value of intrinsic motivation. Kids with high intrinsic motivation are more likely to engage in self-care activities conducive to positive body image. That's because they value activities that help them feel good inside rather than feeling pressured by external influences to meet societal standards or gather appearance-based validation.

I've worked with many children and young people whose symptoms of depression, anxiety and disordered eating are strongly linked to their belief that to be loveable, acceptable and worthy, they have to be the best. The best at sport, the best academically, the best looking, the best all around. And it's an impossibly high bar for any child to begin to live up to. What's really striking about many of these kids, however, is that they frequently report that their parents don't put pressure on them at all. They tell me that their parents encourage them to relax, that they just want them to be happy, and that they should do what they enjoy. I stress this because it's a common misconception that perfectionist kids are the product of pushy parents. While that might be the case in some instances, it's certainly not the case in all, and it's important to recognize that the values and praise patterns of peers, teachers, coaches, media messages and, of course, kids themselves also play a key role.

Embracing imperfection

When working with high-achieving kids who feel a lot of pressure to be perfect, I focus on four main things:

1. **Values:** Clarifying what really matters most to them and why it matters.
2. **Emotional resilience:** Helping them to tolerate uncomfortable feelings when they arise so that they can stay true to their values even if difficult emotions show up.
3. **Self-compassion:** Helping them to be kinder to themselves, often by asking them to think about what they would say to their best friend if they felt the same way.
4. **Joy:** Encouraging them to engage in activities purely for the fun of it, not for the opportunity to impress anyone else or succeed.

Each of these techniques helps kids to disentangle from the need to relentlessly achieve to feel acceptable to the people who matter to them, especially themselves.

We'll continue to discuss praise as it relates to movement, exercise and body image in Chapter 6.

Mirror, mirror on the wall, help me be fair and not compare

In the Brothers Grimm story of Snow White and the Seven Dwarves, we can think of the mirror symbolizing several self-esteem-related themes. Beauty represents the highest power one can possess, and the evil Queen, Snow White's *birth* mother in the original story, turns to the mirror daily to determine whether she is the most beautiful, and therefore most powerful, in the land. She is deeply insecure, a narcissist who tries to self-soothe and boost her low self-esteem by comparing herself to others via her magic mirror.

What I like about this story is that the mirror doesn't just reflect the Queen's physical beauty, but her inner self, too. It symbolizes self-reflection and self-awareness that go beyond the Queen's beautiful exterior to reveal the shadows within. With that, the tale emphasizes the perils of an obsession with physical appearance. It also highlights how a lack of self-awareness and self-acceptance (something that those with narcissistic personality disorder struggle with enormously) leads to the attributing of blame, an indicator of low self-esteem, which, in this story, is represented by the Queen's intolerable jealousy of her own daughter. This not only reminds us to look within to find personal peace, but also that externalizing our pain by blaming it on other people or even simply comparing ourselves to others ultimately leads us further from our own inner contentment.

Self-reflection (literally)

For many people with low self-esteem and/or poor body image, the mirror is often a trigger for anxiety, low mood, frustration and even anger. Yet I would suggest that it's also an incredibly powerful tool for improving your – and your kid's – self-esteem and personal empowerment.

It may not feel like it right now, but looking in the mirror can be an act of profound self-compassion, self-acceptance and self-love. Self-compassion is so fundamental to our self-esteem because the more of it we have, the less space there is for self-criticism, a hallmark not just of a negative self-view but of anxiety and depression, too.[25]

Self-compassion is a way of relating to ourselves. It literally means, 'to suffer with'. It's the kindness, warmth, understanding and care we offer ourselves when we acknowledge our own suffering. It's the urge to want to help ourselves when we're having a hard time. It's a recognition of our humanity, fragility and imperfection. You might say that self-compassion comes from a place of love, whereas self-criticism comes from a place of fear; fear of failure, fear of judgement, and fear of abandonment.[26] That's why so many people who are prone to self-criticism are afraid even to try, and self-criticism is so strongly associated with underachievement and limiting behaviours such as procrastination.[27] I find it interesting how many people are sceptical of self-compassion, believing that you will wither away on the sofa and do nothing with your life if you are too nice to yourself.

But is that really the case?

Pick a coach

Imagine you're learning to play tennis, and you've had your first few sessions with a new coach, Pam. Every time you make a mistake, miss the ball, are in the wrong position, or misunderstand your instructions, your coach comes down on you like a ton of bricks. 'You're useless!' she yells across the court, rolling her eyes and checking her watch to see how much longer she has to endure your incompetence. 'Do it again, and this time, don't mess it up!'

Now imagine you've just had your first few sessions with a different coach, Derek. Despite making the same mistakes, he offers understanding and compassion and reassures you that making mistakes is part of the learning process. Derek tells you he's genuinely impressed with how quickly you're picking the skills up despite being such a new player. 'I know it's frustrating when it feels like you're making mistakes, but you are putting so much effort into this and with a few tweaks to the exercise, I think you'll nail it!'

Which coach do you think you would most enjoy working with? Who would be most likely to help you improve your game? And which coach do you currently have in your head?

Far from being self-indulgent and obstructing performance, research shows that people who talk to themselves in a self-compassionate way are just as ambitious as self-critical people, but their experience is generally more enjoyable and less driven by the avoidance of rejection and ridicule.

Just like with other painful internal experiences, many of us have come to avoid looking at our bodies in the mirror to protect ourselves from the painful thoughts and feelings it evokes, especially self-criticism. As we've discussed, those thoughts and feelings are often rooted in harmful beliefs we've inherited through diet culture and impossible beauty standards. By avoiding looking deeply in the mirror, we may temporarily avoid difficult feelings about ourselves, but we also miss the opportunity to really see ourselves, to offer ourselves compassion, and to realize that we're not as unacceptable as we thought. When we gaze at ourselves in the mirror, we allow ourselves to see and practise appreciating and accepting everything we are, both internally and externally. The emphasis here is on practice, because to notice the treasures in your reflection and whether those flaws you thought you had are all that awful, you must be willing to look. The same is true of our shadow selves, those hidden emotional aspects of ourselves that we don't like to acknowledge and, therefore, repress into the darkness of our subconscious. Those aspects cannot be integrated and healed until we find the courage to shine a light on them.

As pioneering compassion researcher Dr Kristin Neff suggests, 'Be kind to yourself when you look in the mirror. Say kind words, compliment yourself, and appreciate the unique person you see.'

Being willing to look is especially necessary if you've been practising the opposite for years until now: actively avoiding your reflection in the mirror or perhaps going out of your way to look for your flaws. Paradoxically, far from bullying yourself into better shape, talking to yourself in a negative way about your weight leads to an increase in the production of the stress hormone cortisol in our bodies, which in turn contributes to a slowing down of metabolism.[28]

How to cultivate self-compassion

You can develop a more compassionate attitude towards yourself, and help your kid do the same, in several ways. A good place to start is to have a set of phrases to draw on when you notice yourself experiencing emotional pain, whether it's as a result of stress before a big meeting, a fight with your partner, anxiety over climate change, or you feel not good enough in some way. When you notice a difficult thought or feeling show up, place your hand on your heart, or give yourself a gentle hug, and repeat the following phrases:

This is a moment of suffering.
We all suffer at times.
May I be gentle on myself.
May I offer myself the compassion I need.

These phrases, which can be adapted to suit you, encompass the three cornerstones of self-compassion; self-kindness, mindfulness and common humanity. The first phrase reflects mindfulness and present-moment awareness. The second reminds us of our shared humanity and that we are not alone in our suffering. The third encourages us to choose kindness over criticism and judgement, and the final phrase emphasizes that we, too, deserve compassion.[29]

Accepting yourself as perfectly imperfect

Given that you've chosen to read this book, I would hazard a guess that you are a fairly conscientious and internally motivated person. What most people with those attributes have in common is the idea they have in mind of who they 'should' be. For example, you might aspire to be kind, intelligent, loving, trustworthy, attractive, fun, positive or successful. Of course, none of us can be all of those things all of the time, and where we tend to run into trouble is when we expect ourselves to be able to consistently meet this idealized image of ourselves and feel inadequate or guilty when we do not. Unfortunately, what we then do to try to avoid these difficult thoughts and feelings is to strive even harder to become this idealized, perfect person, and so the vicious cycle continues.

To free ourselves from this trap, we have to decide to accept our imperfections, our flawsomeness. That means breaking free from the perfectionist standards we've set for ourselves and embracing ourselves as we are, warts and all.

To help with this, it can be useful to commit to actively taking in the good, and by that I mean allowing other people to compliment you without shrugging it off, disputing or challenging their opinion. Dismissing compliments can become quite habitual but reinforces a negative self-view. I'm not suggesting you suddenly try to agree with the compliments you receive, as that might feel disingenuous, but you can allow other people to have their positive opinion of you without undermining it or insinuating they're lying! In fact, this is an effective way of reminding yourself that there can be more than one 'truth', and that just because your mind comes up with negative thoughts about you doesn't mean that's what everyone thinks.

Body Confident You

My invitation to you is to spend a few minutes each day practising self-compassion in your own mirror. I know this might feel hard or even painful, especially if you've spent years being conditioned to believe fat is bad or your body is wrong in some way. I'm here to remind you that neither of those things is true. In many cultures, large bodies are associated with beauty, fertility and strength; we get to choose what we want to see as beautiful. Healthwise, I also want to remind you that there is no medical condition we see in fat bodies that we don't also see in thin bodies. It's just that the treatment options are often very different. You might also have been conditioned to see other aspects of your body as unacceptable too, such as your body hair. If this resonates, I have so much compassion for you. Stereotypes and stigma around women's hairiness may have had us all shaving and waxing furiously, but there is literally nothing more natural than the hair on your body. The embarrassment and shame women have been made to feel is just another example of how female bodies are policed, shamed, politicized and monetized. So, if you struggle with how you feel about your hairiness, remember that those feelings are likely to be, at least in part, a symptom of patriarchal beauty standards, and you, and only you, get to choose what feels best for your body.

As you look in the mirror, make space for whatever thoughts and feelings that might show up. If you're reading this and thinking, 'There's no way I'm doing that,' I encourage you to lean into those thoughts and do it anyway. Remember, change happens when we step outside of our comfort zone.

Bringing your most compassionate, empathic, non-judgemental part of yourself to the fore, notice what you see in your reflection.

The laughter lines.
The stories in your scars.
The heritage in your skin colour.
The dimples in your cheeks. All of your cheeks.
Your hands and all the things they enable you to do.
The stretch marks you acquired growing your baby, or simply just your body.

Then look closer still.
What's inside?

The curious mind.
The kindness to others.
The determination to keep on trying.
Courage to do difficult things.
A hurting heart that needs and deserves to be held gently.
Someone with a beautiful soul despite everything you've been through.
Glorious imperfection.

Notice what shows up for you as you gaze into the mirror and try to bring a non-judgemental, accepting stance to the thoughts and feelings that emerge. A key component of self-compassion is mindfulness, which means intentionally paying attention to your present-moment experience without trying to hold onto anything or push anything away. It means being aware of your experience and, simultaneously, allowing it to be exactly as it is in the moment. Mindfulness is fundamental to building your capacity for self-compassion, as it's only when we're fully aware of our internal experiences, including self-critical thoughts and negative self-talk, that we can choose to respond to ourselves with kindness and understanding. As we explored when looking at the Choice Point, pressing pause and being mindful gives us the power to be able to recognize our suffering without getting completely enmeshed with it.

EXERCISE

Body Confident Kid: Loving-Kindness Meditation

We can teach kids basic meditation skills to help them develop their capacity for self-soothing and compassion. Meditation helps kids develop self-awareness, emotional resilience, empathy and self-compassion. It also helps them manage stress and be more in contact with the present moment, which means encouraging a deeper connection and appreciation of the world around them and of themselves.

Below is a simple script you can read to your kid or record for them to listen to independently. They may even prefer to record it themselves, creating a soothing inner voice to counterbalance any self-critical thoughts they may experience.

Let's start by finding a comfortable sitting position with your hands placed gently in your lap.

Allow your breath to be exactly as it is right now. Bring your attention to your breath and just notice the air moving through your mouth or nose and filling your lungs. As you do this, notice how your body responds, notice how your lungs expand to make space for the air passing through your body and the lowering of your shoulders and ribcage as you exhale.

As you continue to focus on your breath, imagine that you are breathing in relaxation and letting go of any tension as you breathe out. If there are areas of your body that you notice feeling especially tense or tight, you might think about breathing that sense of relaxation into those areas.

Now imagine you are surrounded by a warm, glowing light, holding you gently like a comforting hug. This light is love and kindness, both towards yourself and others.

This light recognizes the goodness in you. With each breath, imagine that you are taking in that light and feeling a sense of peace and acceptance as you do. That light reminds you that you are worthy of love and acceptance exactly as you are. And that you deserve kindness. There is no need to change or be anyone other than who you are.

Take a moment to appreciate yourself, your uniqueness, and your strengths and qualities. Allow that light to fill you with love and acceptance, knowing you are enough just as you are.

When you're ready, gently bring your attention back to your breath, and again imagine you are breathing in a sense of relaxation and breathing out any tension.

Allow yourself a moment to pause.

When you're ready, you can slowly open your eyes and return your attention to the room.

Once the meditation is over, if you are practising together, it can be useful to reflect on your child's experience. This gives them space to share any thoughts or feelings that they noticed during the meditation and ask any questions they might have. Remember, meditation is a very individual practice; there is no right or wrong way to do it. There will be days when you and your kid feel centred and focused and, if you're anything like me, other days when your mind is flitting all over the place. That said, things that can help us all experience the benefits of meditation include finding a quiet and comfortable place to do it, sitting upright and gently bringing your attention back to the present moment when you notice your mind wandering.

Body Confident You and Body Confident Kid Exercise: A Love Letter to Yourself

Acting from a place of self-compassion and self-love puts you and your child in a better position to enjoy life and your pursuits and feel more content in the person you are than acting from a place of self-criticism ever will.

Writing (or recording) a love letter to yourself is a powerful exercise for you and your kid. Although it will likely be challenging, it's an opportunity to consciously acknowledge your needs and how much you deserve for them to be met. It's a chance to show up for yourself, to give yourself love, acceptance and appreciation for who you are, and to provide an alternative narrative to the autopilot negativity of the inner critic. It's a reminder that the most important person of all approves of you – and that's you.

You might have to lean into some awkwardness in completing this, and there are two ways to go about it. The first is to write it down in a letter and place it in a self-addressed envelope, then ask someone you trust to keep it safe for you and post it back to you at a time that they feel might be helpful. The second option is to record your letter on your phone and play it back to yourself every few days, or whenever you need a reminder of your worth.

Put some time in your diary for a date with yourself, so it feels like a comforting act of self-love rather than a chore. In this letter, I suggest you address all of the aspects you love about yourself, or if that feels really hard at the moment, that someone who really cherishes you would say are loveable about you.

That might include:

* *Your strengths*
* *The ways in which you're kind*
* *Your sense of purpose*
* *The impact you have on those around you and the impact you have yet to have*
* *The ways in which you inspire others*
* *Your uniqueness*
* *The challenges you've overcome*
* *Your achievements*

To give you an example, here is the self-love letter I wrote to myself while I was writing this book:

Dear Charlotte,

I just wanted to say how proud I am of you and how glad I am to be you. I know that I haven't always been there for you in the way you deserve and that I have often been the enemy within, turning on you when you most need me and making it hard for you to appreciate or enjoy any of your efforts or achievements. I know I have often made you feel like you weren't a good person.

I know you are a good person. I know how hard you try to do the right things by others and make a difference in the world even when you are battling your own demons. That takes a lot of strength and determination.

I deeply value your humility, compassion towards others, and appreciation for every opportunity you've been given. You deserve compassion, too. Sometimes, I've undermined who you are and what you've achieved by overemphasizing the blessings you've had and diminishing the challenges you've faced. I've been determined to celebrate everyone but you. That wasn't fair, and I'm sorry.

I love the way you always try to take responsibility when you have been in the wrong and apologize. I am proud of the courage you have shown in looking at your shadows and finding new ways of behaving, even when it feels scary and difficult. I know there is so much more to come, and I believe you can and will leave the positive mark you want to on the world.

I love your tenacity and the space you've made for my immense doubt and criticism. To be honest I'm surprised how you have succeeded in your career despite me. I also know that your drive to achieve often masks the darker thoughts and feelings you have, and I want you to know that you are valuable and loved whether you are achieving or not and whether you look a certain way or not.

Your greatest beauty will come from your own self-acceptance and your greatest achievement will come from recognizing that you are already enough as you are.

I will always try to have your back.

Love,

Me

KEY REFLECTIONS

- We come into the world hardwired to feel safe in our bodies, our environment and ourselves. Our nervous systems are designed to help us do this by assessing safety and risk, but sometimes they become a bit too vigilant and set alarm bells ringing unnecessarily. This can often lead to thoughts about not being good enough and encourage us to go down the sticky path of comparison. Understanding that these thoughts and feelings reflect your nervous system's attempt to keep you safe rather than a sign you are lacking in some way or about to be cast from the tribe can help you and your kid make space for the difficult feelings.

- Exposing both your child and yourself to a rich diversity of body types will help to dismantle stigmatizing attitudes towards marginalized bodies and reduce the pressure you both feel to conform to an idealized appearance in order to feel safe and accepted. This is important even if your kid has a body that is socially revered, because that might not always be the case. Bodies change.

- Model self-compassion and celebrate your flawsomeness! Normalize being kind and respectful towards yourself and accepting of all of the parts of you so that your child learns to do the same. If this feels hard and you find it tricky to move away from ingrained habits such as self-depreciation, having practised the exercises in this book, consider seeking the help of a therapist who specializes in healing body image and practices from a Health at Every Size perspective.

- Using the Choice Point from Chapter 2 (see page 79), notice when hooks such as not being good enough, attractive enough, successful enough or 'should' thoughts show up and ask yourself, 'Is it going to be helpful to me to get enmeshed with this thought?' Then, do a brief check-in with yourself and decide what it is that you need, at that moment, to help you feel connected to your values.

- Notice how your kid responds to praise and adjust your delivery accordingly. Focus on encouraging what is in their control rather than natural ability and be specific about what you're praising them for.

- Use every self-critical thought you notice as a cue to practice self-compassion, whether that be repeating the self-compassion phrases outlined in this chapter, practising a loving-kindness meditation, taking a mindful pause, or doing mirror work.

- Remember, confidence and self-esteem come from accepting yourself and having your own back, not from a relentless quest for self-improvement.

CHAPTER FIVE

Scrolling for Self-Love: Balancing Body Positivity and Pressures Online

'Technology doesn't just do things for us. It does things to us, changing not just what we do but who we are.'
Sherry Turkle, sociologist and
human-technology interaction expert

In 2019, the Mental Health Foundation launched a survey as part of Mental Health Week which found that almost a third of teens felt shame about how they looked, and 40 per cent of them cited social media as a cause for their body image concerns. The survey also found that 35 per cent of respondents reported worrying about their appearance every single day, and the same amount said that they had stopped or heavily restricted their eating due to anxiety about how they looked. Another study exploring US teenagers' online experiences found that 59 per cent had been subjected to cyberbullying, including attacks on their appearance.[1]

As well as teens, social media use is also strongly linked to body image concerns and eating disorders in adults. Studies show that 88 per cent of women compare themselves to the social media images of the people they follow, and over half of them judge those comparisons unfavourably.[2] This is unsurprising given that, for example, while 55 per cent of American women have an endomorph body shape (soft and round with a higher body fat percentage), they are the least represented on social media by a large margin. The most represented are mesomorph body types (lean and muscular), which only 7 per cent of the US population possess. With that in mind, it's not hard to see how social media comparisons can leave us feeling lacking, and that's before we consider the additional issues of filters and doctoring of images.

Meanwhile, in a survey of 2,000 British mums, 63 per cent felt that they compared themselves unfavourably to others online not just in appearance, but also felt under pressure to be a more perfect parent.[3] The influence of social media is clearly formidable, shaping the perceptions of both children and adults regarding their own appearance and self-concept.

It's amazing to think that just a couple of decades ago, social media didn't even exist. MySpace, commonly regarded as the first social media site, didn't reach a million monthly users until 2004. Before that, most of us were happy simply to hear the sound of an internet connection finally being made via the painfully slow dial-up phone line.

Nowadays, whether we like it or not, a child's online world is a legitimate part of their 'real world', as well as potentially yours, so it's helpful to take an interest in it. That's especially true given some of the unique challenges it presents.

Arguably, one of the most problematic features of social networking sites is the constant bombardment of aspirational images we're exposed to, many of which aren't even real. One US social media and body image survey found that nearly 50 per cent of women and nearly 60 per cent of men take between two and five selfies before feeling satisfied enough to post online, with some respondents spending over twenty minutes tweaking each image before sharing.[4] Meanwhile, Girlguiding's annual report found that a third of girls and young women aged 11–21 won't post a selfie online without editing it first. One outcome of this is the emergence of new subsets of body image disorders such as 'Snapchat dysmorphia', a term coined by plastic surgeons to describe the increasing number of patients requesting modifications to make them look like a filtered image of themselves.[5] Even when images are real, they're often posted by people whose full-time job it is to look a certain way and sell products off the back of their content.

One of the major challenges social media presents is its emphasis on online validation and, relatedly, cyberbullying. We might wonder, if we as adults are affected by the number of likes and hearts our online presence attracts and find it difficult not to be impacted by other users' trolling or inflammatory behaviour, how are kids supposed to deal with it?

Safety online

While there isn't specific legislation governing every potentially harmful website, ethical guidelines and best practices do serve minimal standards that web hosts must adhere to. The introduction of the UK Online Safety Act in 2021 aims to regulate online platforms and ensure that web-based companies uphold a duty of care to their users. That means they're obligated to ensure that content likely to be viewed by children doesn't contain potentially dangerous or inappropriate content. In many instances, however, parents facilitate their kids' use of technology that they haven't been cleared to access. For example, many parents will allow their kids to use WhatsApp as a means of communicating with family and friends despite their children being under WhatsApp's minimum age criteria of sixteen. These are muddy waters indeed, especially when certain apps can feel like the lifeblood of your child's social network.

Positively, platforms hosting eating disorder content must now prevent minors from accessing related material. It doesn't, however, protect adults from harmful, pro-eating disorder information. It also doesn't address the problem of celebrities, influencers and everyday social media users who, knowingly or unknowingly, promote harmful dieting and weight loss beliefs and behaviours. What compounds the problem is that sometimes, they even get paid to do so by companies set to benefit from users' body dissatisfaction. This is significant, given that nearly 5 billion people use social media worldwide, with the average person spending 2 hours and 24 minutes on social media platforms every day. Those figures include the 91 per cent of 15–16-year-olds who use social media.[6] That's a lot of exposure for young and impressionable audiences.

Two sides to every coin

Before we go further, though, please don't despair. While there is no doubt social media presents hurdles to overcome and real threats to kids' and our own wellbeing, body image and self-view, it's also an incredible portal for learning, including making psychological information and support more accessible.

Despite its dangers, I would argue that social media isn't all bad, and can be a powerful tool in promoting body acceptance, diversity, personal agency, body positivity and genuine health and fitness. While most studies agree social media has a significant impact on teenagers' body image, they also show conflicting results in terms of whether specific age brackets are more vulnerable. One found that the impact of social media is strongly linked to kids' developmental age, with girls aged 11–13 and boys aged 14–15 reporting a negative link between social media use and life satisfaction. At other ages, it found that that link isn't statistically significant.[7] This suggests that social media may present more of a risk to kids' mental health at specific times during adolescence, which may be useful in identifying times when kids are developmentally more vulnerable and may need additional support. My advice here would be to be guided by your own kid's experience and neither assume that they will be impacted negatively nor assume that they won't be.

Social media can also offer free access to supportive communities of all different types, from those in marginalized bodies, eating disorder sufferers, those with compromised health, and people suffering from loneliness, or as a means of simply bringing more joy into your life. These forums can provide a lifeline and go some way to providing the empathy, understanding, support and encouragement that we all need to reach a place of greater self-acceptance, inner peace and contentment. Social media also offers tremendous potential reach for activists to transmit messages of equality, diversity, disability rights, gender rights and fat acceptance, and provides a platform on which frequently silenced voices can be heard.

More informed parents mean more empowered kids, who are better positioned to build the resilience and security required to withstand negative feedback on or offline. From this perspective, you could say that social media and the internet, more broadly, do create certain problems, but also help us find solutions to them.

Part of the fear around social media use for parents is often the lack of familiarity and invisibility of what goes on on kids' devices. Unless you're an internet whizz, the online world can feel like an abyss of uncertainty in terms of how algorithms, influencers and Big Tech might be pushing your kids one way or another. Those unknowns can be worrying, even in the absence of any behavioural change or distress in your kid. Combined with our innate evolutionary tendency to pay close attention to potential threat, this makes us much more susceptible to worrying about news articles reporting on the negative impact of the digital world on kids, even when our own kid is doing fine. My aim here is to provide sound guidance to help you feel more informed about what you can do to help you and your child have a safe and enjoyable online life while acknowledging that there are some issues to look out for and hold lightly in mind.

I don't know you, but please like me: Virtual validation and self-worth

It's easy for anyone who regularly uses networking sites to start to rely on social media feedback to form their sense of identity and self-esteem, especially kids. That's a concern when feedback via likes, shares and comments is often instantaneous and public in a way that it isn't offline. Even more problematically, many of the people providing feedback are complete strangers who don't even know you. Receiving this constant feedback can lead to an unhealthy obsession with others' opinions and excessive levels of self-evaluation and comparison. In addition, people are more inclined to act maliciously when they feel protected by the anonymity of a keyboard and screen.

Negativity tends to breed negativity, resulting in one person's negative comment spiralling into a potential cascade of online abuse. One reason for this may be our inbuilt negativity bias, which primes us to pay more attention to negative content. This makes us more likely to engage with and share it, which the algorithms – the rules, signals and data that direct a platform's operation and determine how content is shown to its users – love.[8] Inappropriate behaviour online can, therefore, be encouraged by the situation and may not solely be down to the antisocial personality traits of the offender.[9]

Why do we cyberbully?

There are several reasons why people bully others online. These include:

1. **Domination:** An attempt to exert power and control over the victim, often as a defensive means of compensating for their own feelings of powerlessness, inadequacy or insecurity.
2. **Publicity:** Bullying that occurs in public forums can potentially reach a large audience and, therefore, have more potential impact.

3. **Shareability:** Bullying is often repetitive, and this is exacerbated online by the fact that posts have enormous potential longevity due to the capacity for sharing and re-posting by others long after the original post was made.[10] [11]

Wounding words

Many of us grew up with the old adage, 'Sticks and stones may break my bones, but words can never hurt me.' Kids especially use this retort to protect themselves against name-calling and to build resilience, and it works to a point. That is, until they start to believe the words that are being thrown at them.

Contrary to the old adage, words can and do hurt. They may not be physical in the way stick and stones are, but they can have just as an immediate impact on our bodies, and the same brain that allows us to understand what words mean also regulates our nervous system.[12] This explains why our response to words often feels so physical: hair standing on end, heart racing, going weak at the knees, a warm, fuzzy feeling, heart sinking. We experience our nervous system through our bodies.

Words, then, have the power to affect us physically and mentally and can cause lasting damage. They can not only maintain anxious feelings, but actually cause them. Studies have found that our brains respond to negative language, especially when it's directed at us, by releasing stress and anxiety-inducing hormones, including cortisol and adrenaline.[13] And this happens not only when others speak negatively to us, but also when we speak negatively to ourselves.

Thankfully, words can also be protective, and so can insight. Just as we can negatively affect someone's nervous system by raising our voice, leaving a negative comment, or even looking at them in a disapproving way, so too can we positively impact others and our own internal state by speaking kindly. Psychologist and neuropsychologist Lisa Feldman Barrett, a renowned researcher of emotions and the brain's response to stress, identified three key ingredients our brains use to make emotions:

1. **Our basic bodily sensations:** Our fundamental physical feelings, such as our heart rate, butterflies in our tummy, spine tingles, dry mouth and temperature, form the basis of our emotions and provide our brains with clues as to how you should feel (i.e., your emotion). Emotions are essentially our brain's best guess about how we should feel and what we need at any given moment.

2. **Our surroundings:** This includes all aspects of our external environment, including what we experience online. The information we receive via our senses, what we see, hear, taste, smell and touch in the world around us, also helps our brains decide what we should feel at that time. It's where the phrase 'story follows state' comes from, because our thoughts and the way we tend to make sense of our experience are heavily impacted by the state of our nervous system. That's why it's helpful to check in regularly to see how we are feeling so that, if necessary, we can change our surroundings.

3. **Our previous experiences:** Our brains tend to use our past experiences to construct appropriate emotions when facing new situations.[14] For instance, if your beloved pet has died but

you haven't experienced such a loss before, your brain might draw on other 'close enough' bereavements that you've faced or your observations of others grieving to form a new experience of sadness.[15]

The more aware of these three ingredients we are, the more active we can be in recognizing what we're experiencing, adjusting our environment accordingly, and putting in place the support we need. We may not be able to control how we feel sometimes, but knowing why we might be feeling that way gives us more choice about how we want to respond. This recipe is a potential game-changer for protecting your kid and helping them build resilience to all types of online (or offline) verbal abuse or negativity, including concern trolling, outing, name-calling or flaming. The exercises at the end of this chapter will help you and your child develop these skills.

How influencers shape our body image and self-concept

Social media influencers make a living by swaying people's opinions and behaviours. Their skillset lies in building a personal brand that holds weight with their audience and being able to promote either their own or someone else's products or services, thereby generating sales. To achieve this, influencers make exciting, inspiring, shareable and sometimes controversial content. They use specific settings, marketing tactics, scripts and collaborations to entice more followers and encourage engagement.

Sometimes, this entails using very selective representations of their lives (usually only the best bits) to achieve this. The effort that goes into creating specific messages, images and feelings can, however, be hard to decipher, and this is reflected in research findings that 32 per cent of preteens are uncertain about whether what they see online is even true.[16]

Sometimes influencers' impact is positive and sometimes negative, but either way, they're likely to be a feature of your kid's life, and probably yours as well, for the foreseeable future. From a looking-glass perspective, influencers have the power to affect how we see beauty and success and act as more mirrors for us to look at and compare ourselves against. If those depictions are narrow or unrealistic, but we're unaware of that, the impact on our self-concept can be potentially damaging.

'I'll never look like them.' Sally's story

Sally was in her early thirties when she came to therapy in utter disdain about her body. 'It's impacting every area of my life,' she told me. As a mum with a young daughter, she no longer had the time nor energy to exercise rigidly and was angry at herself that she'd been unable to get her pre-baby body back. She was adamant that the only hope she had left was through surgical contouring, and she was saving up for various modifying procedures, including a breast reduction and tummy tuck. 'I'm only here because my partner's worried about me undergoing risky surgeries, and I need you to help me convince him it's in the interest of my mental health,' she explained.

As Sally and I gently unpacked her painful past, it became clear that her poor body image and fragile self-esteem were rooted in her experience of being adopted as a child and her subsequent escape into cyberspace. She believed there must have been something wrong with her to make her biological parents not want her. This was despite understanding logically that they weren't able to care for her sufficiently and her adoptive parents offering a secure, supportive and loving home. She told me that she couldn't remember a time that she'd been herself in a fully spontaneous way, apart from when she was online gaming.

Indeed, Sally's immersion in the online world was striking. Not only did she work in the tech industry, but her social life was almost exclusively built around online gaming networks, and she was an avid social media user. While, for some, the number on the scales dictates what kind of day it's going to be, for Sally it was the number of likes and follows that governed how validated she felt. She revered social media influencers whose perfect appearance awarded them with, in Sally's eyes, love, acceptance and a free ride through life. This was something that she craved, perhaps because her low self-esteem made her doubt whether she would ever be good enough at her job to support herself, and her child self longed to be looked after and taken care of. But she felt she could never match up, and her self-comparisons with online models and influencers ultimately led her to a place where she felt so inadequate that she avoided even looking at herself in the mirror from the neck down.

For Sally, the golden thread that led her away from despair

and towards more healthy self-esteem was understanding how disruption and trauma in her early caregiving experience had manifested in a heightened fear of rejection and abandonment. This insight gave her greater compassion for her child self, who was so vigilant to signs that she might not be good enough and might be abandoned again. Over time, she realized that she didn't need to look or be perfect to be safe and cared for. She started to acknowledge the beauty in others without making it mean that she was unattractive. She recognized that, while she had made some good friends through gaming, playing online several hours a day took her away from her values of being present with her daughter, showing up authentically in the world, spending quality time with her partner and engaging in self-care. She became more able to internalize positive feedback at work and believe that she didn't need to be given freebies, nor validation from strangers online, to have what she wanted in life. She also realized that the social media accounts she held for her pets and creative endeavours supported her self-esteem in a way that her fashion account, which focused solely on her appearance and encouraged negative self-comparison, did not.

How are you influenced?

As always, it's helpful to take a look at how you personally relate to influencer content before thinking about the impact it has on your kid. To do so, ask yourself questions such as:

- *How does looking at influencer content make me feel about myself?*
- *Do I keep in mind that editing and filtering may have been used when looking at influencer content?*
- *Do I feel the need to buy particular products or undergo certain procedures promoted by influencers to enhance my appearance?*
- *Am I following a diverse range of influencers who represent different body types, cultures and lifestyles?*
- *Do I feel inspired and empowered by the influencers I follow, or do they make me feel inadequate?*

To help your kid 'keep it real' and maintain realistic expectations for themselves and others, even when influencers, including picture-perfect AI influencers, are literally at their fingertips, having open and transparent conversations is key. Approaching this in a relaxed, informal and curious way, as opposed to a 'We need to talk . . .'–type opening, is less likely to have your kid running for the hills. Some conversation starters might include questions such as:

- *Who's your favourite influencer, and what do they do?*
- *How do they make money out of their account? Is it through views, likes and follows, product sales, or something else?*
- *Do you think their reels reflect their real life?*
- *How does it make you feel when you watch their videos?*
- *How much time do you reckon they spend making each reel?*
- *Do you notice any influencers that make you feel less positive?*

Parental smartphone use

Social media is designed to impact us below the level of subconscious awareness, and that makes it easy to get sucked down internet rabbit holes before you've even realized it happening. That's not to say that we don't have any responsibility or control over our behaviour. On the contrary, it's important that we consider how aligned our social media usage is with our values, not only for ourselves but because it sets a clear example for our kids. Social media might offer us rewards and reinforcements, but so do many offline activities that may have fewer drawbacks.

With that in mind, here are some proactive steps you can take to set a positive example to your child around social media use:

- Be mindful of what you are conveying to your kid when you're using your phone. While engaging in screen-based activities can be a healthy bonding experience, socializing on your phone while with your child is likely to diminish how present you are in your interaction with them. Multi-socializing in this way will influence how your kid feels in your presence and influence how available they feel you are. When we use our phones to distract ourselves because there's a lull in the conversation or we're feeling bored, it also models a lack of tolerance for less exciting or stimulating emotions. So be aware of what you convey and try to teach your child through your own screen use.
- Be conscious of your own posting behaviour. Do you spend a lot of time editing your images or taking multiple selfies to find one that feels 'good enough' to post? Be kind and

curious about what your kid might infer from your own image-sharing activities.

- Be mindful of your own response to likes on images that you post, and the message that sends to your kids. Complaining that no one has liked that picture of you in your new dress sends the message that external validation is important and that your own opinion, or the opinions of those close to you, aren't enough.

Still-face

In 1972, a study called the still-face experiment[17] was conducted to explore whether caregiver interactions impacted infants' development and thriving. The experiment was pretty simple, and involved mothers sitting in front of their babies while being video recorded. Initially the mothers talk to their babies, laughing, smiling and responding when they point to things around the room. Then, for two minutes, the mothers stop all interaction with their babies; they are still, unsmiling and unresponsive. The babies invariably react by trying to engage their mothers, screeching, pointing and waving their arms; they are confused and eventually become distressed and start crying. When the mothers re-engage and re-establish connection, the babies are initially wary before they recover and resume normal interaction with their mums. This experiment was relatively brief and conducted in a lab setting, but it clearly demonstrates how a lack of or inconsistent engagement can be very distressing for a child and how critically important these early interactions are for kids' social development.

So, what happens when kids experience their parents being non-responsive more frequently, or if their attempts to re-engage their parents are met with frustration? What happens when their parent shifts between being responsive at times and ignoring the child at others? This is often the scenario when parents are on their own digital devices. Dr Elaine Kasket, a counselling psychologist and author of *Reset: Rethinking Your Digital World for a Happier Life*,[18] explains, 'A bored parent looking for connection and looking for entertainment [. . .] lapses into the same kind of facial expression as the parents in the still-face experiment. That's okay if that situation isn't frequent, but if we're habitually on our phone rather than responsive to the child, then that can profoundly affect that child's attachment. It can affect their neuropsychological development.' Being mindful of *our own* relationship with and use of technology is therefore as important for kids' wellbeing and sense of self as their own – perhaps even more so.

Kids' smartphone use

The amount of time kids spend on devices is also relevant, and one of the challenges around it is that hard-and-fast rules are likely to result in pushback. The American Academy of Paediatrics recommends no screen time for kids under two, one hour or less per day of non-educational screen time for kids aged two to twelve, and no more than two hours per day for teens and adults. Now, I don't know about you, but when I was a kid, I would get home from spending the entire day at school with my best friend, Sarah, only to spend two hours chatting with her on the phone.

Kids' friendships are important to their wellbeing and development, and we don't want to stop them just because the medium they use is different. There's a lot of guidance around setting limits on kids' devices, but as Dr Jenny Draisey explains, 'children will naturally reject [imposed limits] because they're not part of the decision-making process'. Collaborative conversations, in which you share your concerns about screen usage and invite your kid to share their concerns, too, are a good place to start in reaching a mutual agreement. Open discussions will also make it less likely that your kid will go behind your back and do what they want to do anyway. They also pave the way for building emotional vocabulary around social media use.

Behind the curtain: Safeguarding kids' body image in the digital age

Social media and its users are rather reminiscent of the characters in *The Wizard of Oz*. The Wizard, residing in the seemingly perfect and idealized Emerald City, is actually just a normal, fallible, everyday older guy in an average place using amplifying technology to appear powerful, when most of it is just smoke and mirrors. As I mentioned in Chapter 3 (see page 119), the character of Dorothy can be seen to represent a journey to find our own sense of home. In a social media context, we can think of this in terms of navigating the online world in search of belonging, acceptance and security. Often, we find ourselves yearning for something more, which can be a result of comparing ourselves to others and finding ourselves lacking, leaving us feeling like we're missing some holy grail or nirvana state that others seem to have attained. We could also see the character of the scarecrow in terms of his quest for acceptance as he finds himself falling short intellectually when he compares himself to others. The lion's longing for courage may reflect the challenge many of us feel in showing up authentically, not just online but generally in a way that might go against the grain of accepted beauty standards. Similarly, in his desperate search for a heart, we may see our desire for validation through likes, comments, shares and followers reflected in the tin man's character.

It doesn't matter if you're an adult or a child: unless you use the internet with your eyes wide open, the likelihood is that you're going to get drawn into a suspension of disbelief – that is, a place where we believe what we see to be true, even though it often isn't. Being digitally conscious means being mindful about what we have showing up in our newsfeeds, because the chances are there'll be some doctored content and injudicious claims, sending us subtle messages about social norms, cultural values, ideologies, trends, consumerism and various other perceptions of what it means to look like and be a worthwhile person.

Fostering digital literacy

To this end, digital literacy, and particularly critical awareness, are now essential skills for kids to learn to help them navigate and safely benefit from the online world. Digital literacy doesn't just mean how to use the internet, which is something the kids of today, who are essentially digital natives born into an online world, may find more intuitive than those of us who are digital immigrants and had to learn how to use the internet later in life.

Being digitally literate actually means several things, including:

- Being able to access information from a variety of sources.
- Evaluating that information in terms of its credibility, accuracy and reliability.
- Being able to distinguish opinion from fact.
- Being able to identify disinformation and fake news.
- Being able to recognize bias, question assumptions and consider ethical and legal issues relative to digital information, including copyright, privacy, security, intellectual property and online etiquette.
- Being aware of our digital footprint.

But why is this so relevant to improving your own and your kids' body image and body confidence? Because being digitally literate and having critical awareness is crucial to feeling empowered around your body in the digital age. Developing these skills will give both you and your kid the ability to evaluate media representations of body ideals critically, recognize who might stand to benefit from certain media messages and advertising, notice when unrealistic or harmful beauty standards are being promoted online, and understand how edited images and filters can be impactful. Such knowledge and awareness helps us all develop a more realistic view of bodies generally. Consequently, this drives a greater appreciation and acceptance of diverse body types, including our own. It also reduces the likelihood of comparing ourselves negatively to digitally altered images, especially as there are no regulations around watermarking modified or AI content at the time of writing.

Through the digital looking glass

According to Cooley's theory of the Looking-Glass Self (see page 31), we develop our self-concept via three main stages:

1. How we think we appear to others, including our appearance and behaviour.
2. How we think others judge us based on their positive or negative perceptions.
3. How we then develop our own self-view based on the perceived judgements we think others have about us and the feedback we receive from them.

How we see ourselves, then, is far from solely based on our internal experience, but also heavily influenced by our interactions with others and how we *think* they think about us. This is somewhat complicated when we consider that we give some feedback more weight than others (for example, you may take your best friend's opinion more seriously than a stranger's) and sometimes misinterpret what others are thinking or saying about us. We also try to match how we see ourselves with how others see us. This can lead us to not take positive feedback seriously if the way we think of ourselves is negative, worsening body image insecurities if we think we fit a bodily ideal but feel others don't see us in that way, or, conversely, boosting body confidence if external validation aligns with our own self-image.

Social media has, therefore, made the process of developing our self-perception infinitely more complex. Whereas, historically, the Looking-Glass Self was developed largely via the people whose paths we crossed in person, in our families and local communities, now we are confronted with a never-ending and ever-increasing number of 'mirrors'.[19] Cyberspace has also created the possibility for each of us to develop a whole new alter ego, a cyber self, a unique version of 'me' that represents our identity in the digital realm. This *can* align with who we are offline, or it can be extremely far removed. It can also vary depending on the platform you're using. For example, my Facebook persona depicts me as a horse, dog and running enthusiast who spends much of my time on holiday. My Instagram page, which I use for work, rarely features the horse, dog, sporting or social aspects of my identity, but shines light heavily on my professional persona as a psychologist. As far as my Instagram identity shows, I rarely leave my office! So far, no real issue, but what happens when your identity isn't fully formed before you start using the internet, or your online identity gets attacked at a young age, or you feel you just don't match up to others' lives, appearances or personalities on social media?

Mary Aiken, a leading expert on how people think and behave online, highlights how this digital Looking-Glass Self, or cyber self, can potentially interfere with kids' development away from screens.

This happens for three main reasons:

1. Their online profiles can be quickly changed based on the opinions of others.
2. Their digital identity can differ considerably across different platforms, potentially leading to a lack of integration of different parts of their identity.
3. Their presence is always available for others to see and comment on, unlike in everyday life offline.

Avatars

Avatars (that is, characters that represent you in the virtual world and are under your control) are another way in which we manipulate our online presence to feel more acceptable to others and ourselves. People respond to avatars' appearances in the same way they respond to people's physical characteristics in person. Depending on the site or game, users are offered varying levels of freedom in creating their own avatar, with some offering full customization and others providing a preset catalogue of avatar options created by the designer.[20]

How kids create their avatars is interesting from a body image perspective, as research shows their customization usually reflects how they see themselves in three ways:

- How they would ideally like to be seen (ideal self)
- What they actually are (real self)
- What they think they should be (ought self)[21]

To this end, your kid's avatar can provide a useful indicator of how they feel about their own appearance. According to research, the extent to which kids create avatars that accurately reflect their real selves seems to correlate with their self-esteem.[22] So, kids with high self-esteem and who are satisfied with their appearance tend to create avatars that look like they do. In contrast, kids with lower self-esteem and psychological well-being tend to create a better version of themselves with more desirable features.[23]

Fortunately, there are lots of things you can do to steer your kid towards developing a coherent, peaceful sense of self that spans both their online and offline worlds.

Unravelling the digital wellness web

Digital literacy and critical awareness become all the more important as we continue to navigate not only diet culture on- and offline but also its fast-growing and equally sneaky relative: wellness culture. This makes being a parent in the digital age tricky in a way no generation has had to contend with before. Whereas, historically, parents' health and wellness practices were largely influenced by their own family traditions and the practices and values of those they were in close contact with, nowadays, we all have to manage the impact of near-constant connectivity and an inevitable barrage of conflicting opinions. Therefore, unless you're someone who has firm boundaries around your online usage, this can often mean that there's an overload of information and disinformation to be sifted through daily, pertaining to all aspects of your life: food, exercise, self-care, mindfulness, stress management and personal development. Given its phenomenal reach, it's unsurprising that wellness culture has hijacked social media platforms so profoundly. Because of this, it's useful to think about how it influences you and how these ideas interact with your own self-view and beliefs about bodies.

Journalist and registered dietician Christy Harrison high-lights how the wellness industry seized on the moment during the Covid pandemic and capitalized on people's health fears. In her book *The Wellness Trap*,[24] she documents how wellness propaganda became so much more prominent in people's lives, sucking us into a wellness pipeline with very little or no evidence base and using social media to give harmful rhetoric considerable traction. 'Wellness culture shares major tenets of diet culture. It worships thinness and equates it to health and moral value, promotes weight loss as a means of attaining higher status, demonizes certain foods and ways of eating while celebrating others, and oppresses people who don't match its supposed picture of health,' Christy explained. She described how many of us become accosted by wellness misinformation and disinformation once we enter innocently via the door of yoga, fitness, nutrition, healthcare or even spirituality. This information is often well intended but misguided and potentially harmful, frequently fuelled by health and wellness influencers with few credentials but large followings and without the integrity of a sound evidence base.

Christy told me that one of the major problems with wellness culture is its tendency to cherry-pick certain aspects of ancient methods or Traditional Chinese Medicine outside the conventional healthcare system that are perceived as being non-Western and, therefore, inherently better. In most cases, however, that is an inaccurate representation of those practices. Their effectiveness, if they have any at all, is most likely through their cultural relevance to a specific population. This is in contrast to actual scientific, physical impacts on people's health, as we would expect to see with evidence-based medicine.

Unconventional medicine is difficult to define, encompassing various philosophies and practices from multiple traditions, histories and beliefs.[25] It includes methods such as homoeopathy,

Ayurveda, acupuncture, reiki and Oriental medicine, and for several reasons wellness influencers are often drawn to advocating these types of approaches. Firstly, promoting more novel medicinal ideas helps them stand out in a crowded online space. Many are not ethically bound to endorse evidence-based practices in the way that registered healthcare professionals are. Some will receive monetary incentives from companies invested in unconventional medicinal products, and others may have personal beliefs about the efficacy of holistic or natural approaches. Part of the problem is that it is often difficult, if not impossible, to decipher the motivations behind an online endorsement and to predict if someone else's personal experience will be the same for you and your family.

Planting peril?
Wellness culture from birth

The impact of both diet and wellness culture starts extremely young, arguably even before birth, when mums are often shamed for gaining too much weight during pregnancy or the baby's size being a point of contention with doctors. In my clinic, I've worked with several parents who have been shamed for having a baby who was deemed to be too big, too small, or premature, and others who have been judged for feeding their infants formula versus breast milk.

In her article '"Breast Is Best" Nearly Cost My Baby Her Life', published on the online platform Medium,[26] Dr Elaine Kasket shared her experience of being shamed by a health visitor for feeding her newborn baby powdered formula. Although she shared observations and evidence that her daughter was getting insufficient milk from breastfeeding alone, her concerns were never seriously considered nor assessed and were disregarded in favour of persisting because 'breast is best'.

Wellness culture shows up in all spaces, including in healthcare, because, ultimately, healthcare experts are human too and not immune to sociocultural norms, beliefs, influences and influencers.

Sharenting

According to Childnet, a resource promoting online safety for young people, 'sharenting' describes a parent or carer using the internet to share information, news, images or videos about their child. I have friends and family who don't post anything about their children online, friends who post the backs of their kids' heads or cover their faces with emojis, and friends who share family life daily. Each of these choices is valid, and if you post pictures of your kid regularly, you're far from alone; one survey found that a third of parents posted pictures of their kids daily, and 92 per cent of two-year-olds in the USA had a digital footprint, many of which began with their sonography before they were even born. Posting content about your child can be a way of sharing joyful moments, keeping loved ones updated, storing precious memories, celebrating and commiserating together.

However, sharenting is an important consideration for your kid's body image for several reasons. It often encourages comparison between children, creating pressure for kids to look a certain way or appear perfect in photos. It places considerable emphasis on their appearance, reinforcing the idea that how they look is an important, if not *the* most important, aspect of their identity. It brings up issues around privacy and consent, as a parent's desire to post images of their kids might conflict with their child's preference not to share their picture. This can put kids in a difficult position where they're encouraged to violate their own boundaries to please others. It also sets up a feedback loop in which social media likes and positive comments reinforce the idea that appearance is strongly linked to personal value, leading to a greater focus on how one looks.

At the time of writing, there is no legislation around producing something using artificial intelligence (AI) without a watermark, which means kids are not only at risk of having aspects of their identity impersonated (voice, image or information), but also that they may find themselves conversing with AI 'kids' without realizing that they are not real.

As much as I would have loved to be a mum, thus far, it hasn't happened for me. I've found other ways to be maternal, including supporting friends and family in raising their kids, having the privilege of being an auntie, God/guide parent to my friends' kids, and writing this book. It feels important to share this with you here because, when it comes to discussing sharenting, I want you to know that I haven't had to make a choice about this for my own kid and, for that part, I am quite thankful; it is a complex decision for any parents.

Safer online posting

Whether you choose to share content related to your kid or not, keeping the following points in mind will not only help to keep your child safe online, but also model respect, privacy, boundaries, consent and open communication, all of which are fundamental aspects of healthy body image and body safety.

- Check your privacy settings to ensure they are up to date and that only people you want to have access can view your posts.

- Be mindful of what personal information you share about your child, including their date of birth, full name, school, sports clubs, etc. Social media can lull us into a false sense of security because the platforms themselves become very familiar, so it can be helpful to think of what you share in terms of whether you'd be happy to share the information you're posting with a stranger on the street.

- Ask your kid if they're happy for you to post pictures of them online, and be respectful if they feel uncomfortable about it. Just as they should seek your permission to post about you, it's also important that they're happy for photos of themselves to be shared. Having open and honest conversations about this will help to establish what feels safe and secure for everyone. If your kid is reluctant to be featured online without consent, but you feel it helps you connect with friends and family, makes you feel proud to share their achievements, or boosts your self-esteem, be compassionate with yourself in wanting those things. They are very human things to desire.

It can be helpful to discuss with your kid whether there are ways you could share aspects of their information that would feel okay for them. That might mean sending photos on a closed family WhatsApp group rather than on public forums or posting a text update only on Facebook.

Body Confident You

Leading from the front and modelling emotional labelling, expression and self-compassion will help your kid learn to notice, name and normalize their feelings. A good starting point for this in the context of internet use is to begin keeping your own social media diary. In this diary, I invite you to note down the following each day for at least a week:

- *The social media platforms you use*
- *The amount of time you spend on each one*
- *How you feel before and after using it, including your basic bodily sensations*
- *What led you to that platform (for example, avoidance of a feeling such as boredom, anxiety, frustration, curiosity or fear of missing out)*
- *Any triggers you noticed while using the platform/s (you might want to think about this broadly, or more specifically, in terms of your body image)*
- *Anything you have learnt, positive or negative, from scrolling that day*

While this exercise requires some commitment in carving out time for reflection, remember it's only for a week, and it can really give useful insights into your own process around your social media use, the function it serves for you, the impact it has on you emotionally, and what you really need; this might be connection, belonging, validation, recognition, escapism, comfort, support or something else. It will also give you a clear indication of the amount of time you invest in social media engagement, which will clarify whether this feels aligned with your values and, if not, what you might like to change. This will differ for everyone; if you run a business and social media is a big part of your marketing strategy, you might spend several hours on digital platforms that feel conducive to your work success. Conversely, if you notice you're frustrated with your life and are spending several hours on social media trying to escape that feeling, only to be left feeling worse at the end of it, that is likely a sign to reassess what's working for you and consider addressing the underlying issues you're grappling with.

EXERCISE

Body Confident Kid

Helping your child build their own emotional vocabulary is beneficial in many ways, not least as they become more engaged with the less controllable online world. Identifying and expressing what they are feeling inside puts them in a better position to seek help and support when they need it, bolsters their resilience, and subsequently develops coping strategies.

Emotion charades, in which the child acts out different emotions while others guess what they are feeling, helps develop their ability to identify and express emotions nonverbally. This can be an especially helpful game for children with speech and language difficulties.

Kids of all ages can also benefit from keeping an emotion journal, where they write about or draw some of the feelings they've experienced that day and any connections they notice between how their body feels and their surroundings. Older kids especially might want to keep their journal private, and it's important to respect that. In this case, agree on privacy boundaries that feel safe for you both, such as agreeing you will not read their journal unless you are worried about the risk of them harming themselves or someone else.

EXERCISE

Body Confident Kid

To help your child see images online more objectively, you can also try this exercise. Ask your kid to take a photo of you and use various filters and adjustments, whether on a platform they use regularly or a face-altering app, to change your appearance in various ways. Then, compare the pictures side by side. This will help your child recognize how pictures can look very natural and yet be extremely far removed from their original source. (I did this with my partner while I was writing this book and the result had us both crying with laughter!)

Body Confident You & Kid

Before we conclude this chapter, I invite you and your child to do an experiment. It entails making a note of each time someone, whether it's either of you or someone inside or outside of your family, asks you to stop what you're doing to pose or smile for the camera, or some other action related to conveying an image for the benefit of a social media audience. Depending on your kid's age, you can explore how comfortable each of you felt about the request, whether you felt reluctant or awkward, whether you felt able to say no if you wanted to, and how your feedback was received.

This exercise will help you and your child set boundaries around whether and how your body and image are shared online and build a sense of autonomy in decisions about what information is communicated about you.

TAKE-HOME ADVICE

- Be curious about what thoughts and feelings lead you to use social media and notice the impact viewing different content has on you. If you feel comfortable doing so, recognize and name those feelings and show yourself compassion openly in front of your kid to model self-awareness, emotional expression and self-kindness.

- Use every opportunity to build on your kid's digital literacy and critical awareness in playful ways.

- Be judicious about health and wellness information online. Notice when you get hooked on dubious claims, especially when they tap into insecurities around your own or your child's appearance. Have a list of trusted resources you go to for family health and wellbeing concerns, and unfollow any accounts that make you doubt yourself or evoke health anxieties.

- Remember, what bleeds leads! Influencers use negative, painful messaging because they know we are biased towards that type of information and are more likely to engage with it. Just because it bleeds and grabs you doesn't mean it's true or helpful; the system is designed to harvest our attention.

- If you're unsure whether your kid's social media use is a problem, trust your personal experience of being with them. Is your kid showing signs of distress? Are they excessively comparing themselves to people online? Are they fixated on screens and unable to redirect their attention? Are they getting very emotional when separated from their device?

Your parental instinct is much more powerful than research statistics or hearsay from other parents or influencers.

- Whether you decide to share content about your child online or not, check your privacy settings are as you want them to ensure both your own and your kid's safety. If you do choose to share photos and information about your child, try to apply the same values around bodies as you would offline, always considering consent, boundaries, and safety. And remember: their body, their choice.

CHAPTER SIX

Power in Motion: Transforming Body Confidence Through Activity

'We all can dance when we find music we love.'

Giles Andreae, children's author

Before I qualified as a psychologist, I was in the fitness industry for over a decade, owned two personal training gyms where I worked with kids as well as adults, was the head strength and conditioning coach to the England lacrosse squad and, as I've already mentioned, was a coach on the UK primetime TV show, *The Biggest Loser* (though I was pretty uncomfortable with the weight-loss emphasis of that show then, and am certainly not an advocate of it now, but we all live and learn). I'm telling you this not to impress you but to impress upon you that I'm fortunate to have experience in both the physical and psychological aspects of health and fitness. When it comes to developing body confidence and a peaceful relationship with your body, these aspects both play crucial and intersecting roles.

We all know that exercise is beneficial for our health and that instilling a good relationship with movement can help kids form healthy habits throughout their lives. Not only are there physical health benefits, but children who participate in sports score higher on scales for happiness and show improved academic performance. Research has also found that exercise can be more beneficial for mental health conditions such as anxiety and depression than psychotherapy or medication.[1]

Neurologically, exercise in adolescence predicts mental capacity in adulthood, indicating that active kids are more likely to be professionally successful. Neuroscientists believe that building cardiovascular fitness in childhood supports the development of brain regions such as the hippocampus, which is responsible for memory, and the prefrontal cortex, which plays a central role in executive functions such as attention, impulse control, memory, anticipating consequences and regulating emotion. Plenty of evidence shows that active kids become active adults,[2] and a wealth of research documents the positive impact exercise has on children's mental health, including how they feel about their bodies. These studies show that improvements in fitness, developing confidence in one's physical capabilities, mastering new skills and being part of a group or team, all have a positive effect on the way kids view their bodies, independent of any physical changes. Even moderate exercise that focuses on how the activity *feels* rather than what your body looks like has been found to improve self-esteem,[3] help people feel more positive about how they look, boost emotional resilience[4] and reduce the likelihood of children suffering from mental health issues such as anxiety and depression.

Exercise quantity

The World Health Organization (WHO) recommends at least an hour a day of moderate or vigorous activity for able-bodied 5–18-year-olds, including a combination of aerobic and strength-building exercises. Pre-schoolers are advised to do three hours of physical activity per day, including active and outdoor play.[5] For younger kids up to five, activities such as clapping, skipping, rough and tumble, dancing, climbing, soft play and outdoor games not only develop coordination, mobility, dexterity, strength and fitness, but also help them learn about what they can and can't do, building confidence in their own abilities.

Risky play activities such as tree climbing, play-fighting, hanging, sliding, building and bouncing are important in promoting a host of psychological skills that will build a kid's confidence, resilience, independence, emotional regulation, social awareness and problem-solving skills. To have body mastery means to have control, understanding and skills related to your own body, and includes things like flexibility, strength, stamina, power and coordination. Mastery over one's body is strongly linked to positive body image,[6][7] and exercise can help children appreciate their bodies for what they can do rather than what they look like or what others think of them.

Team-based activities, whether organized sports or simple play, are also fantastic at building a sense of belonging, camaraderie, team spirit, collaboration and healthy competition. These activities boost kids' confidence and general happiness by helping them develop key life skills that will serve them far beyond the sports field. These include social skills, emotional control, working towards shared goals, compromise, empathy, conflict resolution, teamwork, overcoming self-doubt and fear, and, perhaps most importantly, friendship.

But let's be real: kids' physical activity has diminished dramatically in recent decades, and their lifestyles have become much more sedentary – much like adults'. A 2024 study conducted by the WHO found that British kids were among the least active in the world.[8] Public Health England's 2020 guidance[9] on how to increase children's physical activity in schools reported that only 17.5 per cent of children met the UK Chief Medical Officer's (CMO) recommendations of participating in at least 60 minutes of exercise every day of the week. Boys (20 per cent) were found to meet the guidelines more than girls (14 per cent), and this gender disparity increased from age nine upwards.

While research on the participation of transgender or gender non-conforming children and their attitudes towards or participation in exercise is sparse, studies on trans adults show that they are less active than cisgender folk.[10] Those who are receiving cross-sex hormones are more likely to be physically active than those who are not due to increased body satisfaction.[11]

How to get kids moving

If you weren't aware of the recommended exercise guidelines for kids, you're in good company, as over a third of British parents also report being unaware,[12] suggesting that this information has been pretty poorly distributed.

So, now you know, what can you realistically do if you're concerned your kid would benefit from more exercise? Here are some tips for even the most time-limited families:

- If you already have dedicated family time scheduled at the weekends, consider incorporating some sort of physical activity, such as bike rides, games in the park or walks together, into that time.
- Exercise doesn't have to be costly or scheduled though; impromptu family dance parties can be a fun and spontaneous way to get everyone moving.
- If finances allow, sign your kid up for sports clubs or activities that they'll enjoy and that fit in with your family's schedule.
- Encourage your kid to play in the garden if you have one, or a local park or green space if not. A skipping rope, basketball or netball post, climbing frame, trampoline or football goal all help kids be active on their own as well as with friends or siblings.
- If you and your kid are dog lovers, they can be a great way of helping everyone stay active. Even if you would prefer not to have the responsibility (and additional expense) of owning a dog, plenty of charities are looking for dog walkers, or you may have older neighbours who would appreciate some help exercising their pets.
- Prioritizing time for your own physical activity, in whatever form you enjoy, and involving your kid where you can, also sets a healthy family norm for fun and regular movement. For younger children this might involve doing a yoga or cardio workout in your living room, for example, and for older children going for a brisk walk, run or swim together.

Getting enthusiastic about exercise

There are several factors that influence how willing and motivated kids are to take part in exercise. These include genetics, family attitudes and values around exercise, hormones, peer norms, school and societal views and constructs, role model behaviour, opportunities to take part in activities they enjoy, as well as physical and emotional past experiences.[13] As kids get older, competing demands like homework and revision can get in the way of leisure activities that get them moving. As well as accessibility issues, due to, for example, playing fields being sold off, the tendency for kids to connect with their friends online means that many are more drawn to watching their on-screen avatar race around than actually breaking a sweat themselves.

I want to be clear, though, that this is not a sign of laziness. This is about conforming, belonging, connecting and adhering to social norms, all of which promote a sense of identity and security within kids' friendship groups. How much kids move is also not just about how much time they spend looking at screens.

Personality type and motivation to move

Personality type can also influence your child's experience of movement. An introverted child, who is generally more energized from the inside or with smaller, familiar groups of people, will potentially engage with physical activity in a very different way from that of an extroverted child, who draws energy from those around them and is positively stimulated by being in large groups.

While it's important to recognize that introversion and extroversion are not the same as sociability, it can be useful to think about what type of movement is likely to work best with their personality. For example, an introverted child may be more inclined towards solo sports such as swimming, biking or running, mindful types of movement such as ballet or yoga, or team sports played with friends they are close to and trust.

An extroverted child is likely to be more motivated by high-energy activities that create a buzz around them, perhaps involving energetic music, lots of people, and an opportunity to socialize. Useful questions to ask yourself as well as your kid when they've tried something new are:

- *How do you feel in your body?*
- *How do you feel in your mind?*
- *What was that like for you?*

Media influence and exercise

For children of all ages, the influence of popular TV, film and video game characters can greatly impact attitudes towards exercise. Kids start forming stereotypes from as young as two years old and start expressing them by age four.[14] As we discussed in Chapter 2, bigger-bodied kids are frequently the subject of disparaging humour in the media, they are the ones shown coughing and spluttering with their T-shirts dislodged to show their midriff in an intentional bid to evoke feelings of embarrassment and disgust in the viewer. With stereotypical representations like this, is it any wonder that larger children often shy away from physical activity? It's rare to see higher-weight kids, or adults, happily engaging in sport and exercise in TV and film, even though plenty of bigger-bodied people do exactly that. So, if you are the parent of a bigger kid, it's especially important to ensure they have role models to show them that bigger-bodied people can be athletic, graceful, agile, fast, powerful, fit and physically skilled. This is one area in which social media can be fantastic, as it provides a platform for athletes and performers of all sizes to showcase their skills and inspire others. Hashtags such as #bodyinclusivefitness, #fatathlete, #fatandfit, #healthateverysize, #HAES, #PlusSizeAthlete, #PlusSizeGymnast, #SizeDiverseFitness, #ParalympicAthlete and #BodyPositiveFitness can help you find diverse fitness role models for your kid online, while sports and activity clubs that advocate for body inclusivity, positivity and diversity are a good place to start offline.

Before we go on, I invite you to pause for a moment and just notice what thoughts and feelings showed up for you as you read those last couple of sentences. Doing so will help shine a gentle light on some of the beliefs you might be holding around body size and physicality and what your child may be internalizing. It is absolutely okay if you have doubts, concerns, negative beliefs or other difficult feelings around larger-bodied people exercising, some of which might encompass your own body and relationship with exercise. It's likely that you yourself will have been exposed to fat stereotypes since the day you were born, along with various myths around the health status, ability and worthiness of bigger-bodied people. That's damaging and can take a while to unhook from, but the great thing is, being aware of these stereotypes is the first step towards becoming more informed and being able to make a choice around what feels best for you and your kid.

Remember, one of the most significant role models your child will ever have is you. That doesn't mean you have to pretend to love exercise if you don't. But it does mean being mindful about the messages you convey around your own relationship with physical activity and demonstrating to your kid that, even if you hate running and can't think of anything worse than going to the swimming pool, there are plenty of ways of looking after your physical health and being active that are fun, feel good and are worth committing to.

If you have yet to find that activity for yourself, my invitation is to try one new physical activity a month, whether on your own or with your partner, friend or child, until you find something that you connect with.

Run like a girl: Gender roles in kids' fitness

Encouragingly, there are plenty of examples of both society and the media moving beyond toxic gender stereotypes. Watching *Mulan* again with my niece recently, it struck me how the film clearly stands against insidious gender pigeon-holing in children's filmmaking and made me feel positively 'YAY!' For example, the song 'I'll Make a Man Out of You' near the start of the film outlines the limiting gender stereotypes of old before Mulan smashes them to bits by becoming a supreme warrior.

Similarly, the fabulous 2017 retelling of *Beauty and the Beast*, in which feminist Emma Watson plays a progressive Belle, also defies gender stereotypes by dismantling Gaston's toxic masculinity and egotism, which ultimately lead to his untimely demise.

Production companies are becoming increasingly gender-neutral, and it is up to us to ensure that where unhelpful narratives and representations do slip the net, we point them out to our kids and help them build awareness and resilience to unhelpful messaging.

No pain, just gain: Turning discomfort into strength for kids who hate exercise

Exercise obviously places a strong focus on physicality. For those kids whose bodies don't fit 'the ideal', have sensory differences, or who aren't particularly athletic, are sensitive to loud noises, have a physical disability, or who are already self-critical about their physical abilities or how they look, this can increase feelings of self-consciousness, shame and discomfort. Plus, exercise can be hard work! It can be uncomfortable both physically and emotionally and sometimes even painful, so it's perfectly under-standable that as kids become more self-aware, they often become less inclined to partake.

We're all conditioned to avoid pain to some extent, whether physical or emotional, and for many kids, exercise represents both. This is especially true when the type and intensity of activity are externally dictated, for example, in a structured PE lesson at school, where kids' intuition for what feels good for their body and mind is overridden in service of meeting the curriculum or accommodating the varying needs of a large group of children.

This reminds me of when I was at school and my entire year

group was made to run the 1,500 metres. I was a sporty and competitive kid, similar to my parents, and I relished the thought of being tested in this way. I wasn't academic compared to most of my peers, but sport was a place I could excel, and I was willing to withstand lung burn and exhausted legs for the chance of validation and recognition. What really stands out for me about that 1,500-metre race was lying on my back, heaving, at the finish line, to see some of my classmates ambling around the track having a good old natter with a few laps still to go. Back then, I didn't get it. I was confused by how differently they clearly felt about the challenge to me. In hindsight, it makes a lot of sense. Racing wasn't important to those classmates, and nor was winning. They didn't crave the boost to their egos that competing gave me. They didn't enjoy the feeling of being puffed out or in pain. Refusing to subject themselves to these was an act of defiance that held an important boundary that not only aligned with their values of friendship and camaraderie but also demonstrated a level of self-care.

Just like adults, for kids to experience the benefits of exercise and feel motivated to be active, it must be rewarding. This can be increasingly tricky as they hit puberty and become more aware of what other people might think of them, because attitudes such as 'girls don't sweat', 'exercise isn't very feminine', or 'boys should be lean, muscular and aggressive' start to hold more sway. It's common for girls to drop out of sport in their early teens as their bodies start to change shape and they feel uncomfortable about how they look. A 2022 research report published by Women in Sport found that more than a million teenage girls who once considered themselves 'sporty' stop doing sport after primary school. Some of the reasons for this included low self-confidence, feeling judged, gender inequalities, feeling unsafe playing sports outdoors, and avoidance of being watched by others. A massive 78 per cent of the teenage girls interviewed also said that they avoided sport while on their period.[15]

Here are some ways you can help combat these barriers to exercise for your kid:

- *Expose your child to relatable and positive role models (yourself included!) who will help to inspire and demonstrate the benefits of staying active in a healthy way.*
- *Talk to your kid about their feelings around sport participation so that you can help them navigate their personal concerns.*
- *When encouraging your child to participate in physical activity, emphasize the parts that you think matter most to them, such as enjoyment, feeling good in their body, belonging to a team and time with friends.*
- *As far as your resources will allow, help your kid feel more comfortable taking part by ensuring they have appropriate and comfortable kit to wear, including period-proof swimwear.*

Swimming with confidence

Fortunately, advances in period-proof swim and sportswear mean that girls are more able to take part in activities throughout their menstrual cycle, and the utter dread of a period-related mishap can be largely avoided. But it isn't just girls who struggle. For boys, being muscular, tall, athletic, competitive and even aggressive are considered aspirational qualities strongly associated with what it means to be a man, and for kids who don't conform to these ideals, the sporting domain is often an uncomfortable and vulnerable place to be.[16] Studies show that boys as young as six express a preference for being muscular and thin and that a third of boys want to be more muscular than they are.[17] This is despite the fact that, prior to puberty, boys lack the hormonal profiles required to build significant muscle mass, setting them up to feel disappointed with their bodies from a young age.[18] These unrealistic body ideals and subsequent feelings of inadequacy and disappointment heighten the risk of boys developing body image issues such as muscle dysmorphia (colloquially referred to as bigorexia), where the sufferer becomes preoccupied with concerns that they aren't big or muscular enough. This condition is strongly linked to anxiety, depression and eating disorders.[19]

Research also shows that 11 per cent of boys have taken steroids or supplements to try to increase their muscle mass, and that many feel embarrassed to take their shirts off to go swimming.[20]

Fit to wear

Thankfully, gone are the days when you were made to exercise in your underwear, having forgotten to bring your gym kit to school, or when you were forced to wear a leotard to do gymnastics regardless of your body size or gender identity. But PE uniform is still something many schools insist on, placing conformity ahead of self-care for many kids. For those for whom traditional dress is essential to their faith, rigid school rules around sportswear can be a tricky space to navigate. For many kids, and especially those who are self-conscious about their body shape, exercise clothing can be particularly triggering and can evoke feelings of humiliation.

Obviously, children must wear clothing that's appropriate for the activity they're taking part in and is not likely to trail, catch or trip anyone up. Uniforms can also create a sense of belonging, togetherness, and being on the same team. But for those kids for whom lycra, swimming costumes and other tight-fitting apparel evoke a sense of dread, being made to wear rigid attire can pose a real barrier to exercise.

Why should all kids be made to wear the exact same uniform to work out when their bodies and ways of dressing are so very different? If the school your child attends insists on a specific uniform for sports, it may be worth exploring with the school whether there's a way the school's values of safety and conformity can be respected without ignoring individual differences. Something as simple as a plain navy kit, for example, can ensure conformity while allowing children to choose what shape that takes, providing it meets required safety standards.

Teachers nowadays are often exceptional at understanding the needs of individual children and adjusting their lessons accordingly. Not an easy task, given there may be thirty kids in a class, all with very different needs and preferences. Ensuring that teachers are informed about what your kid enjoys or finds difficult about PE can help them to ensure that structured sports lessons cater for everyone and avoid stereotyping kids because of their appearance, neurodiversity or religious beliefs.

The easiest way to do this is to ask the child themselves, giving them more autonomy and responsibility over what feels right for their body and ensuring that physical activity feels like a positive challenge rather than a humiliating or painful experience that simply has to be endured. While we all have to learn to accommodate some discomfort now and then and can't realistically expect accommodations to be made at every turn if we want to get on in life, exerting too much control over a child is likely to create a power struggle and evoke resistance over one of the few things they have some control over: their body.

'Exercise is not for me.' Zac's story

Zac was a bigger-bodied nine-year-old who I trained back when I was a fitness coach, and it was clear that coming to the gym was 100 per cent his mum's idea, not his. He was self-conscious about his shape, physically unfit – having avoided exercise as much as possible – and extremely accomplished at using chatting as an avoidance tactic.

Who could blame him? Zac's experience of PE lessons had been one of humiliation and embarrassment – the last to be picked for teams, the first to be laughed at if he made a mistake or couldn't keep up, all served with a side portion of physical discomfort.

From the outset, I suspected it would be challenging to get Zac to willingly engage with a standard exercise programme. So, I took a different approach. I spent the first few sessions with him on the mats, gently foam rolling, stretching him myself, but mainly just chatting. Chatting about nine-year-old things like video games, fashion, football, spelling tests and the trials and tribulations of school life. While not a bead of sweat was expelled during those initial sessions, they proved invaluable in giving me an insight into what really mattered to Zac, what he cared about, and, as he gained trust in me, what he worried about, too.

Doing things completely differently also meant our sessions were outside his frame of reference and unrelated to his previous traumatic experiences of physical activity. I discovered that his appearance was really important to him, and he loved styling his hair and following the latest fashion trends. He was also mad about watching football but lacked the confidence and fitness to try to enjoy playing himself. He was worried about living up to his parents' expectations and anxious about not fitting in with his friends. This proved to be a valuable key for us.

We met twice a week, with one session focused on building and then completing an obstacle course (an activity that was new to Zac, but a brilliant one at getting him thinking, lifting, pushing and using his core before he'd even tackled the course!), and the second session practising very specific football-based fine motor skills that didn't overly tax Zac's body and make him sore, but gave him growing confidence and several party tricks to show his friends. It helped that I was the strength and conditioning coach for the England lacrosse team at the time, as having an 'international coach' gave Zac a sense of kudos and confidence in what we were doing. Over time, Zac's strength, mobility, fitness and skill level improved dramatically, and it wasn't long before he asked me if we could include more cardiovascular conditioning to help him run better on the pitch. The last time I saw Zac, two years after we started training together, he strutted in proudly and told me that he had been selected for the school football team. He was still a big-bodied boy, and he was slower than some of the boys on his team, and yet, regardless, he was excited about moving his body and representing his school at sport.

If you have a kid like Zac, who is really resistant to exercise and very self-conscious, it can be useful to think outside the box: tune in to what they like doing and are interested in and match the exercise to that to increase their motivation and change their relationship with physical activity. Depending on their age, that might look like arranging for your child to help out with active chores at the local riding school or petting farm if they like animals, or setting them up with an online dance course if they're an enthusiastic singer or performer.

Breaking barriers, building strength

For children of all ages, normalizing exercise and the body's responses to it (sweating, puffing, increased heart rate, getting red-faced, etc.) will help reduce feelings of body shame and subsequent avoidance.

How do *you* feel about working up a sweat or breathing heavily after exercising? Do you get embarrassed, or do you feel proud and empowered? It can be really helpful to marvel with your child about how brilliant both your body and theirs are at responding to increased exercise and how they can take care of all of these functions for us without us having to think about it. Amazing!

It's similarly important to understand the barriers your child faces towards exercise. Once you do and they realize that you're on their team and not judging them for their resistance, it's time to get curious about what they'll enjoy that doesn't evoke overwhelming levels of anxiety or other difficult feelings for them.

There are several things that can get in the way of kids being able and wanting to exercise, and not all of them will be in your control.

Socioeconomic barriers

Socioeconomic factors undoubtedly play a role in children's opportunities to engage in physical activity and, therefore, whether they experience the benefits of movement on body image. Even in two-parent families, both parents are usually working, which makes having time to ferry kids to and from sports activities tricky. For single-parent families, that can be even tougher. Lack or cost of transport to activities is another factor. Other costs also have an impact, as some sessions are financially unworkable or involve the use of old equipment that doesn't inspire kids to actually use it.

The Active Lives Children and Young People Survey[21] found that 86 per cent of children from lower-income families can't swim a 25-metre length by the time they leave primary school, despite it being part of the National Curriculum. This is compared to 42 per cent of children from more affluent families. From early childhood, kids from low socioeconomic backgrounds are also significantly more likely to be of higher body weight,[22] highlighting how our bodies and our health are not simply a case of personal responsibility but both are influenced by lots of different variables, many of which operate at the individual level but are beyond individual control.[23]

To some extent, at least, health is a privilege that not everyone can afford. Financial hardship often makes it extremely difficult to promote healthy lifestyle choices at home. Fresh produce is often considerably more expensive than processed convenience foods, and very often takes more time to prepare, which is a key concern for parents working multiple jobs or long hours to make ends meet. Food insecurity, where people don't have reliable access to nutritious and affordable food, combined with other financial stresses and strains, also takes a significant emotional toll on family members. As a result, kids from low-income families are more susceptible to the impact of a high-stress home environment, which can contribute to them developing an insecure attachment style, mental health challenges, and unhelpful coping strategies such as binge eating.[24][25] Be compassionate with yourself and focus on the small things you can do to help your kid be active rather than what you can't. Simple choices in your control, such as taking the stairs rather than the lift, playing active family games, walking or cycling to school with your kid or doing some stretches with them before bed are small ways to encourage healthy movement.

Cultural barriers

Cultural practices, language barriers and faith can all impact children's motivation and confidence to participate in physical activity, and this may be particularly relevant for children from ethnic minority groups. Traditional sports facilities and clubs often lack appeal to culturally excluded young people, who may feel uncatered for or unwelcome when participating in traditional dress, for example. Girls from ethnic minority backgrounds may feel particularly influenced by cultural beliefs about women's participation in sports, and children of all gender identities may be hesitant to engage with predominantly white organizations due to fears about not fitting in or being exposed to racism or discrimination.[26]

To support minority ethnic group kids in benefitting from physical activity, creating spaces in which religious commitments such as prayer and fasting, traditional dress and other factors are embraced and normalized is important. This includes classes and sports held in faith-based settings such as mosques, temples, churches and gurdwaras, as well as increased awareness about initiatives such as Swim England's Learn to Swim programme and Swim Safe campaigns, launched in response to a survey released in 2021 that revealed 95 per cent of Black adults and 80 per cent of Black children cannot swim, despite it being considered a key life skill.[27] Even if your child isn't from a minority ethnic community, every child can benefit from understanding more about different cultural identities and practices.

Disability barriers

Disabled people are twice as likely to be physically inactive than non-disabled people,[28] widening health disparities as they age. Disabled kids often have to contend with social perceptions that they're fragile, weak, higher risk or physically inferior to able-bodied peers,[29] which has an effect not only on their body image but also how much they want to participate in physical activity.

For children with physical disabilities, participation in sports can be particularly challenging given that daily activities often already demand a great deal of effort, and suitable sports facilities to cater for specific needs are not always easy to find. Dependency on others, motivation, commitment and family attitudes towards the child's participation in exercise have all been found to be factors influencing how much kids with physical disabilities participate in physical activity.[30]

But, just like most kids, those less physically able are more likely to want to take part if people they know and like are doing the same. They also feel motivated by having fun and how good it feels to move their bodies, as well as the mental and physical health benefits.[31] It's also often assumed that disabled children don't want to be competitive when research suggests this is not the case.[32]

For the first time ever, the UK's Chief Medical Officers published guidelines on supporting physical activity for disabled children and young people in 2022.[33] These guidelines, co-produced by disabled children, their families and researchers, recommend 120 to 180 minutes of moderate to vigorous intensity physical exercise a week, incorporating a range of activities such as rowing, walking or cycling, as well as strength and balance enhancing activities such as yoga or modified sports three times per week.

You can facilitate a disabled child's engagement in physical activities in several ways. Providing a range of activities for kids to choose from is key, from competitive sports (adapted where necessary) to dance and Pilates. Opportunities to develop physical and social skills, often a hallmark of school PE lessons, play a significant part in developing a positive relationship with movement and highlight the key role of schools in helping kids develop specific skills, and that feeling of achievement. Exposing children to active disabled role models, whether via social media, film or TV, will also help to normalize exercising with a disability and reassure kids with a disability that they can enjoy physical activity and compete if they want to.

Competitive sport and body image

Whether or not parents and teachers should encourage competitiveness among kids is a controversial and complex topic. On the one hand, it's human nature to form a hierarchy, and we are evolutionarily hardwired to compete. Competition is part of the adult world, whether we like it or not, and it's an aspect that children need to be prepared for. Those who aren't prepared tend to lack resilience, so some exposure is believed by many to be important. If we consider the animal kingdom, the animals that survive and reproduce are usually the fittest and strongest. Evolution favours dominance. As discussed in Chapter 5, it stands to reason, therefore, that we often feel compelled to compare ourselves to others to see how we match up and ascertain our survival chances. Obviously, nowadays, being fitter than Karen next door is unlikely to mean Karen is cast out of the tribe to perish in the hostile wilderness, but our primal brains don't know that. Historically, being rejected by one's community *did* mean almost certain death, so we are wired to be vigilant to this.

In our society, a lot of emphasis and value is placed on being the best in certain domains, whether that be in sport, art, academia, popularity or business. Consequently, it's easy to see how we might readily link the feeling of excelling at something with being worthy of love, attachment and safety. Sporting competition is an overt way of establishing a hierarchy, at least in that context, which explains why kids who are more athletic tend to thrive off it and those who aren't often absolutely hate it. Unless a child has high self-worth derived from other areas, struggling physically can evoke primal and existential anxiety.

So, while an excessive focus on winning and losing can promote low self-worth in kids who are less physically able, it can induce a hyper-focus on achievement as a source of self-worth for those who are. The latter is equally problematic because no one can win at everything all of the time and it's an impossibly high bar for anyone to pursue. We sometimes refer to this as the 'Golden Child' syndrome – the kid who is exceptional is expected to do brilliantly and is therefore burdened with the task of living up to their role as the one who's good at everything, even into adulthood.

Balance, therefore, is key. Providing kids with opportunities to free play, and to engage in unfamiliar games such as korfball, as well as better-known games such as cricket, netball, hockey or football, facilitates a more level playing field and experience of movement that is focused on trying something new rather than competition. Kids who are less engaged and tend to be put off by feeling compared to others tend to enjoy free play and unfamiliar sports that are new to everyone and they are, therefore, more likely to participate. Children who enjoy competing, on the other hand, tend to experience more familiar sports as being fun.

Whatever your child's personality, encouraging them to make friends through exercise will help to ensure their experience of movement isn't solely laid on the treacherous foundations of simply aiming to win or making a good impression. You can do this by looking online for group activities and sports held in your local park or community centre, attending free public events, organizing informal group activities like rounders in the park with your neighbours, or exploring after-school clubs or programmes your kid might enjoy.

Praising effort

On this note, a word of caution. While almost always well intended, telling children that they've done brilliantly when they've come last or performed badly can be confusing to them. This is especially so when the feedback doesn't align with their personal experience. Kids aren't stupid and are good at picking up when adults are being disingenuous! They also know when they haven't done well at something. Praising kids when they have performed badly also sends the message that failure is such a bad thing we can't even acknowledge it. As we discussed in Chapter 4, this goes against one of the major tenets of self-compassion, which is to accept that we all fail sometimes, and that doesn't diminish our worth as a person. It also creates confusion around lying; on the one hand, kids are told it's wrong to lie, and on the other, they feel they are being lied to by their role models when they are told they have done well when they know they haven't.

A better approach is to ask how kids themselves feel they've done, or how they feel they did compared to last time, or what they enjoyed most about the activity. If they were disappointed with the outcome, it can be useful to ask what they think happened, making space for their full range of feelings. You might recognize the effort they've put in and praise them if they've stepped out of their comfort zone. That way, you encourage trust in their own appraisal, promote comparison with themselves rather than others, and draw attention to their personal experience of reward. In doing so, you are sitting with whatever competitive outcome there was, validating your kid's experience, encouraging them to trust and name their own emotions and drawing attention to the positive aspects of their efforts as well as potential areas for improvement.

Making movement fun and fitness role models

As I've discussed, there are many reasons your kid might be reluctant to get moving, and poor body image may be one of them. The good news is that you can do many things to support your child, and you are not a bad parent if your kid has a bad relationship with exercise. Getting creative, honouring your kid's feelings and finding ways to make movement fun are key to helping them feel more positive about movement and also about their body.

For older kids especially, access to positive role models who participate in sports and exercise and whom they can identify with will help them reframe their view of movement positively. As previously discussed, monitoring social media accounts used by younger children for suitability and encouraging older kids to be conscious of the narratives and body ideals promoted by the fitness influencers they follow will help to nurture a realistic and kind relationship with their own body.

The term 'influence' means to have the capacity to produce an effect. What effect influencers have on your kid's body image, self-esteem, behaviour and view of the world will undoubtedly be steered by who they follow. You can help enormously in shaping your kid's view of truly healthy exercise by being mindful of your own narratives around fitness, being selective about the types of exercise-related media you consume, and being careful not to impose your own relationship with exercise (particularly if it's negative, or indeed something you are hugely devoted to) onto your child.

This may require you to let go of preconceived ideas or hopes you might hold about the types of activities you enjoy and would like your kid to enjoy as well. You may have to accept that they just don't like tennis, or rugby, or swimming, even if you love it. As the famous psychoanalyst Carl Jung stated, 'There is no greater burden on a child than the unlived life of a parent.' I have had many an adult sat in my therapy room sharing sadly how they didn't feel they could live up to their parents' super active lifestyle or how their parents' hatred of exercise made them feel avoidant of it before they'd ever really given it a go.

Developing body autonomy

A key part of ensuring your kid feels comfortable in their body is checking how they feel around people who pat, hug or kiss them without their permission. Giving your kid the chance to say if and how they'd like to interact physically with others gives them a clear message that if they don't feel happy with something, it is absolutely okay for them to say no. Grandma might not love it if her grandchild doesn't want to accept their hugs and kisses, but teaching kids that they should ignore their feelings to please others sets them up to feel obligated to comply in more serious situations and could make them more vulnerable to abuse.[34]

Some might say there's a danger that kids will be ostracized if they refuse to partake in the social norms associated with greetings, but I strongly believe safety and autonomy must come first. If social norms put kids or adults in positions that compromise their boundaries, then it's the social norms that need to change. As kids get older and are better able to distinguish between appropriate and inappropriate touch, it is then up to them to decide whether they're willing to accept a sloppy kiss from a relative even if they'd rather not, but this has to come from a foundation of knowing it is always okay to decline.

Questions such as, 'How would you like to say bye to Granny today?' along with offering some examples, such as, 'Would you prefer to wave, fist bump, hug, high five or something else?', can help give kids a sense of empowerment and choice around touch.

It can also be helpful for kids to see others modelling different preferences as well as how to assess the preferences of others. For example, 'Thomas stepped back when I went to hug him, so I don't think he wants a hug. Let's ask him how he feels about being hugged today or if he'd prefer a different greeting.'

Risky play

Dr Helen Damon, a counselling psychologist and qualified play therapist, advocates allowing children to take part in risky play, including 'violent play', where children are allowed to play with toy weapons such as guns and swords. This is under the proviso that they are played with in a consensual way for all involved and that respects everyone's safety. Play doesn't always have to be enjoyable, though. As kids' primary form of language, it's the broad equivalent of talking for adults, so there are times when children play games that feel difficult or scary. While toy weapons are often banned in schools and nurseries for fear of promoting physical violence, psychologically prohibiting them sends the message that it's not okay for kids to express emotions such as anger or injustice and prevents them from developing boundaries around these internal experiences.

The distinction between playful aggression (which can be helpful in a child's development) and serious aggression isn't always the easiest to distinguish. Playful aggression should not be 'real' in that it shouldn't really hurt, but it may incorporate elements from the 'real world', such as war. If a kid needs to express real-world aggression and isn't able to do so through words or play, providing alternative suggestions such as stomping on cardboard boxes, screaming into a pillow, physically shaking or brushing it off or receiving a big hug, with permission, can teach kids how to safely process difficult or overwhelming feelings.

Risky play also helps children to explore their physical capabilities and build trust in what their bodies can do. For example, a younger kid might enjoy balancing on a beam and will learn from their experience of wobbling around and finding ways to correct and rebalance. Activities like this are a great way to help them build bodily autonomy; for example, you might ask your child if they would like any help, maybe holding onto one or both of your hands, so that they get to dictate the support they need while learning to take and manage age-appropriate risks. Kids are well attuned to what feels uncomfortable for them and it's generally the well-meant interference of adults that socializes this instinct out of them.

If your kid asks if they're allowed to do something that could be considered risky, such as jumping off a wall or climbing a frame (assuming there is no serious risk involved), rather than telling them yes or no, try asking: 'Does it feel safe in your body?'

If the answer is no, ask, 'What do you need to make it feel safe?'

This might be a challenge if you yourself grew up with parents who were constantly telling you to 'be careful!' or helicopter-parented you, as both reinforce the idea that the world isn't a safe place and that you lack the skills to even begin to manage that risk. Allowing your own kid more freedom can feel incredibly anxiety-provoking, so be compassionate towards yourself and take small steps so that neither of you feels overwhelmed. It's important you feel safe, too!

As far as you feel comfortable and assess as appropriate for the situation, show your trust in your kid's intuition and offer whatever help they need, but let them lead the decision if you can. If your child feels safe but you're concerned they might not be, you can validate their feelings while addressing potential risks by saying something like, 'That's great you feel confident and safe, it shows you're being thoughtful about what's around you. But sometimes, as adults, we might see risks that aren't always that obvious. Let's talk about what could happen and ways we can stay safe together.'

As I've previously mentioned with regards to your child's appetite and relationship with food, your job is to support your child's trust in their own judgement and their own assessment of what their body needs, is capable of, and what feels safe. It's also your job to provide help to make it safe if they need it and make space for your own anxiety and inner critical or judgemental thoughts should they arise. Allow your child to think for themselves, and they will usually pause and question instinctively if something doesn't feel right.

Nurturing the mind–body connection: The many benefits of yoga

Activities such as yoga, which emphasize the mind–body connection and encourage focus towards internal experiences in a compassionate way, can be particularly helpful in building a respectful and positive relationship with the physical and psychological self. Compatible with most religious beliefs and adaptable as a spiritual practice, the benefits of yoga include improved flexibility, strength and coordination, relief from physical pain and emotional trauma, improved digestion and sleep, better cognition, and the development of communication and social skills.[35]

Dr Naomi Middleton, a clinical psychologist and yoga teacher, highlights how yoga provides a safe space in which participants can be nourished by the connection and gentle energy of the yoga community while also developing a deeper connection to themselves. She describes how yoga can be particularly helpful for children's mental health, as it teaches students how to make space for uncomfortable or challenging sensations and, rather than avoid them by coming out of a posture, for example, they learn how to use their body and breath to work through those experiences.

In this way, yoga helps build some essential life skills; the ability to expand awareness and be mindful, lean into and accept difficult internal experiences, respect personal boundaries, self-soothe, and regulate emotions. Yoga is therefore an ideal activity for younger and older children alike, and is especially suitable for those who prefer non-competitive forms of exercise. With many yoga tutorials available for free online, it's also very accessible, and there are also several free or low-cost yoga resources designed especially for children, such as the YouTube channel Cosmic Kids Yoga and the Kids Yoga book series by Sarah Jane Hinder.

Thanks to its adaptability and emphasis on relaxation as well as movement, it's well-suited for children with disabilities, and charities such as Special Yoga provide in-person and online courses for children, regardless of the body they were born into. Children as young as two can benefit from basic breathing and simple posture exercises, and Dr Middleton suggests that from four years old, kids are usually able to take part in shorter classes. Such classes might introduce playful, dynamic forms of yoga. This could include practising being a tree, then a snake on the floor, then a lion: active postures that tell a story and promote bodily awareness and being in the moment. They might also incorporate creative elements such as mindful colouring and making different sounds, or relaxing activities such as placing a cuddly toy on their belly and watching its movement up and down. As well as developing physical capacities like strength, balance and coordination, yoga invites kids to be attentive to their natural understanding of what their bodies can do, encourages awareness and curiosity around physical sensations, and promotes an appreciation for what feels good for them personally.

This intuitive knowledge tends to become disconnected as we age, as self-doubt creeps in, information overload overwhelms us, and we feel more and more pressure to conform. As we discussed in the previous chapter, marketing companies also encourage us to mistrust our own sense of what our bodies need so that we're more inclined to look to experts and their products for rescue and buy things in an attempt to feel better.

Yoga and Polyvagal Theory

A major benefit of yoga, especially if you or your kid suffer from anxiety, depression, eating disorders, stress or agitation, is its effectiveness in stimulating the vagus nerve. The longest of our twelve cranial nerves, the vagus nerve plays a central role in our nervous system activation, in turn impacting how we experience our surroundings and, therefore, how we feel. You might recall from Chapter 5 how our brains create emotions using three main ingredients: bodily sensations, surroundings and past experiences (see page 179).

According to Dr Stephen Porges, who developed the Polyvagal Theory, the vagus nerve has two sides: the front (ventral) and back (dorsal). These two bunches of sensory nerve cells are distributed throughout the body and play a key role in the autonomic nervous system, whose role is to scan our environment for cues of safety and danger in a process called neuroception. Both sides of the vagus nerve can be stimulated during this process, which is involuntary and happens *before* conscious perception. The ventral side responds to signals of security in our surroundings and interactions, evoking feelings of physical and emotional safety. The dorsal side, meanwhile, responds to cues of danger, pulling us away from connection and into a state of self-protection.[36]

How the autonomic nervous system responds to signs of safety or danger can be explained in terms of the 'autonomic ladder', pictured opposite. At the top of the ladder, we have our ventral vagal (or 'social engagement') state. This is the state in which we feel safe, connected to others and at ease in our environment. As Dr Porges notes, the story we build around our experience follows our state, so when we're in a ventral vagal response, we experience the world as a safe place and often feel relaxed, happy and interested.[37] This is commonly called the 'rest and digest' part of our nervous system, so called because it aids digestion and promotes a slowing of the heart rate to help us rest.

Further down the ladder is the sympathetic response. This state becomes activated when we detect danger in our environment, such as a negative comment or look from someone, a siren blaring, shouting, or being given the silent treatment. In this state, we go into a sympathetic nervous system state of mobilization associated with the fight-or-flight response. We are ready to dispatch danger either by fighting or fleeing. In this state, we often feel anxious, jittery or angry, and the world around us feels unsafe.

At the bottom of the ladder is the dorsal vagal (or 'shutdown') response. This is activated when we neurologically sense signs of extreme danger. In this state, we are immobilized and go into a freeze response. You might experience this as feeling disconnected, numb, dissociated, hopeless, depressed, despairing, or even faint.

THE POLYVAGAL AUTONOMIC LADDER
Adapted from Deb Dana[38]

VENTRAL VAGAL STATE

I am safe, connected to others and at ease in my environment. I can relax.

SYMPATHETIC STATE

I feel stressed, unsafe and overwhelmed. I am in fight or flight response and I want to get out of here!

DORSAL VAGAL STATE

I feel unable to cope. I am in freeze mode and I am shutting down. I feel numb, disconnected and withdrawn.

Most of us will shift between these three states over the course of a day. Some people will spend the majority of their time in the ventral vagal state, but if you've experienced trauma or adverse experiences, you may have a harder time moving up the ladder and are more likely to be vigilant to threats. Spending too much time in a dorsal vagal response can even contribute to physical symptoms such as irritable bowel syndrome and stomach ulcers.[39]

Yoga's use of diaphragmatic breathing, loving-kindness meditations, singing, chanting, pranayama (the regulation and control of the breath), progressive muscular relaxation and chest-opening postures mean it is particularly effective at stimulating the ventral vagal response.[40] It also helps to reduce our blood pressure and heart rate and instils a feeling of calmness and relaxation.[41]

Polyvagal Theory and body trust

Polyvagal Theory has important implications for what you can do as a parent or caregiver to help your child feel safe and grounded in their body. Babies and young children can't regulate their emotions, so they depend on their primary caregivers to hold, soothe and calm them when they get out of control. By meeting your kid's distress with warmth, compassion and kindness, you're not only modelling emotion regulation skills, which they will gradually internalize for themselves, but also reassuring them that they are safe in their own body and environment. These experiences are fundamental to the development of body confidence. Making space for yourself and investing time in developing your own self-soothing skills is, therefore, a powerful way of supporting your kid's wellbeing as well as your own. Some simple practices that can help include:

1. **Gentle humming**, singing or chanting: activities that use your vocal cords stimulate the vagus nerve by creating vibrations in your throat, which can help instil a feeling of calm and groundedness.
2. **Deep breathing:** Slow, deep breaths, focusing on a longer exhale, activate the vagus nerve by engaging your diaphragm and promoting a more relaxed state.
3. **Meditation:** Listening to a brief, guided mindfulness meditation can help stimulate your vagus nerve and enhance your feeling of safety. Meditation apps such as Insight Timer can be a valuable resource for guided practices.
4. **Cold exposure:** Splashing cold water on your face or taking a cold shower can stimulate the vagus nerve and calm the body's stress response.
5. **Gargling:** Activates the muscles at the back of your throat which stimulates the vague nerve and soothes your nervous system.
6. **Social connection:** Positive, nurturing interactions with others, such as eye contact, laughing, and affectionate touch, all support the vagus nerve by fostering trust and a sense of social safety.

EXERCISE

Body Confident You

The following exercise is designed to help you establish a regular physical activity routine by addressing the psychological issues that have previously got in your way.

1. First, choose an activity you've either enjoyed in the past or are curious about trying. You might do it on your own or with your kid, but the focus here is on you. Schedule a time in your diary, like an appointment, for this activity and treat it as you would any other important engagement, so it doesn't get booked over. This might be a 15-minute walk, 10 minutes of skipping, 20 minutes of an online yoga class, a horse-riding lesson, a bike ride, a jog around the block or a game of badminton with a friend or partner.

2. As you decide what you'd like to try and schedule it, take a few moments to check in with how you are feeling and what thoughts are showing up for you. Are you worried about making time for this activity? Are you wondering about what other people might think? Are you concerned that you won't keep it up? Are you anxious that you won't be as 'good' as you used to be? Notice these thoughts with kind curiosity and try to acknowledge them without judgement and without pushing them away.

3. As you plan your activity and when you actually do it, keep in mind why it's important to you. What values is this activity serving? Is it to be a positive role model for your kid? To look after your health? To feel fit and energized? To spend more time in nature? Or to spend quality time with your family? Remember, there is no right or wrong here. Keeping your values top of mind will help you to stay motivated even if difficult thoughts and feelings show up for you.

4. Remember that it's normal to have mixed feelings when you try something new or return to an activity you haven't done for a long time. If unhelpful thoughts emerge, use the defusion techniques we've covered already, such as the 'I'm

noticing I'm having the thought . . .' exercise on page 47, or imagining your thoughts are like the weather travelling through the sky, allowing them to pass by without getting too enmeshed with them. Stay as present as you can while doing the activity, noticing any physical sensations, thoughts and emotions you experience.

5. Once you've completed the activity, congratulate yourself on leaning into this challenge. The more you can make space for uncomfortable thoughts and feelings and offer yourself compassion, the less they will pull you around and the better you'll be able to act in line with the things that matter most to you. If you enjoyed the activity, book it in again in a few days or for next week. If not, try something else. Either is fine, but keep your values in mind and take committed action.

EXERCISE

Body Confident Kid

Have a think about what your kid already finds fun and challenge yourself to turn it into movement. If your child is arty, perhaps grab some chalk, head outside and make a pavement chalk gallery around the neighbourhood. For musical children, you could encourage dancing while they play their instruments. If your child enjoys playing games, physically active ones such as hopscotch, skittles, bowls, catch and throw, and even activity-based computer games can be easy wins.

For kids that enjoy rough-and-tumble play, games such as

'catch me if you can', play-fighting in pretend combat scenarios or superhero battles where they can spar and dodge attacks, and forms of tumbling such as acrobatics can get kids active as well as using their imagination and social skills. These types of play can also help teach kids about the importance of setting boundaries to ensure safety. Offering toys such as balls, skipping ropes and frisbees is also a great way to encourage active play.

EXERCISE

Body Confident You & Kid

Establish a routine, at least once a week, where you take a few moments with your kid to notice where both of you are on the autonomic ladder (see pages 238–39) and what emotional state you are in. This is a simple but powerful way of helping your kid (and yourself!) tune in to what is going on inside and build confidence that you can influence your own internal state – possibly one of the most impactful life skills any of us can possess.

Remember:

- If you feel *steady and secure*, you're in **ventral vagal activation**.
- If you're feeling *stressed, agitated, anxious, scared or panicky*, then you're in the **sympathetic nervous system state**, or **fight or flight**.

- If you're feeling *shut down, numb, helpless, disconnected or dissociated*, you're in **dorsal vagal activation**, or **shutdown**.

Once you've identified where you are on the ladder, you'll have a clearer sense of what you need to bring you back to a place of safety, if necessary. If you're feeling anxious and need calming, take a few minutes to do an activity that helps you feel more relaxed. This might include:

- **Deep breathing:** Taking long, deep, slow breaths.[42] Box breathing is a simple technique you might like to try. To do it, find a comfortable sitting or lying position, inhale slowly through your nose for a count of 4 until your lungs are full without straining. Hold your breath for a count of 4, staying as relaxed as you can during the pause. Exhale gently through your nose for a count of 4, emptying your lungs. Pause for a count of 4 again, and begin the next cycle.
- **Laughing:** Listening to something funny that makes you and your kid giggle also helps to stimulate your parasympathetic nervous system and promote relaxation.
- **Humming:** You may have already noticed how children often hum to self-soothe. As adults, we can also utilize this to help us return to a state of safety when we're feeling anxious.

If you notice you or your kid are feeling shut down or disconnected, you may require movement or physical connection with trusted others to help move you up the ladder. This might include:

- Small movements, such as rolling your head and neck in

half-circles, rolling your shoulders, gently tilting your ear to touch your shoulder on each side.

- Bigger movements, such as skipping or star jumps.
- Holding hands and taking deep, slow breaths together with your child. This can help you both coregulate, which means utilizing the connection between your nervous systems to promote a shared sense of safety.[43]

Regular practice will not only help you and your kid feel more in tune with your emotional state and what you need to feel safe and secure, but will also help you find the strategies that work best for you both.

KEY REFLECTIONS

- Be curious about what gets in the way of your own physical activity, and use the mindfulness, defusion and acceptance skills you're learning in this book to disentangle from thoughts or feelings that stop you from taking action.

- Commit to trying one new physical activity, or take up something you have previously enjoyed, and schedule it as an unmissable appointment. Make space for the feelings and thoughts this activity evokes for you and keep reminding yourself why it's important for you to lean in and give this a go, even if it's uncomfortable.

- Encourage your child to set personal challenges that will stretch their comfort zone, support a helpful element of competition with themselves, and give them a sense of achievement when they reach a personal best.

- Ask your kid what they enjoy about PE and what they find more difficult. Do they prefer team or individual sports and why? Do they enjoy competing, or are activities that promote inclusion and togetherness, like dance, more fun for them?

- Allow your kid to take the lead on what feels safe for their body and offer assistance as they feel they need it. Be compassionate with yourself. It is natural to want to shout, 'Be careful!' and it is okay if you do.

- Instead of praising your child when they haven't done well, ask them how they think it went, what it felt like for them physically and emotionally, or how it compared to their last try.

- Give your child access to active role models that they will resonate with. Make them aware of negative stereotypes filtering through the media regarding exercise and certain types of body size, colour or ability.

- Create a rule in your home that no one has to engage in physical contact with anyone else unless they want to.

- Try not to overdo exercise or put excessive pressure on kids to move. Physical activity needs to be primarily fun and not horribly painful or completely exhausting for most people to find enjoyable. If you're concerned that your child may be exercising too much (a common symptom of eating disorders), it's important to seek your family GP's guidance.

CHAPTER SEVEN

Be the Change

*'Never doubt that a small group of thoughtful
committed individuals can change the world.
In fact, it's the only thing that ever has.'*
Margaret Mead, anthropologist

One Christmas, my brother bought me a hydroponic growing system. If you haven't heard of one of these, it's a tray that holds little sponges you put seeds in that are submerged in water, with an LED light over the top. Despite being a novice gardener, I've successfully grown more cosmos plants than I could possibly give away, let alone plant in my own garden. As simple as it is, this little contraption provides the perfect environment for seedlings to flourish. They have all the resources they need, including light, nutrients and circulating water. Their environment makes the difference between blossoming into a splendid flowery display for all to enjoy and a withered little sprout hanging limply over the pot's side.

None of us operates in a vacuum. So, while focusing on self-help and the things we can do individually are essential in promoting positive body image, we must also recognize that it's more than just an inside job. With the best will in the world, very few kids will grow up feeling resilient and body confident if the world around them is relentlessly unsupportive. Similar to my cosmos seedlings, we all need the right resources to flourish and feel good in the skin we're in. As we've covered so far, our self-view is strongly influenced by our family environment and beliefs and values, media, advertising, the influence of our friends and colleagues, the education and political systems we're raised in, our cultural norms and values, and our healthcare experience. In this chapter, we'll be exploring ways in which we can all help steer and develop body inclusivity in our communities and society more broadly, as well as improving access to resources that promote positive body image.

As author and disability rights activist Helen Keller once said,

'Although the world is full of suffering, it is full also of the overcoming of it. My optimism, then, does not rest on the absence of evil, but on a glad belief in the preponderance of good and a willing effort always to cooperate with the good, that it may prevail.'

Social support embodies the essence of that goodwill. It's the offering of love, respect and acceptance regardless of appearance. It's the creation and maintenance of spaces in which people of all body types can feel valued and celebrated. It's the willingness to engage with stakeholders, whether educational institutions, healthcare settings, media organizations, workplaces, government, celebrities, influencers or community organizations who have the power to sway aspects of society that drive health and beauty standards.

We must remember that the ability to make healthy lifestyle

changes is a privilege not everyone can afford and that wider systemic issues must be addressed to give everyone the tools they need to flourish. No one can be expected to feel well, behave well, or live well when denied basic human rights or bearing the weight of oppressive systems of control. Happy, healthy parents contribute to making happy, healthy kids. Kids can flourish in many different types of families, such as those with young single parents, or those with two mums or two dads. What's important is that families, whatever their configuration, have the social support they need.

Everyday advocacy

Parenting is a demanding task, and embracing body activism, even if it's something you value, can seem overwhelming. Please be gentle with yourself around this; we are all limited in time, energy and resources, and none of us can do everything we would like to all of the time. The good news, however, is that there are simple ways to advocate for body acceptance and diversity that take little or no extra time, but undoubtedly have a positive impact.

First, however, let's look at why advocacy and activism around body image diversity is so important.

1. We shine a light on the problem

Firstly, while most people have experienced the impact of diet and wellness culture first hand, the ideologies and narratives these systems create have become so ingrained in our society that they are often hidden in plain sight. Consequently, many people are still unaware of the harmful effects unrealistic health and beauty standards have on us. Raising awareness of how restrictive beauty standards and body shaming affect us is a constructive move towards building a community that thrives in both physical and mental wellbeing.

2. We combat stigma and stereotypes

Activism is necessary in dismantling harmful stereotypes and reducing stigma around bodily differences such as weight, disability, skin colour and deformation. Earlier in this book, I mentioned that I spent several years working in NHS weight management and bariatric services, and nowhere in my life has the damage and danger of stigma been more apparent. In those services, I assessed countless high-weight patients, many of whom were in their early twenties and even late teens, who were desperate for weight-loss surgery. Not because they lacked mobility or had a weight-related health issue, but mainly because they just wanted to be treated like a 'normal person'. With dignity and respect. So painful was the dehumanizing treatment they'd received in life that they were willing to undergo the life-changing amputation of a significant part of their digestive tract, with all the risks that entails, just to be treated more kindly. I cannot stress enough the counterproductive nature of weight-stigmatizing behaviour; it perpetuates the very issue it strives to resolve and places enormous stress on people, which we know to be damaging to physical and mental health.

3. We support and encourage others

Advocating for body diversity and acceptance is hugely empowering. It supports people in caring for and loving their bodies, whatever they look like, and gives them the courage to reject harmful societal norms. In doing so, it helps to prevent people from suffering from mental health conditions such as anxiety, depression and eating disorders.

4. We reduce the harmful effects of shame

Challenging myths around appearance, weight and health is essential in reducing damaging behaviours such as fat-shaming and concern trolling, both of which are usually carried out under the misguided belief that if someone just feels bad enough about their appearance or worried enough about their weight, they'll be galvanized to take action to change their body. The research in this area consistently shows that being shamed or constantly told others are worried about your body actually has the opposite effect and leads to people gaining more weight and caring less about themselves. It either exacerbates the perceived problem or encourages people to undertake harmful behaviours that they know don't work, like extreme dieting, just to be seen to be 'doing something about their weight'.

5. We can get real results

Finally, activism and advocacy do create positive change. They lead to more inclusivity, better representation and more equal opportunity. They also hold companies accountable for acting responsibly and considering the wellbeing of the communities they serve, including you, your kids, and the people who matter most to you.

Positive actions that count

You don't have to be marching the streets, nor standing in front of a camera, or have people watching you to be impactful. Activism doesn't always have to be public. Social justice advocate Dr Joy Cox highlights actions we can all take to be part of the change in moving towards a more inclusive, supportive society both on and offline. It could be lending your platform to someone who has an important message but has not been able to get their voice heard, or creating space for someone from a marginalized group to write some pages or take to the stage.

You and your family can start incorporating everyday advocacy into your lives and making a difference in several easy ways. These include:

- Buying your family's clothes from brands that support body positivity and offer clothes in a wide range of sizes, including plus size.
- Stepping away from or diverting conversations that promote stigmatizing attitudes around appearance.
- Calling it out when you hear harmful discussions around weight or shape if you feel comfortable doing so.
- Following more diverse bodies on social media and liking and sharing their content. In doing so you increase the likelihood of others seeing their content, too.
- Giving compliments based on people's personalities rather than looks. I asked my Instagram followers what their most treasured non-appearance-based compliments have been, and they told me:

'It's so good to see you!'

'I've been looking forward to our laughs together!'

'You impact my life just by being you.'

'I always feel I can be myself in your company.'

'You are strong as hell!'

'You are always laughing, and that makes me laugh, too.'

'You're the kindest person I know.'

'You are such an inspiration to me.'

'You have an amazing zest for life!'

- Talking to your friends, family and colleagues about why body diversity and inclusivity matter to you and your child. They might not get it or be comfortable with it right away, but many of us were there once. A single drop can create many ripples, and regular conversations about body acceptance help normalize both the topic and diverse bodies themselves.

Behind-the-scenes activism

The link between body size and other appearance-based characteristics makes a huge difference to the way in which beauty standards are both constructed and experienced in our society. You can possess some idealized characteristics, but lose fundamental rights if you are in a bigger body. For example, how are bigger-bodied people supposed to show up wearing well-fitting, beautiful clothing if fashion stores don't cater for their size? Or feel confident at the gym when they get stared at and ridiculed when they get there? How are large men and women meant to enjoy grooming and personal care to help them look and feel good when there aren't salon chairs to support all bodies? How can bigger-bodied people benefit from social interaction when their friends' homes or restaurants only have chairs with arms on, into which they cannot fit?

These structural limitations prevent larger-bodied people from being able to show up in the world with confidence and perpetuate harmful stereotypes. Whatever industry you work in, including the very real work of being a 24/7 full-time parent, there are many opportunities to make a difference in your corner. Do people of all sizes have access to your home and place of work? Do you have an armless chair around your table? Are you offering the same treatment options to people of all sizes if you work in the health or medical arenas?

This is especially important at this particular time in history, as body size and weight continue to be such a prevalent form of bias. When I was training to become a counselling psychologist, I was fortunate enough to have a supervisor, Professor Martin Milton, who strongly encouraged my colleagues and I to use our psychological expertise to promote political change. This prompted me to lobby for weight to be included as a protected characteristic under the Equality Act 2010. My petition sadly gained little traction at that time but was a central topic in a heated live discussion I took part in on BBC One's popular debate show, *The*

Big Questions. This reinforced just how much work still needs to be done to reach a place where people's rights aren't determined by their dress size and people aren't paid less, harassed or discriminated against because of their size.

Whether verbally or structurally, we can all make a difference to the world by being mindful of the way in which we talk about and cater for diverse bodies. We can call it out when we hear people using stigmatizing, stereotyping or shaming language, and we can also stand up when we see discrimination rearing its ugly head.

The first time I did this was on a hen do in Ibiza, when a member of the party I didn't know very well took a photo of a bigger-bodied girl in a bikini dancing to live music on the beach. She showed the picture to the rest of the group and said, 'That shouldn't be in a swimsuit.' Before I'd even had a chance to think about it, I asked her, 'So she should stop having a good time so that you feel more comfortable?' She looked at me, shocked, before apologizing, and I got the sense that her own thin privilege meant that this was possibly the first time she'd ever had to confront her own weight bias and prejudice. Perhaps the others around us that day thought I was being a bit serious, uptight maybe, or perhaps I said what they wanted to. Either way, if we want to build a society that is kinder to people in all sorts of bodies, if we can, we need to call it out when we see the opposite happening.

Amplifying marginalized voices where you can, including the voices of LGBTQ+ individuals, people of colour, people with disabilities or visible differences, and people of all ages, is a simple way we can all increase representation and showcase the beautiful depth and breadth of human diversity. I follow a number of disabled riders, bigger-bodied gymnasts and fashion influencers with visible differences who not only share brilliant and inspiring content but are helping to break down the stereotypes around what different types of bodies can do.

My invitation to you is to share – by word of mouth, social media or other means of communication – at least one voice a week who is doing something to promote body diversity and a more inclusive world for people of all body types.

Stone Soup

We are wounded in community, and we are also healed in the community. While healing may not come from the same community that caused the harm in the first place, it is necessary for healing nonetheless[1]. The healing power of community in improving body image is symbolized in the European folktale, Stone Soup. It tells the story of a traveller who arrives in a village, desperately hungry, asking for food. But the villagers refuse, claiming that they have too little to share. The traveller begins boiling a large pot of water with a simple stone inside, telling the villagers that he is making 'stone soup'. Curious, the villagers gather around and gradually start to contribute small ingredients – potatoes, leeks, carrots, spices – and before long, the soup becomes a hearty meal that can nourish everyone. The story illustrates how collective effort, generosity, and hopefulness can create abundance from perceived scarcity and reminds us that small actions can transform a culture of hunger and inadequacy into one of nourishment, connection and empowerment.

Environmental impact

Throughout this book we've explored the various ways in which messages about bodies are embedded within our environment, whether it be on billboards, social media, in the magazines you're reading, the music you're listening to, in conversations at the school gates, in the television shows and digital content your kid is watching, at the gym and so on. Messages about bodies are everywhere, and they are unlikely to ever completely go away. What we can all do, however, is be aware of what messages are being conveyed and encouraged around our bodies. What are we being taught it means to be a worthwhile person, both physically and behaviourally? What beliefs, ideas and values are being supported by the political, economic or social systems we're living in? How are things like beauty and ugliness being portrayed in your kid's environment?

Physiognomy (derived from the ancient Greek word *physis* meaning 'nature' and *gnomon* meaning 'judge') refers to how we correspond people's psychological characteristics to their physical features and body structure. We see this in the tendency for popular media to depict heroes and villains using certain physical characteristics, including visible differences. Authors and creators predictably find inspiration for their enemies and villains by exploiting existing cultural fears and, in doing so, reinforce the notion that characteristics largely out of people's control signal moral inferiority along with other negative stereotypes.

Apart from the beautiful, evil woman trope, baddies are pretty much always depicted as unattractive. This is hugely unfair if you share one of the physical characteristics commonly associated with the worst of the worst characters in popular stories. Ask any kid to draw a witch's face, for example, and the likelihood is they will draw someone with a large, hooked nose. It's true that the world isn't always fair, but that doesn't mean we can't all do our bit to ensure that people aren't demonized and denied basic human rights simply because of the way that they look.

Our fascination with beauty and ugliness and how this relates to moral goodness isn't a new thing. It goes way back to ancient times when Plato believed that beauty was a sign of moral purity and a link to the divine. This connection then became more and more pronounced with the evolution of photography in the nineteenth century.[2] Nowadays, we subtly reinforce the notion that attractiveness and moral goodness go hand in hand when we use phrases such as, 'I've let myself go' to describe when we have gained weight. This implies that there is something morally inferior or bad about you, despite the fact that bodily changes, including weight gain, are normal, natural and healthy across the life course.

Being aware of harmful attitudes and behaviours towards certain body types won't necessarily change them right away. But such awareness can and will change their impact on you, your family, and those around you by giving you a conscious choice to accept or reject these ideas as your own and treat your body and yourself accordingly. Never underestimate the ripples that those small actions can create.

Positive changes at home

A really common concern for many parents is that their own history of disordered eating or body image struggles is going to impact their kids. If this resonates with you, please be kind to yourself. You're certainly not alone. We have all grown up in a culture that has pushed body dissatisfaction and glorified extreme dieting; it is not your fault that what you were told would help actually only made the struggle worse. It's also okay if you recognize that diet and wellness culture has made its way into your home. Whether it's banning sugary treats, using moralizing language around certain foods, demonizing certain body types or something else that you recognize isn't conducive to your family having a peaceful relationship with your bodies and food, it's never too late to make positive changes.

It's often helpful to talk to your kid in advance so that they understand why changes are being made in your home. You might explain that you've realized you've been too restrictive around certain foods and that it's important you all feel able to enjoy all types of foods and feel safe and at peace with them. Or that you think it'll be helpful for your kid to be able to decide how much they want to eat, so you'll be serving them a variety of foods at meals and snacks, and it's up to them to listen to their body and decide how much they feel like having.

These conversations will depend on the age of your child, but you might want to share that you want your kid to have a better relationship with their body and food than you did so that they don't feel confused or disorientated if you switch things up and they don't understand why. If they are old enough, conversations around social pressures and stigma relating to different body types can be helpful in teaching your kid that while inequality around bodies isn't fair nor right, their home, your house, is somewhere where all bodies are valued and seen as good.

One degree is all it takes

If a pilot changes the flight path of their plane by just one degree, at first, the difference will seem negligible. The further they travel, however, the more their trajectory changes, and over time, they'll end up in a completely different location to the one they were originally headed.

Making any sort of change can feel clunky and difficult to begin with, so give yourself some grace if it takes a while to create new habits in your home and focus on one degree at a time. As James Clear highlights in his book *Atomic Habits*, forming new ways of being requires a focus on repetition, not perfection. James also stresses that in order to make positive changes, we need to design our environment to work for us.

An exercise that can be useful in creating a home environment conducive to body confidence for both you and your family is to become more conscious about the subtle ways in which body acceptance might be contradicted in your household.

For a couple of days or more, if you feel able, note how your home environment promotes body acceptance and instances that might counter it.

For example, you might notice that you're finding it easy to encourage intuitive eating but that you're still inclined to want your bigger-bodied child to exercise more than their smaller-bodied sibling or friends. You might also notice different food rules for different family members based on their body size. Try to suspend self-judgement as you perform this body acceptance audit, remembering that it isn't easy to find resilience against the pressures of diet culture, including from doctors who are steeped in a weight-biased medical legacy. Keep in mind that you are navigating this difficult tension so that your kid doesn't have to.

'I didn't recognize myself.' Tulsi's story

Tulsi Vagjiani is an international speaker and advocate for those with visible differences. She was just ten years old when she lost her mother, father and brother in a plane crash and sustained second- and third-degree burns to her face and body. Following weeks in the hospital, Tulsi recalled seeing herself in the mirror for the first time: 'It was like somebody had drawn a face on [me]. I literally thought somebody had pranked me because there was no way I could look like that. It was only when the person in the mirror was moving their eyes and mouth I realized, that's me.'

Initially, Tulsi coped with the enormity of what had happened to her by minimizing her injuries and upholding a 'it's no big deal' philosophy. However, on returning to the community, she became the target of name-calling, bullying and rejection. 'There was no one guiding me through this . . . whoever I turned to to tell them I was experiencing this form of bullying made me feel like I was being stupid. They'd tell me I just had to get used to it because of how I looked now. So, I carried on and suffered in silence. That was where the whole vicious cycle of self-loathing started.'

Tulsi's experience of rejection continued through her adolescence and into adulthood, where she recalled feeling constantly overlooked romantically. 'No one looked at me twice. I was the kind of person people would look at and think, *Oh my god*, and then move on. That stayed with me.' Like many people with visible differences, she also found herself being repeatedly rejected for jobs she was perfectly skilled for. She realized, 'This is not about my skills. This is about my scars.' Indeed, research shows that more than 50 per cent of people with a disfigurement feel their condition hindered their job in some way.[3]

The effects of visible difference

Bigger-bodied people also face appearance-based discrimination at work. One study, which collected data from nearly 1,500 UK employees, found that 70 per cent believed weight discrimination was an issue in their workplace.[4] Underneath these discriminatory hiring decisions are stigmatizing attitudes and stereotypes, such as that bigger-bodied people are less competent, lazy, lacking in self-discipline and willpower, and less conscientious,[5] or that certain physical attributes are more valuable than others. Learning to categorize things such as objects, colours, shapes and genders is a natural and fundamental part of kids' development and helps them make sense of the world. To some extent, we are also naturally drawn to those who look similar to us and, therefore, to our parents. But the value and stereotypes they attach to particular characteristics, such as conventionally attractive people being considered more friendly and successful, are generally learnt from those around us.[6]

Tulsi's story highlights not only how important it is for kids with visible differences to receive support in building resilience and self-compassion around appearance-based judgements, but also how imperative it is that, as a society, we raise kids who are kind, curious and accepting of body diversity. To do that, we need more representation, more conversations, more education, more curiosity and more modelling and encouragement of compassionate attitudes. Most people understand that kids are inquisitive and are likely to be intrigued when they see someone who looks different to people they are used to seeing. It's when they are told to be quiet, to look away, to pretend it isn't happening in order to avoid the discomfort, that they learn there's something wrong about difference, that there is something that has to be turned away from, a person's existence denied.

Charities such as Changing Faces do essential work in supporting those with visible differences via their provision of mental health and skin camouflage resources, but they also do a lot of work in schools. Their website, detailed in the resources section on page 286, hosts an array of guidance and training for creating an inclusive school environment and provides classroom and lesson study aids for parents and teachers to use.

School of thought

Body image is one of the few areas in which intentions to do good often result in a lot of harm. In schools, for example, efforts to promote wellbeing and body confidence, such as weigh-ins, food diaries and fitness report cards, often do the complete opposite and contribute to many kids going down a path to body discontent and disordered eating. Indeed, many common practices in schools, whether aimed at wellbeing or not, can have a life-long impact. You might recall from your own childhood those cringy moments when the sporty kids were chosen as team captains on the rounders field and, one by one, they selected other kids for their team until only the least sporty (and often larger-bodied) kids remained. Or having your weight declared in front of your classmates by a school nurse, only for it to be compared and rated against the weights of your peers for days after.

Thankfully, most of these practices have changed significantly since then. The NHS National Child Measurement Program still encourages weigh-ins at school, but these should be carried out sensitively and privately. If you feel this is not beneficial to your child's wellbeing, you are absolutely within your rights to opt your kid out. If weighing doesn't feel helpful, remember there are many other ways to monitor your child's health without using a set of scales.

Zara Allan, a mother of two, teacher, and Equality, Diversity and Inclusion leader at her school, explains that parents should inform their child's school if they're concerned about their kid's body image. 'A child will rarely come and share a concern them-selves, but if a parent tells us they're worried, our family liaison team are there to support them.' Zara highlighted how schools often have nurture programs in place for kids who are struggling with their thoughts or feelings. These often include a walk and talk, where kids can go for a walk with a trusted adult at school, share how they're feeling and explore what contributes to them feeling upset. In schools where this provision has either yet to be implemented or cut due to funding shortages, parents and teachers can still support kids' mental health by putting in place everyday discussions about feelings, practising coping skills such as those outlined in this book, promoting healthy habits such as regular sleep and an enjoyable exercise routine, and seeking professional help when needed.

As a mum of a boy and a girl herself, Zara highlighted how media content and peer norms influence the body image of children of all genders. While kids' interests and concerns aren't universally similar, it's important to be aware of the trends your child is being exposed to, whether it be among their peers or online, if they have access. 'With my daughter, who is eleven, she very much wants that slim body, big eyes and big lips like Kylie Jenner,' Zara shares. 'She's already thinking about wrinkles. It's all about skincare. That is coming from social media. At eleven years old, I wasn't thinking about wrinkles, but I didn't have a whole social media barrage coming through. She gets very swayed by all these influencers doing videos promoting skincare routines and then she and her friends want to emulate those videos and make them themselves. It's all about validation. [My daughter] hates it if I set her videos to private because she doesn't get likes and comments, but she uses my account so I can monitor what she posts. I have to remind her that it's my job to keep her safe. For the boys, it's more about being manly, being bulky, feeling like their muscles aren't big enough or their face isn't attractive. [My son] is very obsessed at the moment with wanting a fit body, a muscular body. A lot of boys start going to the gym at around fourteen, and that's where these ideals come from. They're talking with others who go to the gym, and they want to be the same as them. It creates a lot of insecurities.'

Boys and body image

Much of the body positivity and body diversity activism we currently see centres around size acceptance, particularly as it affects girls and women. But it's important to remember that boys and men suffer too, and, as Zara highlights and I touched upon earlier, there are significant and unrealistic expectations on boys to become muscular and lean in ways that are virtually impossible for the average boy without pharmaceutical assistance such as steroids.

Boys and men are typically underdiagnosed and undertreated for eating disorders, despite evidence that body dissatisfaction among them has steadily escalated in recent years. This has resulted in increased body concerns, excessive exercise, more substance misuse and higher rates of eating disorders.[7] Disordered eating behaviour may look quite different for boys and men, including eating excessive amounts of protein while restricting calories or relying heavily on shakes and supplements over actual food. It's essential that they are also considered in our advocacy efforts, recognizing that the way they experience poor body image and subsequently try to manage it may look quite different to girls and women, but can be equally damaging.

Under the influence: The power of social proof

As we discussed in Chapter 5, how we as adults use media directly impacts how kids use it, too. Zara points out that teachers, for example, now rely on various videos on platforms such as

YouTube to support learning, just as many parents do at home.

Social proof is a psychological phenomenon describing how we are more likely to behave in the way we see others behaving because we assume that, since others are doing it, it must be the right thing for us to do, too.

And this bears relation to another way we can all advocate for body acceptance and diversity, because the resources you use online or select to show your kid essentially give those brands your vote, boost the platform's viewing figures and increase the likelihood of others following suit. However, particularly if the subject matter isn't directly related to body image, it can be helpful to gently consider the more subtle messages these platforms deliver while also taking reasonable care and caution in checking their credibility.

It's also important to be mindful of the subliminal messages conveyed by the media more generally. For example, you might watch reality television programmes like *Love Island*, where there are few, if any, bigger-bodied contestants and the emphasis is very much on attractiveness. Unless the lack of diversity is openly discussed, it's feasible that your kid will receive the message that to be considered attractive and wanted, they have to be slim and toned if they're a girl, and lean and muscular if they're a boy. Simply naming these discrepancies can reassure your kid that the issue is in the lack of representation rather than specific body types not being worthy.

Body image education
and the school curriculum

In England, Scotland, Wales and Northern Ireland, body image is addressed as part of the compulsory curriculum in all schools, particularly in Personal, Social, Health and Economic (PSHE) lessons. These lessons cover an array of topics, including what body image is and the impact it has on mental and physical health. It's typically introduced in primary education (Key Stage 1, ages 5–7) through to secondary school (Key States 3 and 4, ages 11–16).[8] Body image education, however, cannot be left to a few lessons dotted across kids' entire school careers. While PHSE addresses body image specifically from around age nine, schools are expected to promote an inclusive culture from the very early years.

Zara shared how, in her school, kids are encouraged to celebrate differences, whether it be around their appearance, family structure, ability and so on. She noted how kids' comments about what a 'healthy body' looks like, for example, can be used as opportunities to gently challenge perspectives and help children develop both awareness and a questioning mind. Kids can be mean, and appearance-based name-calling is still a regular occurrence in most schools. It is therefore up to parents and staff to allow kids to talk about their experiences, share how they're feeling, and unpack where their feelings are coming from so that they can arrive at their own answers and feel more empowered to handle difficult situations going forward.

Zara emphasizes: 'It's so important not to be dismissive [when kids are name-called]. It's all too easy to tell a kid, "Oh, don't be silly, you're lovely as you are." Teaching is busy, and it'd be so easy to [tell a kid to . . .] "just ignore them". But the message you're then giving them is that it's not important to you. You need to take that moment to stop.' She suggested that teachers can use instances of name-calling as a cue to plan discussions around dealing with scenarios such as body shaming into lesson plans, asking kids what they would do if they saw a particular scenario playing out. Similarly, lesson plans can incorporate today's 'big question' around a displayed image of a person's body to encourage thoughtfulness around body image.

While body image is covered in the curriculum and diversity and inclusion are usually woven into schools' policies daily, there is often less support available for parents who are somewhat left to fend for themselves. Obviously, funding and time are usually constricting factors, so it's important to be realistic about what is achievable. Registering for initiatives such as the Dove Self-Esteem Project UK and encouraging your child's teachers and other parents at their school to do the same is a simple way to support the discovery of new ways of integrating body positivity into the school ethos for the benefit of parents, teachers and kids. Projects such as these offer lots of resources for parents and teachers, including lesson plans, activity sheets and body-positive videos to watch with your child or that they can watch in class.

If your kid's school or Parent Teacher Association (PTA) does have provision for hosting speakers, making a suggestion for presenters who are body-positive activists or educators, whether they be psychologists, dieticians, medics, personal trainers or life coaches, can be a great way of supporting parents and, in turn, kids in building a community in which all bodies are recognized as being good. If you have expertise in this area yourself or know someone who does, you might consider offering to help set this up. I have personally given several unpaid talks for pupils and parents at local schools, so it is possible to find experts willing to help without remuneration, or for a donation to charity or an opportunity to promote their business if funding is a barrier.

Body Confident You

Being an activist can sound like an intimidating idea, but activism essentially means acting with love for the greater good. You don't have to be lobbying outside Parliament, volunteering time you don't have or marching the streets to make a difference, though these things are obviously fantastic if you genuinely have the capacity and inclination. Quite possibly, the most impactful thing any of us can do, and which you have already started as you read this book, is to commit to open-heartedly educating yourself and putting self-love and self-care into practice. By becoming more informed about body acceptance and diversity, you will continue to better understand the issues that contribute to body image difficulties and inequalities, and that will put you in a much stronger position to both model and have conversations with others that sow seeds for positive change. Books, podcasts, articles and body-positive social media accounts are all great ways of staying up to date with new developments and playing your part in creating positive change. A good place to start is to commit to reading one article or book chapter or sharing a social media post that you found useful in the body acceptance arena each week.

Body Confident Kid

Research shows that children who feel they have a voice and believe they can make a difference in the world, even in the face of injustice, tend to be more resilient than those who don't[9]. There are lots of ways you can encourage your child to be active in promoting body diversity and acceptance in the wider community, but, for older kids, one place to start is to encourage them to take part in a writing campaign.

Ask them to consider their local community or the brands or facilities that they use regularly and how inclusive those individuals or companies are.

- *How diverse is their representation?*
- *Do they use inclusive language?*
- *Are their products accessible (i.e. do they cater for various body sizes, skin colours, cultural backgrounds, etc.)?*
- *Do they acknowledge and act on feedback from their customers?*
- *Do they have a diverse workforce?*

From there, you can invite your kid to write a letter or email to a company, government representative, influencer, or media outlet that really stands out to them as needing improvement in the area of body diversity and acceptance. Encourage your kid to advocate in their letter or email for a more inclusive and diverse representation of different bodies in the recipient's media, marketing, and facilities. Depending on your kid's age, they might need some help with this, but once it's sent, make sure you celebrate their courage and assertiveness in advocating for change.

Body Confident You & Kid

A fun and impactful activity you and your child can do together is to take part in social media challenges that advocate for body acceptance and positivity. This is straightforward to do; just search for hashtags relating to body image challenges and share your own post or reel using that hashtag. You could even come up with your own hashtag and encourage both your own and your kid's friends to take part too.

Fundraising for body-positive charities and campaigns is another way you and your kid can make a real impact in the wider world. Not only does this help support charities in making positive change, but it will also boost your kid's self-esteem by giving them the pride of helping others and also give them (and you!) a real sense of belonging to the community, both key ways of improving your self-image. Fundraising activities might include a car boot sale, sponsored silence, a cake sale, car-washing, a run, walk or cycle competition, quiz night or even gaming contest – whatever most appeals to you and your child.

KEY REFLECTIONS

- Whether at your place of work, in your friendship circle or on your social media, create platforms for underrepresented activists to have their voices heard.

- Remember that a one-degree shift can completely change your destination. Focus on making small, sustainable changes.

- If you plan on making changes around how you speak about bodies or how food is served in your home, explain to your kid why you've decided to make changes to avoid them feeling confused.

- Do your due diligence on the credibility of resources or accounts you share on or offline. What you share effectively gets your vote and will increase that resource's visibility. Make sure that's what you really want!

- Encourage your kid's school to host a body image talk for parents to complement what kids are learning about bodies and health in PHSE.

- Normalize discussions around body diversity and inclusivity in your social circles.

- Remember, you have the power to make a difference in the world, and so does your child!

CONCLUSION

A Body Confident Future

*'Develop enough courage so that you can stand up for
yourself and then stand up for somebody else.'*
Maya Angelou, author and human rights activist

While pop psychology has led to the notion that conditions such
as depression, anxiety, body-image distortions and eating disorders are caused by 'imbalances in the brain', the reality is that
there's a myriad of different factors that contribute to these issues,
and most of them can be traced back to the way we live.

Loneliness, insufficient sleep, poor nutrition, lack of agency at
work, stress, financial worries, lack of purpose and high levels of
screen time all make us more susceptible to poor mental health.
Basic human rights are, therefore, essential for our communal
wellbeing. These rights include proper access to healthcare and
support services, autonomy, protection from abuse and neglect,
social connection, education, proper housing, dignity and respect.

Throughout history, every era has in some way helped to
improve human rights, building on the progress made by earlier

generations. Our forebears have already proven how possible real change is. Thanks to the vision, determination and purpose of those who have gone before, I can, as a woman in a same-sex relationship, cast my vote, walk down the street hand in hand with my partner, work in a job that I love, and have had the privilege of working alongside amazing people of all ethnicities and gender orientations.

I believe the twenty-first century can be the era that future generations look back on as the pivotal time in history in which appearance-based discrimination, stigma and bias became unacceptable. An era in which it was no longer considered normal to hate your body, hide it or starve it in a desperate bid to get your fundamental need for love, belonging and safety met. So much amazing work has already been done to change the social and political landscape around what it means to have a good, worthy body, and I have listed some in the resources section on page 285, which you and your kid might find helpful as you continue to make your home and community more body-inclusive. Wounding happens in community, but so does healing.

A vision for change

My hope is that this book has given you the knowledge, tools and confidence to move forward positively, knowing that you can have a loving, respectful and peaceful relationship with your own body, no matter how at war you've felt with it in the past.

I also hope you will close this book with a greater sense of how you can guide your kid towards a future in which their body is something they can appreciate, enjoy and feel at ease with.

I encourage you to keep revisiting these pages as a reminder not only of how to support your kid but also how to support yourself. Because sometimes, amidst the endless noise of diet and wellness chatter vying for our attention, it's easy to forget that you and your body deserve care, love and respect.

We now have an opportunity to educate kids about the importance of body diversity and acceptance from the ground up. To inform them how Big Tech, Big Pharma, diet and wellness culture have historically sought to capitalize on our insecurities. To arm them with the mindfulness and awareness skills outlined throughout this book that will better protect them from those whose intentions might cause harm.

As parents, teachers, counsellors, family members and friends, we can all help kids build a sense of intrinsic self-worth that isn't overly focused on appearance by encouraging them to be present in the moment, in flow and in play. This contrasts the externally led culture of speed, achievement and multi-tasking that has become so commonplace, distracting us from our internal experience and often disconnecting us from our bodies.

We have an enormous array of truly powerful tools available to us that we can use to cultivate body confidence in ourselves and our kids. We just need to normalize using them.

- *We can use praise to boost internal self-worth.*
- *We can model self-acceptance, compassion and flawsomeness.*
- *We can name, and in so doing dismantle, the harmful myths that have steered us into destructive relationships with our own bodies.*
- *We can turn to sound evidence, rather than hearsay or social media noise, for guidance on protecting our own and our family's health.*

- *We can encourage movement based on what your family finds fun, whether competitive, structured sport, or something completely focused on the in-the-moment experience.*
- *We can uncouple our body shape, what we eat and how we exercise from our own and our kids' worth as individuals.*
- *We can encourage intuitive eating.*
- *We can increase our family's exposure to diverse body types and support minority voices to increase representation.*
- *We can normalize talking kindly and positively about all different types of bodies in our homes and hold firm boundaries around diet and wellness talk around our kids.*
- *We can consistently reiterate body autonomy and consent both on- and offline.*
- *We can opt for healthcare providers who practise from a Health at Every Size perspective.*
- *We can keep showing ourselves love and kindness and remind ourselves that we have always done the best we could with the tools and knowledge we have, which is all anyone can ever ask for. We can meet our own shame with the same compassion we would offer to our best friend.*
- *We can promote digital literacy and critical awareness through what we do and teach and also what we don't do, like choosing not to use our electronic devices during family meals and activities.*
- *And, perhaps most importantly, we can keep returning to the root of it all: our own and our kids' need to feel safe, understood, valued and securely attached. That is the basis not only of a positive body image and body confidence, but also of how we see ourselves more generally.*

Finding your why

I've lost track of the number of people I've heard say that parenting is the hardest thing they've ever done. People from all walks of life, including teachers, entrepreneurs, psychologists and Olympic athletes, have all told me the same thing. That's because parenting *is* hard. It presents a whole new ball game of responsibility and physical and emotional exhaustion. In all my years of counselling, I have yet to meet a parent who didn't find it difficult in one way or another. This is why it's important to first go easy on yourself if you're struggling to keep all your balls in the air and, secondly, be clear on why prioritizing self-love, self-care and self-acceptance is important to you.

Understanding your 'why' will help you stay focused and motivated and make good decisions even when confronted with challenging situations. Neither I, nor anyone else, can tell you why this inner work is important to you, but I can share why I believe it's important to me and many of the people I work with.

Freedom.

Body acceptance frees us from all the harmful strategies people use to try to change, deflect or avoid the way we look, including negative self-talk, extreme dieting, excessive or unenjoyable exercise, surgery, substance abuse, social withdrawal or acting the clown.

As a result, proactively accepting ourselves as we are actually improves our mental and physical health. It reduces stress, lowers susceptibility to depression, anxiety and eating disorders, actively buffers against harmful external influences that might otherwise be internalized, allows us to reconnect with and trust the internal body wisdom we were all born with, enables us to reclaim our peace with food, and spend more time engaging with activities that genuinely support our wellbeing rather than detract from it. It also allows us to be guided by our own experience rather than a dodgy BMI scale or other data-yielding device that was either never intended to be used as a measure of health in the first place or is not able to take account of individual nuance.

In my experience, body acceptance leads to greater self-care, resilience to stigmatizing messages, and increased motivation to look after oneself. For kids, it means learning from the outset that their natural shape, weight and appearance are one of many unique and amazing things about them that deserve to be celebrated. Can you imagine how powerful that would have been if that was the message you received when you were a kid? While I don't believe any of us can be happy all of the time, not being at constant war with yourself certainly helps.

A final thought

As you go forward, remember that change is often uncomfortable and outside of your comfort zone. Feeling anxious, awkward, scared or uncertain in this new space is normal. These feelings are part of the human experience and the more you can make space for your full array of feelings, the less they will govern you. Learning new ways of thinking and being and becoming aware of our biases can sometimes evoke feelings of shame for not having known before. Make space for that, too, and be kind to yourself. None of us can know it all, especially in such a complex and multifaceted arena as body image. Keep it simple. Make small changes at a time, starting with yourself. Keep reminding yourself of what matters most to you and that you deserve empathy and compassion as much as anyone else.

As we come to the end of this book, my wish is that we all come to find a place of peace with our bodies. A place in which we can enjoy it without overthinking it and love it because it is our only home and most loyal friend. If we can work towards that and reclaim the freedom we were born with; if we can run or walk or wheel or crawl along the beach, breathing in the sea air, refusing to let beauty ideals steal any more joy away from us; if we can care deeply for our bodies like we would the most precious gift we were ever given because that's exactly what it is, then we pave the way for future generations, your kid, and your kid's kids, to keep their love for their bodies intact and enjoy the body confidence they deserve. That you deserve.

It's time to be the change we want to see in our children, to take our love for ourselves back, to take all the suffering we've experienced, all the self-criticism, all the heartache of being at war with ourselves, to show ourselves the compassion we so deeply deserve and say:

This ends with me.

Resources

Happy Body Org

www.bodyhappyorg.com
An organization dedicated to social change around body acceptance, with free body image resources for parents, teachers and kids.

The Dove Self-Esteem Project

www.dove.com/uk/dove-self-esteem-project/help-for-parents.html
Evidence-based resources designed to support young people in developing and maintaining a healthy body image.

National Eating Disorders Association, Body Activism Guide

www.nationaleatingdisorders.org/sites/default/files/
BodyActivismGuideFINAL.pdf
A body activism guide designed for high-school and college-aged kids for use in the classroom, with friends or family.

Association for Size Diversity and Health

www.asdah.org
Community, educational resources and professional referrals committed to the Health at Every Size (HAES) principles.

Special Yoga

www.specialyoga.co.uk
Special yoga combines breathwork, bodywork and mindfulness to benefit parents, caregivers, adults and children. It offers accessible yoga practices for use at home, school and in healthcare, along with training courses.

Diversity Role Models

www.diversityrolemodels.org
A charity that promotes inclusion, diversity, and acceptance, particularly around LGBTQ+ matters. It offers resources and workshops to create safe spaces for children and young people to explore differences and build empathy and understanding.

Changing Faces

www.changingfaces.org.uk
A UK-based charity that provides support and resources for those with visible differences.

Acknowledgements

They say it takes a village to raise a child, and this book would not have come to fruition if it hadn't been for so many wise, wonderful and inspiring people. My first thank you goes to Dr Elaine Kasket, who has been a guiding light in my career since my first day of doctoral training. Elaine helped me sharpen my vision for a more effective, loving and inclusive approach to health and wellness, sculpt it into a book proposal, take my first step into the magical literary world and share my idea with those who could help give it wings.

This brings me to my fantastic agent, Julia Silk at Greyhound Literature. Thank you for having such faith in me as a first-time author, for giving me the confidence that my idea needs and deserves to be shared, and for ensuring my book found the most amazing home with Bluebird. My dad always used to say you make your own luck, but I feel extremely fortunate to have you on my side and to have benefitted from your depth of experience, reassurance and kindness.

To my fabulous publisher and editor, Jodie Lancet-Grant and Bluebird, thank you for your wholehearted and infectious enthusiasm for this project since day one. From our first meeting, I knew you understood why this book was so important, and it has been a dream to have your guidance, support and positivity throughout this journey. I could not have asked for a better team to work with.

To my friends and family, thank you for having such relentless faith in me, for your enthusiasm, for celebrating each little milestone along the way and for cheering me on in those fretful moments when the muse wouldn't come.

To all the amazing people who have shared their personal experiences and expertise with me for this book, it is so much richer for your contribution, and I am so grateful to each and every one of you for taking the time to work with me on this project. I learnt so much and was inspired by you in so many ways.

To my therapist, Sarah, thank you for your unwavering support, compassion and encouragement, which have been instrumental in helping me find greater self-acceptance and the confidence to share my work with the world.

To my brother, Nick, thank you for your generous support in proofreading and for consistently offering insightful, thought-provoking and good-humoured feedback. You never cease to inspire and amaze me with your breadth of knowledge.

Finally, to my wonderful partner, CJ, I am so deeply grateful for your love, understanding and support during my writing journey and in general. Your willingness to discuss ideas, challenge my perspective and offer honest feedback has helped make this book what it is.

About the Author

Dr Charlotte Ord is a Counselling Psychologist and runs a private psychology practice specializing in helping both adults and adolescents with issues around body image, self-esteem, food, eating and more.

She was twice named UK Personal Trainer of the Year, owned two bespoke personal training gyms under the umbrella Charlotte Ord Academy, was strength and conditioning coach to the England lacrosse team, and produced a fitness DVD, Back to Basics, aimed at encouraging people of all shapes, sizes and abilities to enjoy movement, which continues to sell worldwide. Charlotte regularly features as an expert in health and weight issues across broadcast, print and online media platforms.

References

Introduction

1 Linardon, J., McClure, Z., Tylka, T. L., & Fuller-Tyszkiewicz, M. (2022). Body appreciation and its psychological correlates: A systematic review and meta-analysis. *Body Image*, 42, 287–296. https://doi.org/10.1016/j.bodyim.2022.07.003

2 Knafo, H. (2016). The development of body image in school-aged girls: A review of the literature from sociocultural, social learning theory, psychoanalytic, and attachment theory perspectives. *The New School Psychology Bulletin*, 13(2), 1–16.

3 Be Real (2017). *Somebody Like Me: A report investigating the impact of body image anxiety on young people in the UK.* https://www.berealcampaign.co.uk/research/somebody-like-me

4 Beech, M. (2020). *COVID-19 Pushes Up Internet Use 70% And Streaming More Than 12%, First Figures Reveal.* https://www.forbes.com/sites/markbeech/2020/03/25/covid-19-pushes-up-internet-use-70-streaming-more-than-12-first-figures-reveal/

5 Bacon, L. (2010). *Health at Every Size: the Surprising Truth About Your Weight.* BenBella Books.

6 The Association for Size Diversity and Health (2020). *Health at Every Size® (HAES®) Professionals Guidelines.* https://asdah.org/health-at-every-size-haes-approach/

Chapter 1: What Is Body Image?

1 İsmail, N., & Tekke, M. (2015). Rediscovering Rogers's Self Theory and Personality. *Journal of Educational, Health and Community Psychology*, 4, 2088–3129.

2 Villines, Z. (2023). *What is shadow work? What to know*. www.medicalnewstoday.com/articles/what-is-shadow-work

3 Journal Psyche (1994). *The Jungian Model of the Psyche*. https://journalpsyche.org/jungian-model-psyche/

4 Bowlby, J. (1958). The nature of the child's tie to his mother. *The International Journal of Psychoanalysis*, 39, 350–373.

5 Heshmati, R., Pellerone, M., Esfandi, M. R. N., Yeganeh, N., Jafari, E. (2023). Interpersonal Attachment Styles and Body Dysmorphic Symptoms in Adolescent Girls: The Mediating Role of Body Image. *Journal of Clinical Neuropsychiatry,*. 20(2), 141–150. doi: 10.36131/cnfioritieditore20230206.

6 Lewis, R. G., Florio, E., Punzo, D., & Borrelli, E. (2021). The Brain's Reward System in Health and Disease. *Advances in Experimental Medicine and Biology*, 1344, 57–69. https://doi.org/10.1007/978-3-030-81147-1_4

7 Woodhouse, S. S., Scott, J. R., Hepworth, A. D., & Cassidy, J. (2020). Secure Base Provision: A New Approach to Examining Links Between Maternal Caregiving and Infant Attachment. *Child Development*, 91(1), e249–e265. https://doi.org/10.1111/cdev.13224

8 Leigh, B. (2016). *The Good Enough Parent*. Centre for Perinatal Psychology. https://www.centreforperinatalpsychology.com.au/good-enough-parent/

9 Winnicott, D. W. (1960). 'Ego distortion in terms of true and false self'. In *The Maturational Process and the Facilitating Environment: Studies in the Theory of Emotional Development*, 140–57. International Universities Press, Inc.

10 Craparo, G., Magnano, P., Zapparrata, M. V., Gori, A., Costanzo, G., Pace, U., & Pellerone, M. (2018). Coping, attachment style and resilience: the mediating role of alexithymia. *Mediterranean Journal of Clinical Psychology*, 6(1). doi:10.6092/2282-1619/2018.6.1773

11 Monteleone, A. M., Castellini, G., Ricca, V., Volpe, U., De Riso, F., Nigro, M., Zamponi, F., Mancini, M., Stanghellini, G., Monteleone, P., Treasure, J., & Maj, M. (2017). Embodiment Mediates the Relationship between Avoidant Attachment and Eating Disorder Psychopathology. *European Eating Disorders Review: The Journal of the Eating Disorders Association*, 25(6), 461–468. https://doi.org/10.1002/erv.2536

12 Bonev, N., & Matanova, V. (2021). Adult attachment representations and body image. *Frontiers in Psychology*, 12, Article 724329. https://doi.org/10.3389/fpsyg.2021.724329

13 Hudson, N. W., Chopik, W. J., & Briley, D. A. (2020). Volitional Change in Adult Attachment: Can People Who Want to Become Less Anxious and Avoidant Move Closer towards Realizing those Goals? *European Journal of Personality*, 34(1), 93–114. https://doi.org/10.1002/per.2226

14 Yoshida, S., & Funato, H. (2021). Physical contact in parent-infant relationship and its effect on fostering a feeling of safety. *iScience*, 24(7), 102721. https://doi.org/10.1016/j.isci.2021.102721.

15 Neves, C., Cipriania, F., Meirelesa, J., Morgadob, F., Ferreira, M. (2017). *Body Image in Childhood: An Integrative Literature Review.* Zeppelini Publishers. http://dx.doi.org/10.1590/1984

16 Sparknotes LLC (2024). *Alice's Adventures in Wonderland.* https://www.sparknotes.com/lit/alice/themes/#:~:text=In%20Chapter%201%2C%20she%20becomes,grows%20and%20changes%20during%20puberty.

17 Knafo, H. (2016). The Development of Body Image in School-Aged Girls: A Review of the Literature from Sociocultural, Social Learning Theory, Psychoanalytic, and Attachment Theory Perspectives. *New School Psychology Bulletin*, 13.

18 Hayes, S. C., Luoma, J. B., Bond, F. W., Masuda, A., & Lillis, J. (2006). Acceptance and Commitment Therapy: Model, Processes And Outcomes. *Psychology Faculty Publications*, 101. https://scholarworks.gsu.edu/psych_facpub/101

19 Harris, R. (2019). *ACT made simple: an easy-to-read primer on acceptance and commitment therapy* (2nd edition). New Harbinger Publications.

20 Your Fat Friend (2019). *The Bizarre and Racist History of the BMI*. https://elemental.medium.com/the-bizarre-and-racist-history-of-the-bmi-7d8dc2aa33bb

21 Gasperino, J. (1996). Ethnic differences in body composition and their relation to health and disease in women. *Ethnicity & Health*, 1(4), 337–47. doi:10.1080/13557858.1996.9961803.

22 Flegal, K. M., Graubard, B. I., Williamson, D. F., & Gail, M. H. (2005). Excess deaths associated with underweight, overweight, and obesity. *JAMA*,. 20, 293(15), 1861–7. doi:10.1001/jama.293.15.1861

23 Sabrina, S. (2019). Fearing the Black Body: The Racial Origins of Fatphobia. NYU Press.

24 Jacquet, P., Schutz, Y., Montani, J. P., & Dulloo, A. (2020). How dieting might make some fatter: modeling weight cycling toward obesity from a perspective of body composition autoregulation. *International Journal of Obesity*, 44(6), 1243–1253. https://doi.org/10.1038/s41366-020-0547-1

25 McConville, R. (2019). *Positive Body Image in the Early Years: A Practical Guide*. Jessica Kingsley Publishers.

Chapter 2: Fit Your Own Mask First

1 Miller, W. R., C'de Baca, J., Matthews, D. B., & Wilbourne, P. L. (2011). *Personal Values Card Sort*. Guildford Press.

2 Whitman, A., De Lew, N., Chappel, A., Aysola, V., Zuckerman, R., & Sommers, B. D. (2022). *Addressing Social Determinants of Health: Examples of Successful Evidence-Based Strategies and Current Federal Efforts*. ASPE Report. https://aspe.hhs.gov/sites/default/files/documents/e2b650cd64cf84aae8ff0fae7474af82/SDOH-Evidence-Review.pdf

3 Simmonds, M., Burch, J., Llewellyn, A., Griffiths, C., Yang, H., Owen, C., Duffy, S., Woolacott, N. (2015). The use of measures of obesity in childhood for predicting obesity and the development of obesity-related diseases in adulthood: a systematic review and meta-analysis. *Health Technology Assessment*, 19(43), 1–336. doi:10.3310/hta19430

4 Sinclair, U. (1935). *I, Candidate for Governor*. Upton Sinclair, Pasadena, CA.

5 Musher-Eizenman, D., Holub, S., Barnhart Miller, A., Goldstein, S. E., & Edwards-Leeper, L. (2004). Body Size Stigmatization in Preschool Children: The Role of Control Attributions. *Journal of Pediatric Psychology*, 29(8), 613–620. https://doi.org/10.1093/jpepsy/jsh063

6 Heider, F. (1958). *The Psychology of Interpersonal Relations*. Wiley. doi:10.1037/10628-000

7 American Psychological Association (2023). Habituation. In *Dictionary of Psychology*. https://dictionary.apa.org/habituation

8 Park K.Y., Hwang HS, Cho K.H., Han K., Nam G.E., Kim Y.H., Kwon Y., Park Y.G. Body Weight Fluctuation as a Risk Factor for Type 2 Diabetes: Results from a Nationwide Cohort Study. *Journal of Clinical Medicine* 2019 Jun 30;8(7):950. doi: 10.3390/jcm8070950. PMID: 31261984; PMCID: PMC6678837.

9 Glassman, S. (2020). *How an Obscure Japanese Marketing Strategy Created a Global Standard for Fitness*. https://bettermarketing.pub/how-an-obscure-japanese-marketing-strategy-became-a-global-standard-for-fitness-24ca265a41f6

10 Borja del Pozo Cruz, M. N., & Ahmadi, I., et al. (2022). Prospective Associations of Daily Step Counts and Intensity With Cancer and Cardiovascular Disease Incidence and Mortality and All-Cause Mortality. *JAMA Internal Medicine.*, 182(11), 1139–1148. https://jamanetwork.com/journals/jamainternalmedicine/fullarticle/2796058

11 Harcombe, Z. (2012). *Five a day: The truth*. https://www.zoeharcombe.com/2012/03/five-a-day-the-truth/

12 Memon, A. N., Gowda, A. S., Rallabhandi, B., Bidika, E., Fayyaz, H., Salib, M., Cancarevic, I. (2020). Have Our Attempts to Curb Obesity Done More Harm Than Good? *Cureus*, 12(9), e10275. doi:10.7759/cureus.10275

13 Griffin, M., Bailey, K. A., Lopez, K. J. (2022). #BodyPositive? A critical exploration of the body positive movement within physical cultures taking an intersectionality approach. *Front Sports Act Living*. 1(4), 908580. doi:10.3389/fspor.2022.908580

14 Gundersen, K., & Suduiko, A. (2024). *Charlie and the Chocolate Factory Themes*. GradeSaver. https://www.gradesaver.com/charlie-and-the-chocolate-factory/study-guide/summary

15 Jirků, V. (2020). *Fat Shaming in Children's Literature*. Masaryk University, . Faculty of Education. https://is.muni.cz/th/jzogo/Fat_Shaming_in_Children_s_Literature.pdf

16 Gailor, R. (2021). *Fatphobia in 'Charlie and the Chocolate Factory' and 'Matilda'*. https://rosiegailor.com/2021/10/22/fatphobia-in-charlie-and-the-chocolate-factory-and-matilda/

17 Sutin, A. R., Stephan, Y., & Terracciano, A. (2015). Weight discrimination and risk of mortality. *Psychological science*, 26(11), 1803–1811.

18 Quinn, D. M., Puhl, R. M., & Reinka, M. A. (2020). Trying again (and again): Weight cycling and depressive symptoms in US adults. *Plos one*, 15(9), e0239004.

19 Wu, Y-K., & Berry, D. C. (2018). Impact of weight stigma on physiological and psychological health outcomes for overweight and obese adults: A systematic review. *Journal of Advanced Nursing*, 74, 1030–1042. https://doi.org/10.1111/jan.13511

20 Cao, V., Makarem, N., Maguire, M., Samayoa, I., Xi, H., Liang, C., & Aggarwal, B. (2021). History of weight cycling is prospectively associated with shorter and poorer-quality sleep and higher sleep Apnea risk in diverse US women. *The Journal of Cardiovascular Nursing*, 36(6), 573.

21 Harris, R. (2017). *The Choice Point 2.0: A Brief Overview*. https://www.actmindfully.com.au/free-stuff/worksheets-handouts-book-chapters/

Chapter 3: Body Talk

1 Andersen, H. C. (1873). *The Ugly Duckling*.

2 Puhl, R. M., Heuer, C. A. (2010). Obesity stigma: important considerations for public health. *American Journal of Public Health*, 100(6), 1019–28. doi: 10.2105/AJPH.2009.159491

3 Vadiveloo, M., & Mattei, J. (2017). Perceived Weight Discrimination

and 10-Year Risk of Allostatic Load Among US Adults. *Annals of Behavioral Medicine: A Publication of the Society of Behavioral Medicine*, 51(1), 94–104. https://doi.org/10.1007/s12160-016-9831-7

4 Barakat, S., McLean, S. A., Bryant, E., et al. (2023). Risk factors for eating disorders: findings from a rapid review. *Journal of Eating Disorders*, 11(8). https://doi.org/10.1186/s40337-022-00717-4

5 Sole-Smith, V. (2023). *Fat Talk: Coming of age in diet culture.* Ithaka.

6 Gordon, A. (2020). *What We Don't Talk About When We Talk About Fat.* Beacon Press.

7 Matz, J., & Frankel, E. (2024). *Beyond a Shadow of a Diet: The Comprehensive Guide to Treating Binge Eating Disorder, Emotional Eating, and Chronic Dieting* (3rd edition). Routledge.

8 Rychter, A. M., Zawada, A., Ratajczak, A. E., Dobrowolska, A., & Krela-Kaźmierczak, I. (2020). Should patients with obesity be more afraid of COVID-19?. *Obesity Reviews: An Official Journal of the International Association for the Study of Obesity*, 21(9), e13083. https://doi.org/10.1111/obr.13083.

9 Fitch, J. (2023). *Tips for teaching children about body boundaries and safety.* Contemporary Paediatrics. https://www. contemporarypediatrics.com/view/aap-tips-for-teaching-children-about-body-boundaries-and-safety

10 Klebl, C., Rhee, J. J., Greenaway, K. H., et al. (2022). Beauty Goes Down to the Core: Attractiveness Biases Moral Character Attributions. *Journal of Nonverbal Behavior,*. 46, 83–97. https://doi.org/10.1007/s10919-021-00388-w

11 Feingold, A. (1992). Good-looking people are not what we think. *Psychological Bulletin*, 111(2), 304–341. https://doi.org/10.1037/0033-2909.111.2.304

12 Chavez-Ugalde, Y., et al., Manuscript title: *Ultra-processed food consumption in UK adolescents: distribution, trends, and sociodemographic correlates using the National Diet and Nutrition Survey* 2008/09 to 2018/19. medRxiv, 2023: p. 2023.06.05.23290977

13 Reed, D. R., & Knaapila, A. (2010). Genetics of taste and smell: poisons and pleasures. *Progress in Molecular Biology and*

Translational Science, 94, 213–240. https://doi.org/10.1016/B978-0-12-375003-7.00008-X

14 Harrison, C. (2019). *Anti-Diet: Reclaim Your Time, Money, Well-Being and Happiness Through Intuitive Eating*. Yellow Kite.

15 Harrison, C. (2022). *Sugar and Your Health*. Podcast. https://christyharrison.com/foodpsych/9/sugar-and-your-health

16 Omiyama, A., & Mann, T. (2013). If Shaming Reduced Obesity, There Would Be No Fat People. *The Hastings Center Report*, 43(3), 4–5. http://dx.doi.org/10.1002/hast.166 Retrieved from https://escholarship.org/uc/item/2nx1p3hs

17 Wolraich, M. L., Wilson, D. B., White, J. W. (1995). The Effect of Sugar on Behavior or Cognition in Children: A Meta-analysis. *JAMA*, 274(20), 1617–1621. doi:10.1001/jama.1995.03530200053037

18 Hoover, D. W, & Milich, R. (1994). Effects of sugar ingestion expectancies on mother-child interactions. *Journal of Abnormal Child Psychology*, 22(4), 501–15. doi:10.1007/BF02168088.

19 Spring, B., Chiodo, J., & Bowen, D. J. (1987). Carbohydrates, tryptophan, and behavior: A methodological review. *Psychological Bulletin*, 102(2), 234–256. https://doi.org/10.1037/0033-2909.102.2.234

20 Benton, D., & Stevens, M. K. (2008). The influence of a glucose containing drink on the behavior of children in school. *Biological psychology*, 78(3), 242–245. https://doi.org/10.1016/j.biopsycho.2008.03.007

21 Wolraich, M. L., Lindgren, S. D., Stumbo, P. J., Stegink, L. D., Appelbaum, M. I., & Kiritsy, M. C. (1994). Effects of diets high in sucrose or aspartame on the behavior and cognitive performance of children. *The New England Journal of Medicine*, 330(5), 301–307. https://doi.org/10.1056/NEJM199402033300501

22 Schiltz, F., & De Witte, K. (2022). Sugar rush or sugar crash? Experimental evidence on the impact of sugary drinks in the classroom. *Health Economics*, 31(1), 215–232. https://doi.org/10.1002/hec.4444

23 *Guideline: Sugars intake for adults and children*. Geneva: World Health Organization; 2015

24 NHS (2023). Sugar: The Facts. https://www.nhs.uk/live-well/eat-well/ food-types/how-does-sugar-in-our-diet-affect-our-health/

25 Intuitiveeating.org (2019). *10 Principles of Intuitive Eating.* https:// www.intuitiveeating.org/10-principles-of-intuitive-eating/

26 Forde, C.G., Mars, M. and de Graaf, K. (2020). Ultra-processing or oral processing? A role for energy density and eating rate in moderating energy intake from Processed Foods, *Current Developments in Nutrition,* 4(3). doi:10.1093/cdn/nzaa019.

27 Powell, P., Simpson, J., & Overton, P. (2015). Self-affirming trait kindness regulates disgust toward one's physical appearance. *Body Image,* 12, 98–107. https://doi.org/10.1016/j.bodyim.2014.10.006.

28 Lee, A., Cardel, M., & Donahoo, W. T. (2019). *Social and Environmental Factors Influencing Obesity.* In K. R. Feingold (Eds.) et. al., Endotext. MDText.com, Inc.

29 Cox, J. (2020). *Fat Girls in Black Bodies.* North Atlantic Books.

30 LeCuyer, E. A., & Swanson, D. P. (2017). A Within-Group Analysis of African American Mothers' Authoritarian Attitudes, Limit-Setting and Children's Self-Regulation. *Journal of Child and Family Studies,* 26(3), 833–842. https://doi.org/10.1007/s10826-016-0609-0

31 Smith, E.P., Yzaguirre, M.M., Dwanyen, L. et al. Culturally Relevant Parenting Approaches Among African American and Latinx Children and Families: Toward Resilient, Strengths-Based, Trauma-Informed Practices. *ADV RES SCI* 3, 209–224 (2022). https://doi. org/10.1007/s42844-022-00059-9

32 Finlay, L. (2015). *Relational Integrative Psychotherapy: Process and Theory in Practice.* Wiley.

33 Gray, N. (2022). *The Dark Truth Of The Wizard Of Oz's Feminist Themes.* Corner of Film. https://corneroffilm.com/2022/08/11/ wizard-of-oz-feminist-theme-dark-sad/

34 Peterson, A. M. (2011). Orphanhood and the Search for Home in L. Frank Baum's 'The Wonderful Wizard of Oz' and Boris Pasternak's 'Doctor Zhivago'. Graduate Student Theses, Dissertations, & Professional Papers, 725. https://scholarworks.umt.edu/etd/725

35 Harris, R. (2017). *ACT for adolescents.* https://www.actmindfully.com.au/ upimages/Making_Self-As-Context_Relevant,_Clear_and_Practical.pdf

36 Harris, R. (2007). *The Happiness Trap*. https://thehappinesstrap.com/
upimages/2007%20Introductory%20ACT%20Workshop%20
Handout%20-%20%20Russ%20Harris.pdf

Chapter 4: Self-Esteem and Body Image

1 Nicholson, N. (1998). *How Hardwired is Human Behaviour?* https://
hbr.org/1998/07/how-hardwired-is-human-behavior

2 Tiggemann, M., & Lynch, J. E. (2001). Body image across the life
span in adult women: The role of self-objectification. *Developmental
Psychology*, 37(2), 243–253. https://doi.org/10.1037/0012-
1649.37.2.243

3 Neumark-Sztainer, D., Paxton, S. J., Hannan, P. J., Haines, J., & Story,
M. (2006). Does body satisfaction matter? Five-year longitudinal
associations between body satisfaction and health behaviors in
adolescent females and males. *Journal of Adolescent Health*.
doi:10.1016/j.jadohealth.2005.12.001

4 Get Real Barbie Fact Sheet. https://www.chapman.edu/students/
health-and-safety/psychological-counseling/_files/eating-disorder-
files/13-barbie-facts.pdf

5 Maine, M. (2000). *Body Wars*. Gurze Books.

6 Bates, C. (2016). *How does 'Curvy Barbie' compare with an average
woman?* https://www.bbc.co.uk/news/magazine-35670446

7 Harriger, J. A., Schaefer, L. M., Kevin Thompson, J., & Cao, L.
(2019). You can buy a child a curvy Barbie doll, but you can't make
her like it: Young girls' beliefs about Barbie dolls with diverse shapes
and sizes. *Body Image*, 30, 107–113. https://doi.org/10.1016/j.
bodyim.2019.06.005

8 Simpson, C. C., & Mazzeo, S. E. (2017). Skinny Is Not Enough: A
Content Analysis of Fitspiration on Pinterest. *Health Communication*,
32(5), 560–567. https://doi.org/10.1080/10410236.2016.1140273

9 Harrison-West, E. (2023). *Barbie may have a fantastically diverse cast
– but we need an actual fat doll in real life*. https://metro.co.
uk/2023/07/24/barbie-may-have-an-amazingly-diverse-cast-but-we-
need-a-fat-doll-irl-19180687

10 Harriger, J. A., Schaefer, L. M., Kevin Thompson, J., & Cao, L. (2019). You can buy a child a curvy Barbie doll, but you can't make her like it: Young girls' beliefs about Barbie dolls with diverse shapes and sizes. *Body Image*, 30, 107–113. https://doi.org/10.1016/j.bodyim.2019.06.005

11 Ibid.

12 de la Haye, K., Dijkstra, J. K., Lubbers, M. J., van Rijsewijk, L., & Stolk, R. (2017). The dual role of friendship and antipathy relations in the marginalization of overweight children in their peer networks: The TRAILS Study. *PloS one*, 12(6), e0178130. https://doi.org/10.1371/journal.pone.0178130

13 Williams, J. (2017). *When Kids Are Fat, They Are Less Likely to Have Friends, Study Finds.* https://www.newsweek.com/overweight-kids-child-obesity-friends-623645

14 Wang, F., & Veugelers, P. J. (2008). Self-esteem and cognitive development in the era of the childhood obesity epidemic. *Obesity reviews : an official journal of the International Association for the Study of Obesity*, 9(6), 615–623. https://doi.org/10.1111/j.1467-789X.2008.00507.x

15 Changing Faces (2024). *Confidence and Self-Esteem.* https://www.changingfaces.org.uk/advice-guidance/confidence-self-esteem/

16 Haig, M. (2015). *Reasons To Stay Alive.* Canongate Books Ltd.

17 OpenAI. (2024). 'Conversation with ChatGPT'.

18 Bastian, B., Jetten, J., & Ferris, L. J. (2014). Pain as Social Glue: Shared Pain Increases Cooperation. *Psychological Science*, 25(11), 2079–2085. https://doi.org/10.1177/0956797614545886

19 Dewar, G. (2024). *The effects of praise on kids: 10 evidence-based tips for better outcomes.* https://parentingscience.com/effects-of-praise/

20 Kelley, S. A., Brownell, C. A., & Campbell, S. B. (2000). Mastery motivation and self-evaluative affect in toddlers: longitudinal relations with maternal behavior. *Child Development*, 71(4), 1061–1071. https://doi.org/10.1111/1467-8624.00209

21 Morris, B. J., & Zentall, S. R. (2014). High fives motivate: the effects of gestural and ambiguous verbal praise on motivation. *Frontiers in Psychology*, 5, 928. https://doi.org/10.3389/fpsyg.2014.00928

22 Nagaoka, D., Tomoshige, N., Ando, S., Morita, M., Kiyono, T., Kanata, S., Fujikawa, S., Endo, K., Yamasaki, S., Fukuda, M., Nishida, A., Hiraiwa-Hasegawa, M., & Kasai, K. (2022). Being Praised for Prosocial Behaviors Longitudinally Reduces Depressive Symptoms in Early Adolescents: A Population-Based Cohort Study. *Frontiers in Psychiatry*, 13, 865907. https://doi.org/10.3389/fpsyt.2022.865907

23 Henderlong, J., & Lepper, M. R. (2002). The effects of praise on children's intrinsic motivation: A review and synthesis. *Psychological Bulletin*, 128(5), 774–795.

24 Dewar, G. (2024). *The effects of praise on kids: 10 Evidence-based tips for better outcomes.* https://parentingscience.com/effects-of-praise/

25 Blatt, S. J. (1995). Representational structures in psychopathology. In D. Cicchetti & S. Toth (eds.), *Emotion, Cognition and Representation*, 1–34. University of Rochester Press.

26 Neff, K. D. (2012). *The science of self-compassion*. In C. Germer & R. Siegel (eds.), *Compassion and Wisdom in Psychotherapy*, 79–92. Guilford Press.

27 Powers, T. A., Koestner, R., & Zuroff, D. C. (2007). Self-criticism, goal motivation, and goal progress. *Journal of Social and Clinical Psychology*, 26, 826–840.

28 Jung, F. U., Bae, Y. J., Kratzsch, J., Riedel-Heller, S. G., & Luck-Sikorski, C. (2020). Internalized weight bias and cortisol reactivity to social stress. *Cognitive, Affective & Behavioral Neuroscience*, 20(1), 49–58. https://doi.org/10.3758/s13415-019-00750-y

29 Neff, K. D. (2012). The science of self-compassion. In C. Germer & R. Siegel (eds.) *Compassion and Wisdom in Psychotherapy*, 79–92. Guilford Press.

Chapter 5: Scrolling for Self-Love: Boosting Body Confidence With Social Media

1 Anderson, M. (2018). *A Majority of Teens Have Experienced Some Form of Cyberbullying.* Pew Research Center. https://www.pewresearch.org/internet/2018/09/27/a-majority-of-teens-have-experienced-some-form-of-cyberbullying/

2 Blackford, M. (2020). *Body Image and Social Media Questionnaire.* FHE Health. https://fherehab.com/survey/bodypositive-image-social-media

3 Peanut (2023). *New Study from Peanut and Tommee Tippee Finds 95% of Mothers Experience Guilt and 62% Face Loss of Identity.* https://www.prnewswire.co.uk/news-releases/new-study-from-peanut-and-tommee-tippee-finds-95-of-mothers-experience-guilt-and-62-face-loss-of-identity-301784913.html

4 Blackford, M. (2020). *Body Image and Social Media Questionnaire.* FHE Health. https://fherehab.com/survey/bodypositive-image-social-media

5 Ramphul, K., & Mejias, S. G. (2018). Is 'Snapchat Dysmorphia' a Real Issue? *Cureus*, 10(3), e2263. https://doi.org/10.7759/cureus.2263

6 Anderson, M. (2018). *A Majority of Teens Have Experienced Some Form of Cyberbullying.* Pew Research Center. https://www.pewresearch.org/internet/2018/09/27/a-majority-of-teens-have-experienced-some-form-of-cyberbullying/

7 Orben, A., Przybylski, A. K., Blakemore, S. J., & Kievit, R. A. (2022). Windows of developmental sensitivity to social media. *Nature Communications*, 13(1), 1649. https://doi.org/10.1038/s41467-022-29296-3

8 Adisa, D. (2023). *Everything you need to know about social media algorithms..* https://sproutsocial.com/insights/social-media-algorithms/

9 Schöne, J. P., Garcia, D., Parkinson, B., & Goldenberg, A. (2023). Negative expressions are shared more on Twitter for public figures than for ordinary users. *PNAS Nexus*, 2(7), pgad219. https://doi.org/10.1093/pnasnexus/pgad219

10 Cuncic, A. (2023). *The Psychology of Cyberbullying.* https://www.verywellmind.com/the-psychology-of-cyberbullying-5086615

11 Zhang, W., Huang, S., Lam, L., Evans, R., & Zhu, C. (2022). Cyberbullying definitions and measurements in children and adolescents: Summarizing 20 years of global efforts. *Frontiers in Public Health*, 10, 1000504. https://doi.org/10.3389/fpubh.2022.1000504

12 Horton, L. (2019). *The Neuroscience Behind Our Words.* Business

Relationship Management Institute. https://brm.institute/neuroscience-behind-words/

13 Ibid.

14 Richter, M., Eck, J., Straube, T., Miltner, W., & Weiss, T. (2010). Do words hurt? Brain activation during the processing of pain-related words, *PAIN*, 148(2), 198–205. https://doi.org/10.1016/j.pain.2009.08.009.

15 Feldman Barrett, L. (2018). *The Science of Making Emotions.* https://lisafeldmanbarrett.com/wp-content/uploads/sites/4/2020/11/ScienceOfMakingEmotions.pdf

16 Internetmatters.org (2024). *Online Safety for Pre-teens.* https://www.internetmatters.org/advice/11-13/

17 Tronick, E., Als, H., Adamson, L., Wise, S., & Brazelton, T. B. (1978). The infant's response to entrapment between contradictory messages in face-to-face interaction. *Journal of the American Academy of Child Psychiatry*, 17(1), 1–13. https://doi.org/10.1016/s0002-7138(09)62273-1

18 Kasket, E. (2024). *Reset: Rethinking Your Digital World for a Happier Life.* Elliot & Thompson.

19 Jones, J. (2015). The Looking Glass Lens: Self-concept Changes Due to Social Media Practices. *The Journal of Social Media in Society.* 4, 100.

20 Media Smarts (2024). *Body Image-Digital Media.* https://mediasmarts.ca/digital-media-literacy/media-issues/body-image/body-image-digital-media#_ftn5

21 Park, J. (2018). The effect of virtual avatar experience on body image discrepancy, body satisfaction and weight regulation intention. *Cyberpsychology: Journal of Psychosocial Research on Cyberspace*, 12(1), Article 3. https://doi.org/10.5817/CP2018-1-3

22 Burke, L. R. (2017). Relationship between Self-Esteem in Adolescence to Avatar Creation of Actual and Idealized Selves. (unpublished doctoral thesis). Fordham University.

23 Paleczna, M., Ilczuk, E., & Szmigielska, B. (2023). *Adolescent–avatar similarity and its predictors: global self-esteem, gender or personality?* https://journals.pan.pl/Content/127817/PDF/2023-01-PPB-01.pdf

24 Harrison, C. (2023). *The Wellness Trap*. Yellow Kite

25 Gevitz N. (1995). Alternative medicine and the orthodox canon. *The Mount Sinai Journal of Medicine*, 62(2), 127–162.

26 Kasket, E. (2019). *'Breast Is Best' Nearly Cost My Baby Her Life*. Medium. https://humanparts.medium.com/lucky-babies-25a888a0b53b

Chapter 6: Power in Motion: Transforming Body Confidence Through Activity

1 Singh, B., Olds, T., Curtis, R., Dumuid, D., Virgara, R., Watson, A., Szeto, K., O'Connor, E., Ferguson, T., Eglitis, E., Miatke, A., Simpson, C. E., & Maher, C. (2023). Effectiveness of physical activity interventions for improving depression, anxiety and distress: an overview of systematic reviews. *British Journal of Sports Medicine*, 57(18), 1203–1209. https://doi.org/10.1136/bjsports-2022-106195

2 Ha, A. S., Ng, J. Y. Y., & Lonsdale, C., et al. (2019). Promoting physical activity in children through family-based intervention: protocol of the 'Active 1 + FUN' randomized controlled trial. *BMC Public Health*, 19, 218. https://doi.org/10.1186/s12889-019-6537-3

3 Furnham, A., & Greaves, N. (1994). Gender and locus of control correlates of body image dissatisfaction. *European Journal of Personality*, 8(3), 183–200. https://doi.org/10.1002/per.2410080304

4 O'Donahue, T. (2016). *Regular Exercise and Emotional Resilience is Associated with Improved Body Image*. https://esource.dbs.ie/items/edc44f52-adbe-4a72-a4c5-70532fad3697

5 NHS (2022). *Physical activity guidelines for children (under 5 years)*. https://www.nhs.uk/live-well/exercise/physical-activity-guidelines-children-under-five-years

6 Foley Davelaar, C. M. (2021). Body Image and its Role in Physical Activity: A Systematic Review. *Cureus*, 13(2), e13379. https://doi.org/10.7759/cureus.13379

7 Grogan, S., & Richards, H. (2002). Body image: Focus groups with boys and men. *Men and Masculinities*, 4(3), 219–232. https://doi.org/10.1177/1097184X02004003001

8   World Health Organization (2024). *Health Behaviour in School-aged Children (HBSC) study.* https://www.who.int/europe/initiatives/ health-behaviour-in-school-aged-children-(hbsc)-study/highlights

9   Public Health England (2020). *What works in schools and colleges to increase physical activity?* https://assets.publishing.service.gov.uk/ media/5e7cd4b486650c7440889ff2/Guidance_to_increase_physical_ activity_among_children_and_young_people_in_schools_and_ colleges.pdf

10 Lightner, J. S., Schneider, J., Grimes, A., Wigginton, M., Curran, L., Gleason, T., & Prochnow, T. (2024). Physical activity among transgender individuals: A systematic review of quantitative and qualitative studies. *PloS one*, 19(2), e0297571. https://doi.org/10.1371/ journal.pone.0297571

11 Jones, B. A., Haycraft, E., Bouman, W. P., & Arcelus, J. (2018). The Levels and Predictors of Physical Activity Engagement Within the Treatment-Seeking Transgender Population: A Matched Control Study. *Journal of Physical Activity & Health*, 15(2), 99–107. https:// doi.org/10.1123/jpah.2017-0298

12 IPSOS (2001). *British Kids Say Parents Are To Blame For Couch Potato Lifestyle.* https://www.ipsos.com/en-uk/british-kids-say- parents-are-blame-couch-potato-lifestyle

13 Cozett, C., et al. (2016). Factors influencing participation in physical activity among 11–13 year old school children in the Western Cape, South Africa. *African Journal for Physical Activity and Health Sciences*, 22(4:2): 1100–1107. http://hdl.handle.net/10520/ EJC200148

14 Weinraub, M., Clemens, L. P., Sockloff, A., Ethridge, T., Gracely, E., & Myers, B. (1984). The Development of Sex Role Stereotypes in the Third Year: Relationships to Gender Labeling, Gender Identity, Sex-Types Toy Preference, and Family Characteristics. *Child Development*, 55(4), 1493–1503. https://doi.org/10.2307/1130019

15 Women In Sport (2022). *Reframing Sport for Teenage Girls: Tackling Teenage Disengagement.* https://womeninsport.org/wp-content/ uploads/2022/03/2022-Reframing-Sport-for-Teenage-Girls-Tackling- Teenage-Disengagement.pdf

16 Hargreaves, D., & Tiggemann, M. (2006). 'Body Image is for Girls':
A Qualitative Study of Boys' Body Image. *Journal of Health
Psychology*, 11, 567–76. https://doi.org/10.1177/1359105306065017

17 McLean, I., Wertheim, E., Paxton, S. (2018). Preferences for being
muscular and thin in 6-year-old boys. *Body Image*, 26, 98–102.
https://doi.org/10.1016/j.bodyim.2018.07.003

18 Markey, C. (2022). *Boys Are Unhappy With Their Bodies, and We
Need to Talk About It*. https://www.psychologytoday.com/us/blog/
smart-people-don-t-diet/202209/boys-are-unhappy-their-bodies-and-
we-need-talk-about-it

19 Murray, S. B., Rieger, E., Hildebrandt, T., & Karlov, L. (2012). *A
comparison of eating disorder symptomatology and comorbidity in
men with muscle dysmorphia and men with an eating disorder*. Body
Image, 9(2), 193–200

20 Glazer, K., Ziobrowski, H., Horton, N., Calzo, J., & Field, A. (2021).
The Course of Weight/Shape Concerns and Disordered Eating
Symptoms Among Adolescent and Young Adult Males. *Journal of
Adolescent Health*, . 69 (4), 615–621.. https://doi.org/10.1016/j.
jadohealth.2021.03.036

21 Sport England (2018). *Active Lives Children and Young People
Survey*. https://sportengland-production-files.s3.eu-west-2.
amazonaws.com/s3fs-public/active-lives-children-survey-academic-
year-17-18.pdf

22 Hemmingsson, E. (2018). Early Childhood Obesity Risk Factors:
Socioeconomic Adversity, Family Dysfunction, Offspring Distress,
and Junk Food Self-Medication. *Current Obesity Reports*, 7(2),
204–209. https://doi.org/10.1007/s13679-018-0310-2

23 Bacon, L. (2010). *Health At Every Size: The Surprising Truth About
Your Weight* (Revised and updated). BenBella Books.

24 Hemmingsson, E. (2018). Early Childhood Obesity Risk Factors:
Socioeconomic Adversity, Family Dysfunction, Offspring Distress,
and Junk Food Self-Medication. *Current Obesity Reports*, 7(2),
204–209. https://doi.org/10.1007/s13679-018-0310-2

25 Haushofer, J., & Fehr, E. (2014). On the psychology of poverty.
Science, 344(6186), 862–867. https://doi.org/10.1126/science.1232491

26 Sporting Equals (2013). *Culturally Excluded Guide.* https://www.
    activehw.co.uk/uploads/38736-sporting-equals-culturally-excluded-
    a4-18pp-v5-12.pdf

27 Obe, D. (2023). *Finding your place in the water.* Sport England.
    https://www.sportengland.org/blogs/finding-your-place-water

28 Sport England (2024). *Research: Disabled People.* https://www.
    sportengland.org/research-and-data/research/disabled-people

29 Gerber, C (2020). *The Unique Body Image Challenges Related to
    Disability.* Verywell Health. https://www.verywellhealth.com/
    the-unique-body-image-challenges-related-to-disablity-1094483

30 Jaarsma, E. A., Dijkstra, P. U., de Blécourt, A. C. E., Geertzen, J. H. B., &
    Dekker, R. (2015). Barriers and facilitators of sports in children with
    physical disabilities: a mixed-method study. *Disability and Rehabilitation*,
    37(18), 1617–1625. https://doi.org/10.3109/09638288.2014.972587

31 Jaarsma, E. A., Dijkstra, P. U., de Blécourt, A. C. E., Geertzen, J. H. B., &
    Dekker, R. (2015). Barriers and facilitators of sports in children with
    physical disabilities: a mixed-method study. *Disability and Rehabilitation*,
    37(18), 1617–1625. https://doi.org/10.3109/09638288.2014.972587

32 Shields, N., & Synnot, A. (2016). Perceived barriers and facilitators
    to participation in physical activity for children with disability: a
    qualitative study. *BMC pediatrics*, 16(9). https://doi.org/10.1186/
    s12887-016-0544-7

33 Department of Health and Social Care (2022). *New guidelines to
    support disabled children to be more active.* Press Release. https://
    www.gov.uk/government/news/new-guidelines-to-support-disabled-
    children-to-be-more-active

34 Morin, A. (2022). *Why You Should Never Make Your Child Hug
    Anyone.* Verywell Family. https://www.verywellfamily.com/why-you-
    shouldnt-make-your-child-hug-anyone-1095081

35 Woodyard, C. (2011). Exploring the therapeutic effects of yoga and
    its ability to increase quality of life. *International Journal of Yoga*,
    4(2), 49–54. https://doi.org/10.4103/0973-6131.85485

36 Clarke, J. (2023). *Polyvagal Theory: How Our Vagus Nerve Controls
    Responses to our Environment.* https://www.verywellmind.com/
    polyvagal-theory-4588049

37 Dana, D. & Porges, S. (2018). *The Polyvagal Theory in Therapy: Engaging the Rhythm of Regulation*. W. W. Norton and Company.

38 Ibid.

39 Ibid.

40 Sullivan, M. B., Erb, M., Schmalzl, L., Moonaz, S., Noggle Taylor, J., & Porges, S. W. (2018). Yoga Therapy and Polyvagal Theory: The Convergence of Traditional Wisdom and Contemporary Neuroscience for Self-Regulation and Resilience. *Frontiers in Human Neuroscience*, 12, 67. https://doi.org/10.3389/fnhum.2018.00067

41 Seymour, T. (2023). *Everything You Need To Know About Polyvagal Theory*. https://www.medicalnewstoday.com/articles/318128

42 Wang, S. Z., Li, S., Xu, X. Y., Lin, G. P., Shao, L., Zhao, Y., & Wang, T. H. (2010). Effect of slow abdominal breathing combined with biofeedback on blood pressure and heart rate variability in prehypertension. *Journal of Alternative and Complementary Medicine*, 16(10), 1039–1045. https://doi.org/10.1089/acm.2009.0577

43 Bornstein, M.H.; Esposito, G. (2023). Coregulation: A Multilevel Approach via Biology and Behavior. *Children*, 10, 1323. https://doi.org/10.3390/children10081323.

Chapter 7: Be the Change

1 Vanier, J. (1989). *From Brokenness to Community*. Paulist Press.

2 Levy, A. (2024). *Why do we see beauty as virtuous and ugliness as a problem to be fixed? Two philosophers explain*. The Philosophers Zone. https://www.abc.net.au/news/2024-02-04/morality-and-pathologising-ugliness-and-beauty/103258672

3 Changing Faces (2017). *Disfigurement in the UK*. www.changingfaces.org.uk/wp-content/uploads/2021/05/disfigurement-in-the-uk-report-2017.pdf

4 Kandola, P. (2023). *Weight Discrimination At Work*. https://pearnkandola.com/app/uploads/2023/08/Weight-Discrimination-At-Work-2023-1.pdf

5 Zacher, H., & von Hippel, C. (2022). Weight-based stereotype threat

in the workplace: consequences for employees with overweight or obesity. *International Journal of Obesity*, 46(4), 767–773. https://doi.org/10.1038/s41366-021-01052-5

6 Changing Faces (2024). *Ending Appearance Related Discrimination*. https://www.changingfaces.org.uk/about-visible-difference/ending-appearance-related-discrimination/

7 Chukwuemeka, N., & Spinn, B. (2024). *Eating Disorders Don't Discriminate*. Jessica Kingsley Publishers.

8 PSHE Association (2024). *Planning PSHE Education*. https://pshe-association.org.uk/guidance/ks1-5/planning-pshe-education

9 Lerner, R.M., Almerigi, J. B., Theokkas, C., & Lerner, J. V. (2005). Positive youth development: A view of the issues. *The Journal of Early Adolescence*. 25(1), 10-16.